TRUST IN INTERNATIONAL POLICE AND JUSTICE COOPERATION

The use of extra-territorial intelligence is growing among security, border, and public agencies. Internationally, rapidly evolving efforts to tackle transnational crime entail the exchange of intelligence across jurisdictions and state borders as well as the 'linking' of law enforcement operations. This book provides a number of different perspectives from across Europe, Australasia and Canada to examine recent cooperation experiences and the challenges faced in practice.

The book brings together scholars from a range of legal and criminological fields to examine the legal imperatives and social parameters that shape international police and justice cooperation, and highlights the importance of both trust and clear legal rules to ensure effective cooperation. It focuses on areas where cooperation is now mandated, but where significant issues are raised, including: the international and regional methods of information and intelligence exchange and challenges to human rights protection; the coordination of international and regional exchange of evidence, such as forensic bioinformation; police cooperation in international investigations and the added value of formalising investigative strategies across jurisdictions regionally and internationally; and the operation, accountability and legitimacy of organisations and institutions of 'cooperation' in law enforcement and specific international policing 'missions'.

Oñati International Series in Law and Society
A SERIES PUBLISHED FOR THE OÑATI INSTITUTE
FOR THE SOCIOLOGY OF LAW

General Editors
Rosemary Hunter   David Nelken

Founding Editors
William L F Felstiner   Eve Darian-Smith

Board of General Editors
Carlos Lugo, Hostos Law School, Puerto Rico
Jacek Kurczewski, Warsaw University, Poland
Marie-Claire Foblets, Leuven University, Belgium

Recent titles in this series

**For the complete list of titles in this series, see
'Oñati International Series in Law and Society' link at
www.hartpub.co.uk/books/series.asp**

Trust in International Police and Justice Cooperation

Edited by
Saskia Hufnagel and Carole McCartney

Oñati International Series in Law and Society

A SERIES PUBLISHED FOR THE OÑATI INSTITUTE
FOR THE SOCIOLOGY OF LAW

·HART·
OXFORD · LONDON · NEW YORK · NEW DELHI · SYDNEY

HART PUBLISHING
Bloomsbury Publishing Plc
Kemp House, Chawley Park, Cumnor Hill, Oxford, OX2 9PH, UK

HART PUBLISHING, the Hart/Stag logo, BLOOMSBURY and the Diana logo are
trademarks of Bloomsbury Publishing Plc
First published in Great Britain 2017

First published in hardback, 2017
Paperback edition, 2019

A catalogue record for this book is available from the British Library.

Library of Congress Cataloging-in-Publication Data

Names: Hufnagel, Saskia, editor. | McCartney, Carole, editor.

Title: Trust in international police and justice cooperation / edited by Saskia Hufnagel
and Carole McCartney.

Description: Oxford [UK] : Portland, Oregon : Hart Publishing, 2017. | Series: Oñati international
series in law and society | Includes bibliographical references and index.

Identifiers: LCCN 2016045783 (print) | LCCN 2016046048 (ebook) | ISBN 9781849467681
(hardback) | ISBN 9781509911295 (Epub)

Subjects: LCSH: International police. | Security, International.

Classification: LCC K3465 .T78 2017 (print) | LCC K3465 (ebook) | DDC 344.05/2—dc23

LC record available at https://lccn.loc.gov/2016045783

ISBN: HB: 978-1-84946-768-1
PB: 978-1-50992-979-5
ePDF: 978-1-50991-130-1
ePub: 978-1-50991-129-5

Series: Oñati International Series in Law and Society

Typeset by Compuscript Ltd, Shannon

To find out more about our authors and books visit www.hartpublishing.co.uk. Here you will find
extracts, author information, details of forthcoming events and the option to sign up for our
newsletters.

Contents

1

Introduction

SASKIA HUFNAGEL AND CAROLE McCARTNEY

Our legal system is here to protect our citizens, and that protection should be given up only if we can really trust the legal systems of other states.[1]

ALL FORMS OF human cooperation and collaboration require mutual trust. It is integral to maintaining stable relationships and is fundamental to ensuring effective cooperation between individuals and groups, large or small. Sociologists have long attempted to define and conceptualise trust, along with economists, philosophers and latterly, lawyers. O'Neill explains that trust is 'a matter of judgement and action, in conditions of less than perfect information'.[2] Bauer meanwhile conceives of trust as 'The subjective judgement that a trustor makes about the likelihood of the trustee following through with an expected and valued action under conditions of uncertainty'.[3] Trust is widely considered formed on the micro level and concerns expectations and predictions of future behaviour, hence individuals rely on trust in order to take a 'leap of faith' about present and future performance of roles. Legitimacy meanwhile is a property possessed by an institution, when others believe that the institution holds and exercises power rightfully.[4]

Both trust and institutional legitimacy are closely intertwined and equally essential within the process of building cooperative relationships within criminal justice systems. Public trust in the state is vital to ensure compliance and maintain law and order through governance by consent, rather

---

[1] David Cameron MP, HC Deb 25 March 2003, vol 402, col 196, emphasis added by the authors.

[2] O O'Neill, *Autonomy and Trust in Bioethics* (Cambridge, Cambridge University Press, 2001).

[3] PC Bauer, 'Conceptualizing and Measuring Trust and Trustworthiness' (2015) Political Concepts: Committee on Concepts and Methods Working Paper Series 61, 1.

[4] J Jackson and J Gau, 'Carving up Concepts? Differentiating Between Trust and Legitimacy in Public Attitudes Towards Legal Authority' in E Shockley, TMS Neal, L Pytlik Zillig and B Bornstein (eds), *Interdisciplinary Perspectives on Trust: Towards Theoretical and Methodological Integration* (New York, Springer, 2015).

than by force. Accordingly, the study of trust has focused on public trust in authority both at the individual and institutional level. So while we have witnessed in the last two decades 'a surge in research devoted to the role of legitimacy in governance',[5] the focus has been on the legitimacy of institutions and the trust that they elicit from citizens. For example, a recently launched (European Union) EU Barometer on Justice asks citizens of Members States how well informed they feel about their national justice system, and the level of trust they have in it.[6] Yet, there has been barely any equivalent consideration of trust between those wielding and exerting authority— such as police officers and policing and judicial agencies. This is despite the fact that police and judicial cooperation is not novel and EU Member States started to evolve cooperation strategies after the 1950s, culminating in the 1985 Schengen Agreement.

Today, the 1990 Schengen Convention can be regarded as the most comprehensive regional cooperation framework. Since Schengen, many more 'soft' and 'hard' law instruments have been created in the EU context with a view to supporting police and justice cooperation. The 'Principle of Availability' under the Hague Programme advocated the automatic sharing of law enforcement data between agencies across the EU by 2008. Such access relies on enhanced mutual trust between competent authorities. Further, the 2009 Stockholm Programme promised 'An Open and Secure Europe Serving and Protecting Citizens', with the EU Council stressing that mutual trust was the basis for 'efficient cooperation in this area. Ensuring trust and finding new ways to increase reliance on, and mutual understanding between, the different legal systems in the Member States will thus be one of the main challenges for the future'.[7] The establishment of trust is thus recognised as necessary between operational law enforcement agents to enable cooperation, coupled with the legitimacy of institutions. For example, with policing bodies, 'true legitimacy also encapsulates the conviction that police can be trusted to use [that] authority judiciously and for the greater good'.[8] Consequently, criminal justice cooperation, such as that required within the EU judicial area and the EU Area of Freedom, Security and Justice promulgated by the 2009 Treaty of Lisbon, cannot be accomplished without trust.

It is undeniable that the policing of cross-border crime demands collaboration between law enforcement authorities from multiple jurisdictions, and an efficient system of information exchange. However, while efforts to ensure effective cooperation are laudable, and may increase the safety of

---

[5] ibid, 49.

[6] Flash Eurobarometer 385, *Justice in the EU Report*, November 2013, available at europa. eu/public_opinion/flash/fl_385_en.pdf.

[7] EU Council, The Stockholm Programme—An Open and Secure Europe Serving and Protecting Citizens [2010] OJ C115/1, para 1.2.1.

[8] Jackson and Gau, above n 4, 51.

citizens, human rights protection can be put at risk. Commentators since 9/11 have warned of the serious threat to civil liberties by an overbearing concern with securitisation policies. In addition, there has been 'a move towards de-territorialisation and securitisation beyond borders ... On top of this, the discourse of insecurity seems to have proliferated and security actions that used to be considered as exceptions to the rule are now more widely used'.[9]

This move from exception to rule in the area of security has been criticised for creating a slippery slope into justifications of human rights abuses.

Internationally, police cooperation relies predominantly on the creation of 'trusted' relations and practitioner networks, such as formalised 'liaison' networks, but more frequently informal police-to-police contacts. However, increasingly there are mandated exchanges of information and obligations upon law enforcement bodies to collaborate and coordinate with bodies from beyond their operational borders. Furthermore, cross-jurisdictional police and justice cooperation has become a central part of many criminal investigations in particular in the areas of organised crime and terrorism. With such collaboration it is recognised that 'Mutual trust and mutual recognition are an essential condition for the exchange of law enforcement information'.[10] To outbalance potential negative effects upon civil liberties, the increase in international cooperation needs to be coupled with an increase in domestic accountability, judicial control and efficient decision-making processes.[11] However, despite the efforts of legal regulation in the EU context, both European and international policing networks are frequently established outside governance and accountability frameworks. While some EU and international 'soft' data protection measures are in place, there is yet to be any systematic consideration of the multifaceted issues raised by direct access and/or exchanges of intelligence. As stated with specific regard to the EU:

> So far, there has been a lack of European peer review/evaluation mechanisms as regards for example the quality of justice ... These elements, however, have huge repercussions concerning some of the essential AFSJ ingredients, such as the functioning of European cooperation on criminal justice as well as to the quality of the exchange of information between law enforcement authorities.[12]

---

[9] European Commission, *Crime and Deviance in the EU—Key Findings from EU Funded Social Sciences and Humanities Research Projects* (Luxembourg, Publications Office of the EU, 2011) 11.

[10] N Scandamis, F Sigalas and S Sofoklis, 'Rival Freedoms in Terms of Security: The Case of Data Protection and the Critierion of Connexity' CHALLENGE Research Paper No 7/2007, 11.

[11] E Guild and F Geyer, 'Justice and Home Affairs Issues at European Union Level' (2006) November *CEPS—Written Evidence to the Select Committee on Home Affairs*, available at www.ceps.eu/system/files/book/1404.pdf, 6.

[12] E Guild, S Carrera and AF Atger, 'Challenges and Prospects for the EU's Area of Freedom, Security and Justice: Recommendations to the European Commission for the Stockholm Programme' CEPS Working Document No 313/2009, 9.

In light of such laxity, in 2013 the EU introduced 'Judicial Scorecards' to attempt some preliminary monitoring of the preconditions for trust, such as creating a committee to oversee the application of the Schengen *Acquis*. There are encouraging signs too, that the neglect of inter-institutional and interpersonal trust among law enforcement agents and judicial personnel is moving up the political agenda. In 2013 the EU Justice Commissioner stated that the 'whole EU legal system ... is based on mutual trust'.[13] The 2014 'EU Justice Agenda for 2020—Strengthening Trust, Mobility and Growth within the Union', posited 'enhancing mutual trust' as the most urgent goal of the EU:

> Mutual trust is the bedrock upon which EU justice policy should be built. While the EU has laid important foundations for the promotion of mutual trust, it needs to be further strengthened to ensure that citizens, legal practitioners and judges fully trust judicial decisions irrespective of the Member State where they have been taken.[14]

The EU Commission aims to bring about a 'fully functioning European area of justice' via a combination of consolidating what has already been achieved, codifying EU law and practice, and complementing existing frameworks.[15] There remain major challenges ahead however, even with this acknowledgment that mutual trust must be strengthened: 'with only 24% of people trusting their own national justice system for example in Slovenia, or 25% in Slovakia, it appears hardly possible to continue presuming a sufficient level of trust, let alone mutual trust'.[16] Is the 'bedrock' of mutual trust still more myth than reality?[17] What is clear is that the belief that mutual trust is fundamental to policing and judicial cooperation is now so widely held and high enough on political and public agendas that its neglect by academia cannot continue. While research on citizen–authority trust continues to be relevant and important, the inter-institutional and interpersonal trust of agencies and actors within international criminal justice systems is vital if truly international policing and law enforcement can be at all effective.

This book addresses the potential contradiction between effectiveness and respect for human rights when policing agencies are cooperating across

---

[13] EU Justice Commissioner Viviane Reding, European Commission—Press release, Building Trust in Justice Systems in Europe: 'Assises de la Justice' forum to shape the future of EU Justice Policy (Brussels, 21 November 2013).

[14] European Commission, 'The EU Justice Agenda for 2020—Strengthening Trust, Mobility and Growth within the Union' (Communication) COM (2014) 144 final, 3.

[15] ibid, 4.

[16] M Weller, 'Enhancing Mutual Trust—Codification of the European Conflict of Laws Rules: Some of the EU Commission's Visions for the Future of EU Justice Policy' (2014) *Conflictoflaws.net*, available at conflictoflaws.net/2014/enhancing-mutual-trust-codification-of-the-european-conflict-of-laws-rules-some-of-the-eu-commissions-visions-for-the-future-of-eu-justice-policy/.

[17] M Weller, 'Mutual Trust: In Search of the Future of European Union Private International Law' (2015) 11(1) *Journal of Private International Law* 64.

jurisdictional boundaries, while ascertaining the place of 'trust' between the policing agencies, and between the police and citizens. The continued existence of exclusions to criminal justice cooperative strategies and priorities, and the sustained demand for greater safeguards however, demonstrates 'the limits of mutual trust'.[18] Yet without mutual trust, the principle of mutual recognition, essential to EU judicial cooperation if resisting full harmonisation of systems

> is doomed as the latter builds on the first. It is furthermore not enough that mutual trust is gained between judicial authorities and their officials. In order to realise the common area of freedom, security and justice, trust into each others' legal systems that guarantee civil liberties, fundamental freedoms and rule of law must exist between the citizens of Europe.[19]

As not particularly eloquently put by British MP Dominic Raab in relation to the EU exchange of data:

> Of course we want to exchange criminal records information, but we do not want the personal data of innocent British citizens washing around Europe, particularly with Governments—let us be honest about this—whom we would not trust to safeguard it. I have to say that I am not sure about trusting our own Government and Whitehall with lots of our personal data. If we do not trust Whitehall, what hope is there when it gets shipped off to Warsaw, Sofia and places like that?[20]

As this book reveals, significant obstacles to ensuring mutual trust and engaging in effective cross-border policing cooperation have yet to be overcome. Immediate practical difficulties such as language differences, time limits and technical legal constraints (eg, the doctrine of double criminality in extradition law) preoccupy policymakers, at the expense of more fundamental considerations of proportionality, necessity and public acceptability. The Stockholm Programme did acknowledge that '[i]n order to improve cooperation based on mutual recognition, some matters of principle should also be resolved'.[21] Yet principled considerations have largely been absent from much subsequent debate. This book not only addresses the benefits and downsides of formalising police cooperation networks inside and outside the EU, but discusses issues relating to international law enforcement data exchange. It also evaluates the added benefit of legal regulation to international police and justice cooperation. Considering that the process of formalisation is already advanced in the EU, its regional strategies are used to assess the advantages and challenges of legal regulation in this area.

---

[18] V Mitsilegas, 'The Third Wave of Third Pillar Law: Which Direction for EU Criminal Justice?' (2009) 34(4) *European Law Review* 523, 541.
[19] Guild and Geyer, above n 11, 11.
[20] Dominic Raab MP, HC Deb 15 July 2013, vol 566, col 828.
[21] EU Council, The Stockholm Programme, above n 7, para 3.1.1.

The complex interrelationship between trust, professional discretion and legal regulation in the area of police and justice cooperation and the significant role that these relationships have in ensuring integrity of data and processes are rarely discussed in parliamentary debates or academic literature. The European Commission often advocates the alignment of national initiatives with international standards and protocols. Yet in most instances relevant international standards are scarce, minimalist and lack enforcement. The recently announced EU–US Privacy Shield, which took two years of negotiation before another two years is expected for implementation, is intended to ensure high data protection standards for data transfers across the Atlantic for law enforcement purposes. At its launch, the EU Vice-President Ansip claimed that 'Trust is a must', while Commissioner Jourová declared: 'These strong safeguards enable Europe and America to restore trust in transatlantic data flows'.[22]

Further, there has been a dearth of academic scrutiny of new international security regimes with regard to integrity and ethics: 'There is an academic void as far as ethics research into emergent hybrid and transnational security practices is concerned'.[23] Yet, integrity is essential to create trust among law enforcement agencies, as well as the wider public. Recent research emphasises the necessity of trust in judicial bodies and systems in order to maintain commitment to the rule of law and normative compliance with social order.[24] The Euro-Justis project confirms that an effective justice system 'must assess itself not only against narrow criteria of crime control, but against broader criteria relating to people's trust in justice and their sense of security'.[25] This potentially rich seam of research now requires mining:

> There is an urgent need to expand the scope of ethics research to new security arenas, including international intelligence-led policing, cross-border policing, peacekeeping missions, international counter-terrorism, co-operation and information sharing between different intelligence organisations and security reform projects. There is also the need for specific research into the European context.[26]

The first part of this book focuses on the concept of trust in international policing. It establishes the concept in three different contexts in particular: the interrelationship between individual police officers across jurisdictional borders; the cooperation at national and agency level; and last, the

---

[22] European Commission—Press release, Restoring trust in transatlantic data flows through strong safeguards: European Commission presents EU–US Privacy Shield (Brussels, 29 February 2016).

[23] J van Buuren, 'Security Ethics: A Thin Blue-Green-Grey-Line' (2009) November No 1 WP3 *INEX Policy Brief* 3.

[24] M Hough and M Sato, *Trust in Justice: why it is important for criminal policy, and how it can be measured: Final report of the Euro-Justis project* (London, Institute for Criminal Policy Research Birkbeck, University of London, 2011).

[25] European *Commission, Crime and Deviance in the EU*, above n 9, 7.

[26] van Buuren, above n 23, 3.

cooperation between police and policed in environments of international policing. The different jurisdictions assessed encompass the EU and other regions of the world as well as the truly 'international' policing context, such as cooperation with jurisdictions outside border or political regions and international peacekeeping missions. The admissibility of evidence in extraterritorial jurisdictions may be open to question, particularly when evidence may have been gathered in breach of human rights. It remains the responsibility of states to prevent harm and if attempting to prosecute cross-border crime, evidence must be fit to be admitted in courts in all jurisdictions. This book thus informs the search for a 'balance' between harnessing the power of international policing cooperation, and at the same time, ensuring it is viable, legitimate and accepted by the public. The first three chapters thus refer to the sociological and psychological trust literature, while also taking into account policing and legal research.

In the first chapter, Ludo Block explores the impact of trust on cross-border police cooperation practice. This contribution focuses in particular on the police-to-police cooperation and trust between individual officers and addresses their relationships with a view to risks that need to be balanced against the gains of international cooperation. International Liaison Officers (ILOs) are highlighted in this context as they embody an important 'go-between' for agencies, even if the trust between jurisdictions is relatively low. Counter-intuitively, he concludes that the trust between nations or agencies at the macro level is not necessarily reflected at the micro level where individual officers can in fact establish trust independent of common (negative) perceptions of the relevant agencies.

The next chapter by Saskia Hufnagel addresses trust and legitimacy constraints on a number of different systems. These include Greater China, Australia, the EU and the international community at large. While academic literature in the fields of law, politics, criminology and sociology has frequently focused on international police cooperation and specific mechanisms applied in the EU, few authors have addressed (at least in the English-speaking literature) cooperation strategies in other parts of the world. Cooperation within federal states has also rarely been discussed.[27] This chapter is the first socio-legal comparative analysis of cross-border legal regulation and its relationship to trust and legitimacy in the area of police cooperation in the three different systems. Similar to the chapter by Block it is concluded that the trust at the personal level can differ from the trust at institutional level, but the formation of regulation will be influenced significantly by the perceived legitimacy of the respective other system.

The last chapter of the first part of this book by Andrew Goldsmith and Vandra Harris sheds light on trust in international policing from a significantly

---

[27] See S Hufnagel, 'Cross-Border Cooperation in Criminal Matters' in T Carty (ed), *Oxford Bibliographies in International Law* (Oxford, Oxford University Press, 2014).

different perspective, that of international peacekeeping missions. While all chapters in this part of the book address the predominant trust literature, the chapter by Goldsmith and Harris goes beyond applying the concept of trust to police-to-police cooperation and also looks at the relationship between the cooperating agencies and the citizens policed by them. This is particularly complex in the international peacekeeping environment as peacekeepers and the local police can form a relationship that is not particularly conducive to trust by and/or towards citizens. If cooperation works very well, it might even jeopardise policing by the local police after the peacekeepers move on. The authors shed light on this very complex interaction through extensive empirical data and in particular interviews with Australian officers involved in peacekeeping missions.

The second part of the book deals with trust and international policing agencies. It moves away from the concept of trust as described in the relevant (theory) literature and focuses on institutions, strategies and security mechanisms of international police cooperation and the trust invested in them. The institutions discussed in this part encompass international and regional mechanisms of police cooperation, such as Interpol, Europol and Eurojust. The strategies this part of the book deals with are non-operational police and judicial cooperation networks, which are often informal, but can be formalised, for example in the EU context. A particular branch of cooperation that is highlighted is international forensic data exchange. Light is also shed on a probably less well-known security mechanism, the 'trusted traveller'. This part of the book deals with the trust invested into institutions and strategies by citizens and police as well as inter-institutional trust, which makes data exchange between institutions possible.

The second part of the book starts with Chapter 5 by Monica den Boer on the concept of the 'trusted traveller'. This mechanism is employed to make it easier for some people to travel, while others are subject to more intrusive security screening. A number of 'trusted traveller' initiatives and how they operate are highlighted. Steps to become 'trusted' and the security objectives behind them are discussed. It concludes by pointing out the discrimination that is involved in trusting some and not trusting others and calls for trusted traveller programmes to evolve into a rights-based direction in which the free movement of persons principle is the rule, rather than the exception.

The next chapter by James Sheptycki looks into the trust invested in the international police cooperation mechanism Interpol. He does so through the lens of the sociology of 'branding'. In particular, this chapter discusses the question whether Interpol is what it wants us to believe it to be. The history, legal set-up and strategic and operational (if any) capacity of Interpol are outlined in depth and contrasted with often diverging popular beliefs. The chapter concludes that trust is most likely invested in Interpol on the basis of the persuasive capacity of the brand itself that has put world order under the influence of a policing power with no democratic basis. Brand Interpol accomplishes something at the symbolic level that does not exist at the practical level of political reality.

After the discussion of an international police cooperation mechanism Celine Cocq and Francesca Galli discuss the trust invested in two regional—EU—policing and judicial cooperation agencies, Europol and Eurojust. While analysing in depth the applicable accountability mechanisms pertaining to the initiatives and whether they deserve the trust of citizens and EU Member States, the chapter goes further into the actual relationship between the two mechanisms and whether there should be trust in inter-agency cooperation. Another rarely discussed aspect, the interrelationship between Europol and external agencies, is also investigated. The chapter concludes by pointing out that the lack of trust towards Europol in particular is the most important hurdle to overcome for the agency to work efficiently.

Moving away from the 'formalised' international and regional institutions and agencies, Toine Spapens provides insight into the work of informal regional networks. The chapter addresses the different 'circles of trust' and whether informal transnational networks fall within any of the conceptual categories.[28] Particular examples discussed with regard to policing networks include the European Tispol, Aquapol and Envicrimenet. The potential impact of informal networks on formalised legal frameworks is discussed. The chapter concludes that informal networks contribute to a widening of the circles of trust as defined by Sztompka and are a crucial building block to trust between EU Member State police organisations and officers more generally.

The last chapter of the second part of this edited volume is by Carole McCartney and addresses the exchange of forensic information in particular within the EU. This chapter focuses on the compliance of evidence exchanges with applicable human rights requirements. The question of trust is addressed in two ways. First, whether the citizen can trust in the legitimacy of forensic data exchanges and second, whether police can trust the data received as well as that the data they provide to other agencies is treated within the necessary legal safeguards. The chapter concludes that more attention needs to be paid to the benefits/risk analysis in the increasingly complex field of exchange of forensic information and that the existing EU databases in particular need to be compliant with human rights safeguards.

The third part of the book provides three more in-depth case studies of international policing and cooperation. The first chapter most specifically

[28] P Sztompka, *Trust. A Sociological Theory* (Cambridge, Cambridge University Press, 1999).

looks at a case study of international police cooperation between the United States and New Zealand. The second chapter addresses North American cases of police cooperation and the last chapter investigates yet another category of cases—intelligence exchange.

In the first chapter of this part of the book, Neil Boister sheds light on the legally extremely complex case of Kim Dotcom. In this case US law enforcement had been cooperating with New Zealand police to extract evidence for a prosecution in the United States. The evidence included a high volume of data from Kim Dotcom's computers. This episode provides a very good example of an extension of domestic policing power under external influence and how securitisation of law enforcement cooperation can remove existing domestic legal barriers and penetrate the enforcement of domestic law and order. A very interesting aspect highlighted in the context of the Kim Dotcom case is that trust itself might not be an issue in international policing, but the lack of knowledge of legal and procedural requirements in the respective other country can lead to vague warrants and police actions, leaving the decision as to the legality of cross-border policing up to the courts to decide.

In her comparative chapter on police cooperation in Europe and North America, Chantal Perras uses her empirical research from a previous study to highlight 'what works' in international policing. Two concepts that are highlighted are flexibility and trust. Counter-intuitively, major databases, such as Interpol and Europol were not at the focus of practitioner attention in international policing, while flexibility and trust are perceived as the essential tools required to complete investigations of international reach like those in drug-trafficking operations. The chapter highlights the differences, but more impressively the similarities of police cooperation in North America and the EU.

The final chapter by Denise Sulca focuses on police cooperation and trust with regard to forensic data. The case study used here is Switzerland as a non-EU country. It highlights the problems of databases used at an international and transnational level and in particular the complexity of data exchange. Without discriminating from which countries data is requested (within a multinational database) Sulca argues, responses will overflow and it will be difficult to decide which responses may or may not be useful. She therefore advocates a more intelligence-led approach to data processing and requests to receive better police investigation outcomes.

Part I

The Concept of Trust in International Police Cooperation

2

Establishing Trust Despite the Risk? An Analysis of the Need for Trust in Police Cooperation

LUDO BLOCK

I. INTRODUCTION

WHILE 'MORE POLICE cooperation' has long been the European Union (EU) policymakers' mantra, the new buzzword today seems to be 'trust'. Trust is seen by the European Commission as one of three key elements—the others being 'tools' and 'training'—in European police cooperation, and as a commodity that can be 'built' and 'promoted'.[1] Another illustration of the emphasis laid on trust can be found in the police cooperation programme under the European Neighbourhood and Partnership Instrument,[2] in which building trust among the police forces of the EU and Eastern Partnership countries is a primary aim. Furthermore, in policies of the Council of the EU on police cooperation 'trust' is now a recurrent concept.[3] However, none of these EU policy documents offer an explanation on what is actually understood to be 'trust' and how and why this is an apparently important element in police cooperation. Generally it is also not specified who should be trusting whom, and why.

Also, in the literature on police cooperation trust is frequently mentioned as a requisite for police cooperation and a lack of trust is generally attributed to different backgrounds of police officers,[4] or malpractice such

---

[1] See C Malmström, 'European Police Cooperation: Tools, Training and Trust' (14th European Police Conference, Berlin, 16 February 2011 (Brussels, Commission of the European Union, 2011).

[2] European Commission—Press release, EU to support police cooperation with Eastern Partnership countries (Brussels, 21 December 2012).

[3] See, eg, Council of the EU, *The Hague Programme: strengthening freedom, security and justice in the European Union* Doc No 16054/04 (Brussels, Council of the European Union, 2004).

[4] See, eg, J van Buuren, 'Runaway Bureaucracy? The European Police Chiefs Task Force' (2012) 6 *Policing* 284; M Deflem, 'Global Rule of Law or Global Rule of Law Enforcement?

as (a perception of) corruption.[5] However, a more in-depth analysis of the concept of trust in relation to police cooperation and how the mechanisms of (dis)trust in police cooperation actually work has not been published so far. With some exceptions[6] the concept of 'trust' is generally taken for granted. This is rather unfortunate as there is a wealth of sociological litera-ture on trust, for example, by Coleman,[7] Luhmann[8] and Sztompka,[9] who each provide a theoretical perspective that may serve to advance our under-standing of the aspect of trust in police cooperation.

Against a background of these sociological perspectives on trust, as well as practical police cooperation practices, this chapter analyses the need for trust in police cooperation. The key question this chapter aims to answer is why trust is needed to establish police cooperation. To that end, the next section first presents theoretical perspectives on trust, using mainly the work of Coleman, Luhmann and Sztompka, illustrated with practical examples from police cooperation situations. The section will arrive at a definition of trust and will above all consider the intimate relation between trust and risk. Section III thereafter examines the risks in police cooperation and intro-duces six categories of concrete situations that may lead to a breach of trust, which could derail cooperation between police.

The penultimate section is dedicated to the strategies that police use to mitigate the risks in cooperation and will map these strategies to the theories discussed in section II. The final section brings together the different insights uncovered throughout this chapter.

II. TRUST AND RISK

As Harrison McKnight and Chervany argue the large, unwieldy topic of trust has been hard for researchers to grasp for at least two reasons.[10]

International Police Cooperation and Counterterrorism' (2006) 603 *The ANNALS of the American Academy of Political and Social Science* 249.

    [5] See, eg, W Bruggeman, 'Transformation of internal security in Europe. Reflections on how to bridge the gap between political ambitions and police reality: able and willing?' Section 20, 'The transformation of internal security' (SGIR–ECPR Conference Constructing World Orders, The Hague, 2004) 8; C Fijnaut, 'The Problem of Corruption of Police Officials' in M Anderson and J Apap (eds), *Police and Justice Cooperation and the New European Borders* (The Hague, Kluwer Law International, 2002).
    [6] See J Apap, 'Towards Closer Partnerships. Requirements for More Effective JHA Cooper-ation in an Enlarged EU' CEPS Working Document No 211/October 2004; Fijnaut, above n 5.
    [7] J Coleman, *Foundations of Social Theory* (London, Harvard University Press, 1990).
    [8] N Luhmann, *Trust and Power* (New York, John Wiley, 1979).
    [9] P Sztompka, *Trust. A Sociological Theory* (Cambridge, Cambridge University Press, 1999).
    [10] D Harrison McKnight and N Chervany, 'Trust and Distrust Definitions: One Bite at a Time' in R Falcone, M Singh and Y Tan (eds), *Trust in Cyber-societies* (Berlin, Springer-Verlag, 2001).

First, much of the confusion about trust results from the divergent perspectives and viewpoints of various intellectual disciplines that contemplate the notion of trust.[11] Second, trust is conceptually extremely rich in terms of the meanings it conveys. In everyday usage, trust has more dictionary definitions than the related terms 'cooperation', 'confidence' and 'predictable' combined.[12] As a result, trust is by nature hard to narrow down to one specific definition.

Harrison McKnight and Chervany arrive at a simple definition of trust as 'a social mechanism for dealing with risk',[13] a definition shared with most other authors. Sztompka, for example, explains very concisely that when our dependency on the cooperation of others grows, the importance of trust in their reliability increases.[14] The time asymmetry in social transactions—ie, the time between investing resources and the return on that investment—introduces a risk: will the trustee keep the trust or breach the trust? If the trustee breaches our trust, all investments may have been made in vain. Trust is thus a crucial strategy for dealing with an uncertain and uncontrollable future.[15] Coleman describes the incorporation of that risk in the decision of whether or not to engage in a transaction—and thus make an uncertain investment—by the single word 'trust'[16] or in other words, trust is a bet about the future actions of others.

Luhmann similarly describes trust as a solution for specific problems of risk and argues that trust builds on two specific elements, ie, expectations and commitment.[17] Only when the expectations of how another will act in the future makes a difference to the decision, is trust needed. At the same time, a commitment is involved, because without commitment there is no risk of a potential loss, hence there is no need to trust.[18] Like Luhmann, Sztompka also emphasises the importance of commitment in relation to a need for trust. The commitment made may be stronger or weaker, depending on the range of consequences, the expected duration of the relationship, the possibility of withdrawal from a commitment, the scope of losses incurred by a breach of trust, the presence and assurance of a back-up and the value of the object of commitment.[19]

The importance of commitment is further explained by Coleman, who argues that losing control over resources to another increases one's vulnerability

---

[11] Ibid, 29.
[12] R Mayer, J Davis and F Schoorman, 'An Integrative Model of Organizational Trust' (1995) 20 *Academy of Management Review* 709.
[13] Harrison McKnight and Chervany, above n 10, 29.
[14] Sztompka, above n 9, 12.
[15] Ibid, 25.
[16] Coleman, above n 7, 91.
[17] Luhmann, above n 8, 95.
[18] Ibid, 24.
[19] Sztompka, above n 9, 28–29.

to that other.[20] Coleman—under the assumption that both parties in a trust relationship (ie, the trustor and trustee) are purposive with the aim of satisfying their interests—describes trust as a decision under risk with three essential elements: p, which is the probability that the trustee is trustworthy; L, which is the potential loss; and G, which is the potential gain.[21] The decision of the trustor to place his trust in the trustee is positive if:

$$\frac{p}{(1-p)} > \frac{L}{G}$$

The information that the trustor may have about p, L and G in many cases may be limited. In some types of transactions—such as financial transactions—the potential gain and loss may be well known. In most social transactions, such as in police cooperation, however, the loss as a result of misplaced trust—or similarly the forfeited gain as a result of failing to place trust—may be less precisely calculable. Still a subjective value can be placed upon these elements. For example, in a criminal investigation it may very well be possible to assess the dependency of information to be obtained from across borders and what effect the failure to obtain that information in a timely way may have on the potential outcome of the investigation.

Most difficult to determine when deciding to trust or not to trust is the probability that the trustee will deserve the trust, in other words his trustworthiness.[22] In the above example of a criminal investigation, it is necessary to assess the probability that the cooperation partner is willing and able to deliver in a timely way the requested information and not disclose the content of the request to the wrong people. So how would police be able to determine the trustworthiness of their cooperation partners across borders?

Sztompka distinguishes two types of information that may be sought to assess trustworthiness.[23] The first type is information about immanent traits of the trustee, which may serve as a base to estimate their primary trustworthiness. Information of this type falls in three categories, the first of which relates to the substance and consistency of past deeds, simply put: reputation. The second category contains information about present conduct and currently obtained results. Sztompka argues that although current actions may be a less reliable cue than reputation, if past deeds are not known, current actions may be extrapolated into the future.[24] The third category of signals that are used to assess the immanent traits of the trustee relate to appearance, which can include many external features such as dress, body language, manners etc.[25] External characteristics of individuals are

[20] Coleman, above n 7, 100.
[21] Ibid, 99.
[22] Ibid, 102.
[23] Sztompka, above n 9, 71.
[24] Ibid, 77.
[25] Ibid, 79.

indicators of underlying personality, identity and status and provide some cues of trustworthiness. As an example from police cooperation practice, the European police liaison officers in Moscow used to take thorough notice of the suits, personal jewellery and cars displayed by their counterparts from the Russian law enforcement agencies. Knowing that the base salary for a police officer in Russia around the year 2000 was only a few hundred dollars, they understood expensive Western suits and watches as indications of potential transgression into corrupt practices.[26] In this respect it is important to note that people are more likely to trust others who are similar to them and distrust those dissimilar to them, possibly because 'we are merely better at predicting the behaviour of those like ourselves'.[27]

The second type of information sought to assess trustworthiness relates to features of the external context in which the actions take place.[28] The extent to which the trustee may be held accountable for his actions, whether formally or informally, is one indicator.[29] As Sztompka argues, accountability changes the trustee's calculation of interests and adds an incentive to keep the trust placed in him. Coleman notes in this respect that it is thus in the interest of the trustor to 'create social structures in which it is to the potential trustee's interest to be trustworthy rather than untrustworthy'.[30]

A different way of looking at the probability that the trustee will keep or break the trust is to question what interests—other than 'internalised moral constraint'—might keep the trustee from breaking it. As Sztompka notes, generally speaking, 'betting on the moral virtues of others is more risky than believing in their basic rationality'.[31] Coleman argues that it is often most important that 'the trustee may have something to gain from being trusted in the future either by the trustor or by another to whom his actions may be communicated'.[32] As a result, Coleman continues, a close community among potential trustors leads to greater trustworthiness.[33]

A vivid example of such a closed community in police cooperation can be found in the cooperation between counterterrorism units connected through the Police Working Group on Terrorism. As one officer notes with regard to his cross-border colleagues: 'It has become a very solid group of working colleagues. We trust each other implicitly and pass information to each other without question'.[34] Within this community, reciprocal trust

---

[26] Personal observations of the author; see also L Block, 'International Policing in Russia. Police Cooperation between the European Union Member States and the Russian Federation' (2007) 17 *Policing & Society* 367.

[27] Sztompka, above n 9, 80.

[28] Ibid, 87.

[29] Sztompka also discusses pre-commitment and a situational facilitation of trust as features of the external context, which are left out here for the sake of brevity.

[30] Coleman, above n 7, 111.

[31] Sztompka, above n 9, 54.

[32] Coleman, above n 7, 108.

[33] Ibid, 109.

[34] F Bresler, *Interpol* (London, Sinclair-Stevenson, 1992) 162.

relationships emerge that lead to an efficiency in operations that facilitates actions across borders within as little as 20 minutes,[35] a speed unmatched by any formal system of police cooperation.

Beyond the one-on-one relations between trustor and trustee, there are other structures where trust is exchanged. An important role is reserved for the intermediary of trust who acts simultaneously as a trustee and trustor.[36] Coleman distinguishes advisers, guarantors and entrepreneurs as intermediaries, but the most pervasive form of an intermediary of trust are the advisers who are found in any aspect of social life. It is the judgement of the adviser that is trusted.[37] In police cooperation the liaison officer is perhaps the most prominent example of an intermediary in trust; this example will be discussed in depth in section IV.

As a final point in this section, it is important to note that two levels of trust, a micro and a macro level may be distinguished.[38] Social action between individuals deciding to place or withdraw trust, or to break or keep trust, takes place at the micro level. The macro level refers to the larger system in which individuals reside. Between the two levels transitions take place. On the one hand, micro-to-macro, meaning that the actions of individuals result in (perceived) behavioural characteristics of a larger system; on the other hand, macro-to-micro, whereby the state of the system influences the decision of individual actors. For example, as noted above, effective systems of accountability may influence individuals' decisions.

The distinction between a micro and macro level of trust is especially important in relation to the use of 'trust' in the EU policy vocabulary because both policy documents, as well as different authors writing about the need for trust in police cooperation, in fact appear to use trust as a characteristic at the macro level. Take, for example, The Hague Programme where it says that 'Strengthening police cooperation requires focused attention on mutual trust and confidence-building. In an enlarged European Union, an explicit effort should be made to improve the understanding of the working of Member States' legal systems and organisations'.[39] Other examples can be found in Bruggeman, who argues in relation to justice and home affairs cooperation in the EU that the level of trust created between different systems should lead to a more intense cooperation,[40] and in Apap who argues

---

[35] Personal interview conducted for the PhD research of the author with a senior police officer, counterterrorism expert (Paris, 27 September 2005).
[36] Coleman, above n 7, 180.
[37] Ibid, 181, 184.
[38] Ibid, 175; See also Sztompka, above n 9, 45, who distinguishes seven types of trust (personal, categorical, positional, group, institutional, commercial and systemic). A further discussion of these types falls outside the scope of this chapter.
[39] Council of the EU, *The Hague Programme*, above n 3, 23.
[40] Bruggeman, above n 5, 7.

that a high level of trust in police cooperation 'cannot be separated from wider issues of building a genuine European community'.[41]

Nonetheless, although macro-to-micro transitions influence an individuals' behaviour when it comes to placing trust—and more specifically provide information that alters one's estimate of the probability of gain[42]—their influence may vary. It is therefore not carved in stone that the macro state of the system influences transactions at the micro level. A vivid example of incongruence between the macro and micro level in police cooperation may be found in the cooperation between police of the EU Member States and Belarus. Belarus has been termed Europe's last dictatorship[43] and the EU Council has imposed sanctions on the Belarus leadership.[44] Also the decision of EU Member States' governments to stop their police officers from participating in the 35th Interpol European Regional Conference, held in May 2006 in Minsk, the capital of Belarus,[45] illustrates the lack of trust at the macro level in the Belarus governmental system. Meanwhile, at the micro level intensive police cooperation takes place between Belarus law enforcement and police from different EU Member States. Liaison officers from the different Member States regularly visit the law enforcement agencies in Minsk and the German Federal Criminal Police Agency (Bundeskriminalamt) even has (had) a long-time liaison officer permanently stationed in Minsk.[46] In my personal experience[47] the officers of the Belarus law enforcement agencies were a trustworthy cooperation partner in the sense that they were professional in their conduct, kept their promises and showed relatively little indications of transgression into corrupt practices. In contrast, possibly because of all the legal restrictions imposed by the Dutch Ministry of Justice on my ability to interact with Belorussian law enforcement at the time, in their eyes I might very well have been a much less trustworthy cooperation partner.

Now that the theoretical background has been mapped with a view to which aspects of trust in police cooperation may be analysed, the next section will focus on risks in police cooperation and situations that could result in a breach of trust for police when they cooperate across borders.

---

[41] Apap, above n 6, 4.

[42] Coleman, above n 7, 103.

[43] S Rausing, 'Belarus: inside Europe's last dictatorship' *The Guardian* (7 October 2012).

[44] European Commission, *Restrictive measures (sanctions) in force*, list of 5 June 2013, available at eeas.europa.eu/cfsp/sanctions/docs/measures_en.pdf.

[45] See Interpol, Interpol Media Release, Letter from Interpol's President and Secretary General to all National Central Bureaus regarding the 35th European Regional Conference in Minsk, Belarus (12 May 2006).

[46] Still, also in Germany police cooperation with Belarus remains a sensitive subject and after newspapers published in early 2012 about training received by the Belarusian police from the German Federal Police, the head of the Federal Police was dismissed; see 'Innenminister: Friedrich wirft Chef der Bundespolizei raus' *Der Spiegel* (28 July 2012).

[47] The author was stationed as the Dutch police liaison officer for Russia and surrounding countries in Moscow between 1999 and 2004.

III. 'RISK' IN POLICE COOPERATION

In the introduction the call for trust in police cooperation was discussed and in the previous paragraph it was shown that trust may be seen as a solution for specific problems of risk. And there are certainly—real and perceived—risks of potential loss in police cooperation.

The discussion of these potential losses in this paragraph will be limited to actual operational police cooperation, or what Benyon et al identify as the 'micro level' of police cooperation.[48] This level involves cooperation in the investigation of specific offences, and the prevention and control of particular forms of crime; in other words, day-to-day operational police cooperation.[49] The micro level as defined by Benyon et al coincides with the micro level of individuals deciding whether to place trust or not, as discussed in the previous section. The other two levels of police cooperation defined by Benyon et al are the 'meso' level and 'macro' level. They can best be compared with what Coleman defines as the wider social structures (meso level) and the state of the system (macro level), in which the cooperation takes place.[50]

Nowadays serious and organised crime almost by definition involves activities in more than one jurisdiction. The criminal links between the different countries could, for example, be direct contacts between the subject of the investigation with other suspects abroad; the use of foreign mobile telecommunication; the use of overseas or offshore bank accounts; the use of foreign registered vehicles or foreign corporate structures. As a result, successfully combating crime requires police to seek partnerships across borders in order to obtain intelligence and information on the criminal activities, structures and individuals they are facing and investigating.[51] However, involving police from across borders in an investigation does result in a decreased control over the investigation for two reasons.

The first reason is that sharing information about the investigation effectively means that the investigator becomes vulnerable in the sense that he loses (full) control over what may be the single most important resource

---

[48] J Benyon, L Turnbull, A Willis, R Woodward and A Beck, *Police Cooperation in Europe: An Investigation* (University of Leicester, Centre for the Study of Public Order 1993).

[49] To add further clarity, police cooperation is used here as a term to describe cooperation between police from different countries, often defined either as 'international police cooperation', 'transnational police cooperation', or 'cross-border police cooperation'. Although these terms could indicate different types of operational police cooperation, for the purpose of this chapter these nuances are of little relevance. See for a further discussion, L Block, *From Politics to Policing: The Rationality Gap in EU Council Policy-Making* (The Hague, Eleven International Publishing, 2011) 28–29.

[50] Coleman, above n 7, 111, 175.

[51] L Block, 'Combating Organized Crime in Europe: Practicalities of Police Cooperation' (2008) 2(1) *Policing: A Journal of Policy and Practice* 74.

in a criminal investigation: information. It is important to understand that not only sharing specific information about the investigation increases the vulnerability of the investigator, but also, for example, whether a certain individual or group is the focus of an investigation or what investigative methods are being applied. It is therefore also important to control such meta-information from which the focus and capabilities of an investigation team can be inferred.

If any of the information about an investigation prematurely became public and/or ended up in the hands of the subject(s) of the investigation, all further investigative activities would be in vain. In particular, the disclosure of applied methods, such as the use of specific technical surveillance capabilities or of a covert human intelligence source (informer) in a particular criminal environment, could set investigations back years and even cause personal danger to the informer.[52]

The second reason for a decreased control over the investigation as a result of involving police from across borders is that engaging in cross-border cooperation entails a strategic choice in the investigation with direct consequences for the way in which resources are allocated. Resource constraints make priority setting in any criminal investigation necessary[53] and when the choice is made to pursue an avenue that involves cooperation across borders, this likely means that resources are diverted from other (domestic) options in the investigation. When the cooperation partner fails to deliver (in a timely manner) the expected results, significant resources invested in the investigation may be lost and the prosecution may even be put at risk.

Thus, for police to take the decision to seek cooperation across borders not only brings potential gains, but also involves commitment. Sharing information with, and depending on the response of colleagues from across borders is a bet on the future contingent actions of their colleagues abroad. Do they deserve the trust and provide the requested information and actions in a timely manner? Or do they break the trust as a result of which, for example, nothing happens, or worse, the investigation becomes compromised? The question that emerges is hence why police from across borders would want or need to break the trust vested in them?

A wide variety of situations may lead to a breach of trust in police cooperation and in order to provide a structural framework for further research and analysis, the following six categories (detailed below) have been created: (i) corruption; (ii) diverging interests; (iii) legal obligations; (iv) resource constraints; (v) bureaucratic impediments; and (vi) different standards.[54]

---

[52] See for the use of informers and risks, C Harfield, 'Police Informers and Professional Ethics' (2012) *Criminal Justice Ethics* 1.

[53] Block, 'Combating Organized Crime in Europe', above n 51, 81.

[54] This classification combines examples from the personal experience of the author and the academic literature. Being a first attempt at tackling the issue of trust in international policing,

A. Corruption

Although there are little transparent or comprehensive statistics on the amount of corruption among police officers, police corruption no doubt exists and compromises investigations.[55] The stereotype idea may be that police corruption is mainly an issue in certain regions of the world, such as Africa, Asia and Eastern Europe. Nonetheless, media accounts show that police corruption happens everywhere.[56] However, there are countries where history and circumstances—such as low police salaries—increase the chance of corruption and where corruption is certainly not a remote risk. For example in Russia, where corruption in society has been ubiquitous in the last century,[57] structural corruption in law enforcement has been widely documented. However, as Sztompka argues, 'If there is widespread corruption, then public officials, police officers, politicians may fall into the class of the a priori distrusted'.[58] In other words, where it concerns police cooperation, distrust in the macro level may cause unfounded negative bias towards the micro level. This contrast illustrates the complexity in assessing trustworthiness in police cooperation.

B. Diverging Interests

A legitimate interest diverging from the interests of the police that sought the cooperation can be a second reason why the counterpart may intentionally break the trust. This is different from corruption, which may be regarded as an illegitimate diverging interest. A diverging legitimate interest may exist at agency level or at the level of the individual officer and examples are the so-called 'controlled' deliveries. In these operations drug shipments, instead of being confiscated upon discovery, are kept under police control and followed to their final destination with the aim to identify all involved individuals in the smuggling operation. When multiple jurisdictions are involved, it may happen that, contrary to the agreement, police in one of the jurisdictions decides to confiscate the drugs anyway.

---

this classification may not yet be exhaustive, sufficiently precise and conceptually sound, but a first framework in this area.

[55] Fijnaut, above n 5.

[56] See, eg, ABC News, 'Dutch police "shattered" by Standen corruption case' (15 August 2011), available at www.abc.net.au/news/2011-08-15/standen-four-corners/2839156; V Dodd and S Laville, 'Scotland Yard admits Daniel Morgan's killers shielded by corruption' *The Guardian* (11 March 2011).

[57] V Brovkin, 'Corruption in the 20th Century Russia' (2003) 40 *Crime Law & Social Change* 195.

[58] Sztompka, above n 9, 43.

Performance targets expressed in the number of arrests, rivalry with another domestic law enforcement agency, or the amount of drugs involved, may let agencies decide to let these (bureaucratic) interests prevail over the agreed cooperation and thus break the trust of the cooperation partner. Also, some countries offer personal bonuses for individual police officers who confiscate drugs, which may offer another incentive to break the trust.[59]

C. Legal Obligations

One very high risk for police when they cooperate with police from other jurisdictions is that their counterpart becomes at some point legally obliged to abandon the agreement. Police in the requested country may have to act against the interests of the requesting police, for example, as a result of disclosure regimes or obligations to act in certain situations. They do not want to breach the trust of the requesting party, but are legally obliged to do so. One concrete example can be found in the Netherlands where police in situations of human trafficking have a legal obligation to intervene as soon as they are aware of the location of victims.[60] By acting prematurely police in the requested country may blow a whole international operation; however under their national law they may not have another choice. Cooperation partners are often insufficiently aware of the differences in legal systems.[61]

D. Resource Constraints

The demand for police capacity is almost by definition larger than the capacity available and as a result police have to prioritise.[62] Therefore, it should not come as a surprise that at some point in an investigation the counterpart may as a result of resource constraints be unable to (continue to) make resources available to execute the request for cooperation. In particular, surveillance operations require considerable resources and generally can be maintained only for a limited period of time. In fact, cooperation requests from abroad have to compete with national and local priorities to

[59] See, eg, Turkish Monitoring Centre for Drugs and Drug Addiction, *2010 National Report to the European Monitoring Centre for Drugs and Drug Addiction* (Ankara, Turkish Ministry of Interior, 2010).

[60] Letter from the Dutch Minister of Justice to the Parliament of 12 April 1999 (TK 1998–99, 25403, nr 35).

[61] P Tak, 'Bottlenecks in International Police and Judicial Cooperation in the EU' (2002) 8 *European Journal of Crime, Criminal Law and Criminal Justice* 343.

[62] See, eg, Block, 'Combating Organized Crime in Europe', above n 51; M Hewitt and D Holmes, 'Overview of Problems Facing Police Investigation of Transnational Crime' in Kent Criminal Justice Centre, *Investigating and Prosecuting Transnational Crime* (Canterbury, University of Kent, 2002).

get resources allocated and, as Deflem convincingly argues, even in success-ful international police cooperation national interests remain paramount.[63]

E. Bureaucratic Impediments

It requires no great stretch of the imagination to understand public police institutions as bureaucracies,[64] which in itself has many advantages. How-ever, the nature of bureaucratic systems also brings certain tardiness with it. In relation to police cooperation, such tardiness could manifest itself in the police organisation itself but also in the legal processes. Within the police organisation the handling of requests for cooperation may need to follow certain 'formal' routes, a vivid example of which can be found in the Anglo-French police cooperation across the Channel before the establishment of a more efficient cooperation platform.[65] But also the time needed to obtain formal judicial approval where necessary to initiate the requested actions could be significant. In particular, in investigations into organised crime that often involve complex and time sensitive operations,[66] a lack of timely responses from across the border is a break of trust and may derail (part of) an investigation.

F. Different Standards

There are no European standards in policing, and what is labelled as 'good policing' in one country may differ significantly from what is considered good practice in another.[67] Criminal investigations can be logistically and legally complex[68] and some types of police operation, such as undercover operations, require very specialist knowledge. Police in the requested coun-try may have agreed to cooperate without having all the requested expertise available, or may have a different notion as to how to execute the request.

The fact that different standards, also in seemingly straightforward inves-tigative practices, may influence the investigation can be illustrated with an

---

[63] M Deflem, *Policing World Society. Historical Foundations of International Police Coop-eration* (Oxford, Oxford University Press, 2002).

[64] Ibid, 15.

[65] F Gallagher, 'Sheer Necessity: The Kent Experience of Regional Transfrontier Police Cooperation' (2002) 12 *Regional & Federal Studies* 111.

[66] See, eg, the detailed descriptions in C Harfield, 'Process and Practicalities. Mutual Legal Assistance and the Investigation of Transnational Crime in the EU from a UK Perspective 1990–2004' (PhD dissertation, University of Southampton, 2005).

[67] P Hobbing, 'Uniforms without Uniformity: A Critical Look at European Standards in Policing' in E Guild and F Geyer (eds), *Security Versus Justice—Police and Judicial Coopera-tion in the European Union* (Aldershot, Ashgate, 2008).

[68] eg, Hewitt and Holmes, above n 62; Harfield, 'Process and Practicalities', above n 66.

example from a Dutch–Belgian Joint Investigation Team. When some suspects in the investigation were arrested in Antwerp they were put together in the same holding cell and interviewed one by one. After each interview the suspects were again locked in the same cell with their co-conspirators while they were provided with a copy of their statement. While this practice inevitably leads to coordination of the statements between the suspects—thus rendering these useless in the investigation—it appeared to be a standard practice in Belgium, much to the surprise of the Dutch cooperation partners.[69]

The six categories of risk in police cooperation as introduced above show that risks of breaching trust are very real. Investigations into serious and organised crime that may run for months, if not years, and represent significant investments in time and resources can, in particular, be significantly damaged when the cooperation partners across the borders breach the trust and do not deliver as promised, regardless of the exact reason. It is therefore only rational that police will try to avoid or mitigate these risks. The next section will examine some of the mitigation strategies that are applied in practice.

IV. MITIGATION

There are several strategies that police may use to avoid or mitigate the risks they run in cross-border information sharing and cooperation. These strategies are discussed below, grouped by the theoretical notions on commitment and assessing trustworthiness as presented in section II.

Theoretically, police could avoid all risks by not cooperating, either by only looking at domestic investigative avenues or unilaterally executing operations across the border. Such a strategy would eliminate any commitment. However, given the current borderless era, where serious and organised crime almost by definition involves activities in more than one jurisdiction, especially within the EU, it is questionable whether such investigations are at all possible without obtaining information from across borders. Also, unilateral police activities on the territory of another state would imply a breach of that state's sovereignty, which is unacceptable for most, if not all, states. Nevertheless, breaches of sovereignty as a result of unilateral police actions do happen,[70] and a well-documented example of unilateral action clearly as a result of a lack of trust can be found in the arrest of an Austrian surveillance team on Slovenian territory. In a criminal

---

[69] Dutch Police Academy, 'Evaluatierapport. Het Joint Investigation Team in onderzoek Amsterdam' (Apeldoorn, Nederlande Politieacademie, 2009, unpublished).

[70] See, eg, E Nadelmann, *Cops Across Borders: The Internationalization of US Criminal Law Enforcement* (Pennsylvania State University, Penn State University Press, 1993) 8, 226.

investigation in Austria there was a need for cross-border surveillance into Slovenia, However, the Austrian team did not trust the head of the surveillance unit in Slovenia. Consequently, the Austrian undercover surveillance team decided that it was better to risk arrest while performing an—illegal, because in violation of sovereignty—operation on Slovenian territory rather than to involve the Slovenian surveillance unit.[71]

Another strategy would be for police to limit their commitment by restricting the amount and type of information exchanged. As Walker notes in relation to information sharing via, for example, the Schengen Information System (SIS), it takes trust to have confidence in the willingness and capacity of others to use information competently and legally.[72] However, some types of information can be easily shared because investigations are not at risk when such information is not used competently and legally. Most of the information shared through Interpol, the SIS and the Prüm channel consists of what may be called 'database information', in other words, static information such as ownership of cars, criminal records, DNA profiles, wanted persons, fingerprints, arrest records, phone subscriptions etc. Of course a request for such information itself discloses the focus on a specific person or group of persons, but it does not have to reveal the specifics of an ongoing investigation, used methods or any other types of information of which premature disclosure could compromise the investigation. Against this background it is easy to understand why information exchange via Interpol, the SIS, Prüm and the Police and Customs Cooperation Centres thrives.[73] At the same time it can also explain why the principles for information exchange as formulated in the so-called Swedish Framework Decision[74] in practice are difficult to implement,[75] especially in relation to criminal intelligence.

A third strategy deployed by police to minimise the risks in information sharing and cooperation is limiting the cooperation to a circle of trusted, personal contacts. Time and time again police researchers have found that, in spite of multiple channels for cooperation, bilateral personal contacts (still) form the backbone of policing in Europe.[76] By building relationships

---

[71] Council of Europe, *Cross-border cooperation in the combating of organised crime. Organised crime—Best Practice Survey No 5* (Strasbourg, Council of Europe, 2003).

[72] N Walker, 'In Search of the Area of Freedom, Security and Justice: A Constitutional Odyssey' in N Walker (ed), *Europe's Area of Freedom, Security and Justice* (Oxford, Oxford University Press, 2004) 30.

[73] Block, *From Politics to Policing*, above n 49, 54, 62 and 68.

[74] Council Framework Decision 2006/960/JHA of 18 December 2006 on simplifying the exchange of information and intelligence between law enforcement authorities of the Member States of the European Union [2006] OJ L386/89.

[75] Operation of the Council Framework Decision 2006/960/JHA of 18 December 2006 ('Swedish Initiative') SEC(2011) 593 final (Brussels, Commission of the European Communities, 2011).

[76] See eg, Benyon et al, above n 48; L Guille, 'Police and Judicial Cooperation in Europe: Bilateral versus Multilateral Cooperation' in F Lemieux (ed), *International Police Cooperation: Emerging Issues, Theory and Practice* (Collumpton, Willan Publishing, 2010).

and cooperating preferably with trusted contacts police avoid the need to (again) determine the probability that the trustee will deserve the trust, in other words, his trustworthiness. The reliance on bilateral contacts can be observed throughout all fields of policing and especially in sensitive areas. In counterterrorism, where absolute secrecy is paramount, cooperation takes places mostly in closed circles of personal contacts.[77] Also, in less sensitive but very specialist areas of policing, such as art crime policing, where reliance on specialist knowledge is of high importance, cooperation takes place within a narrow circle of trusted contacts.[78] These examples fit very well in Coleman's observations that a close community among potential trustors leads to greater trustworthiness.[79]

Taking this argument one step further, long-term cooperation is organised in (regional) platforms such as the Baltic Sea Task Force or the Police Working Group on Terrorism, as discussed in section II, which are what Benyon et al call the meso-level structures. As Coleman notes, such social structures could be seen as accountability structures providing the participants with an (extra) incentive to be trustworthy.[80]

A fourth strategy to avoid risks that can be observed in police cooperation is the use of intermediaries of trust who act simultaneously as a trustee and trustor and in particular in the form of liaison officers. This strategy is widely used in police cooperation inside and outside the EU.[81] Liaison officers are law enforcement officers who are—often on a temporary basis—stationed in another territorial jurisdiction. They act in a formal diplomatic capacity on behalf of their nation state and do not exercise executive or operational powers. In the daily practice of police cooperation, the police liaison officer acts on behalf of agencies that are located in different countries with completely divergent legal and cultural systems and values.[82] Their role is also described as somewhat ambiguous in that they act as official representatives of their agency, but also as informal 'fixers', facilitators, or go-betweens[83] or simply as the 'human interface' between police forces.[84] The informal part of this ambiguous role especially generates a range of benefits. Building a privileged partnership in the law enforcement context means that information

---

[77] Block, *From Politics to Policing*, above n 49, 58–59.

[78] L Block, 'Policing Art Crime in the European Union' in D Chappel and S Hufnagel (eds), *Contemporary Perspectives on the Detection, Investigation and Prosecution of Art Crime* (Farnham, Ashgate, 2014).

[79] Coleman, above n 7, 109.

[80] Ibid, 111.

[81] See Block, *From Politics to Policing*, above n 49, Ch 8; see also contributions in M den Boer and L Block (eds), *Liaison Officers: Essential Actors in Transnational Policing* (The Hague, Eleven International Publishing, 2013).

[82] See den Boer and Block, above n 81, 9.

[83] Nadelmann, above n 70, 153.

[84] D Bigo, 'Liaison Officers in Europe: New Officers in the European Security Field' in J Sheptycki (ed), *Issues in Transnational Policing* (London, Routledge, 2000) 67.

is easier to come by, intelligence can be within reach, treacherous negotiations may be avoided, and all kinds of operational actions can be facilitated and accelerated. In other words, a liaison officer can manage to overcome bureaucratic hurdles and political sensitivities by acting as an intermediary in trust.[85] One of the key roles of liaison officers in police cooperation is the assessment of the trustworthiness of the cooperation partner as they have a more direct access to information and the substance and consistency of past deeds of the cooperation partners.

While these strategies to avoid or mitigate the risk that the cooperation partner breaches the trust appear rational, a side effect is that the potential result of the cross-border actions is limited, thus increasing the risk of forfeited gain.[86]

V. CONCLUSION

When it comes to cooperation across borders, police are in a constant balancing act between trusting too much and trusting too little. When they trust too little they may forfeit the potential gain and have to endure criticism that they are not 'willing to cooperate' even though, as was demonstrated in section III, there are very real risks involved in cooperation across borders. When police trust too much they risk losing their investment which, especially in investigations into serious and organised crime, could represent a significant loss of time and resources. This dilemma, which is a central theme in the practice of police cooperation, however, has hardly received any in-depth attention in policing literature up to now.

This chapter aims to create a foundation for a more structural discussion of the aspect of trust in police cooperation and has shown that sociological theories offer rich insights into the concept of trust and its different manifestations in human interaction. Alongside different examples, it was shown that practices of police cooperation can be very well understood in the light of these theoretical insights on trust. Subsequently, the different reasons why in police cooperation the cooperation partners across the border would have an interest—or a legal obligation—to breach the trust have been mapped and classified. While this classification still may be somewhat rudimentary it does show that police are confronted with very real risks when they choose to cooperate across borders. This perspective may shine a new light on the often heard criticism that police are not willing to cooperate and are 'cocooning' their intelligence.[87] However, in today's globalised world it makes no sense to limit criminal investigations to a single jurisdiction, and

---

[85] den Boer and Block, above n 81, 191.
[86] Coleman, above n 7, 100.
[87] See, eg, Bruggeman, above n 5.

the different strategies developed and employed by police to mitigate the risks show that, despite the risk, they are willing and able to cooperate.

While these insights shed some new light on the dynamics of police cooperation, at the same time they also raise all kinds of questions on the nature of trust relationships. These are not only very practical questions like how do police assess trustworthiness, and to what extent the characteristics of the larger system in which the cooperation takes place influence the cooperation at the micro level, but also more normative questions come to mind, for example, the extent to which legal and democratic safeguards in the criminal justice system may be eroded in situations such as the Police Working Group on Terrorism where police trust each other implicitly and act without question. Also, from that perspective the dynamic of trust in police cooperation represents a delicate balancing act that is worth further research.

3

Police Cooperation in Europe, China and Australia: Does Trust Depend on the Political System?

SASKIA HUFNAGEL

I. INTRODUCTION

THE REGULATION OF police cooperation across national and international jurisdictional boundaries differs significantly around the world. It ranges from formal, legally binding international treaties and agreements to informal customs between agencies. While these are the two most extreme cases of formality and informality, many types of regulation are situated somewhere on a continuum between these two points, such as Memoranda of Understanding (MOU) between agencies or Associations of Chiefs of Police. There are hence different 'stages' of formalisation and enforceability of regulation. A customary good relationship between two police officers, two police stations or two agencies or departments can result in frequent exchange of information, mutual assistance and even joint investigations at an informal, unregulated level. In some instances, such informal cooperation has led to the establishment of more formalised initiatives, such as MOU between agencies, departments and nation states, or even to legally binding bilateral and multilateral treaties and agreements. Nation states have also established international regulations governing police cooperation not instituted subsequent to developments in policing practice. This 'top-down' regulation can equally influence transnational policing. This chapter tries to determine what influences the different developmental stages of regulation and how they relate to levels of trust and legitimacy.

Police cooperation strategies between Member States of the European Union (EU), between Mainland China, Taiwan and the special administrative regions of Hong Kong and Macau, and between Australian federal, state and territory jurisdictions are an important aspect of their fight against crime. While the abolition of controlled borders is still a recent phenomenon in the EU, Australian states and territories effectively abolished border controls with the advent of Federation in 1901. Taiwan and—despite their return to Chinese sovereignty in the late 1990s—the two special administrative regions of Hong Kong and Macao participate like autonomous nation states in police cooperation in China. While formal police cooperation frameworks have evolved at EU level in recent years, police cooperation in Australia and China still relies predominantly on informal police-to-police strategies in border regions. This chapter explores whether formalisation of police cooperation (as in the EU) is a sign of trust, or whether formalisation might be spurred by a lack of trust. Different levels of influence of trust on the three (very) different systems that all require internal law enforcement cooperation within them are determined. The existence (or not) of trust will furthermore be linked to the concept of legitimacy and in particular whether the perception of an agency or system as legitimate influences the readiness to cooperate with it and whether systems cooperating on the grounds of legitimacy tend to formalise their interactions or not.

With a view to the regulation of cooperation strategies, such as cross-border incursions, information exchange and joint investigations, each region examined in this chapter has developed differently. Australia has no formalised legal framework guiding law enforcement activity across borders, but a federal police with powers across all jurisdictions for a select number of offences. The EU has developed a significant number of rather detailed cooperation frameworks, whereas Greater China, as one nation state, still relies predominantly on international informal strategies, such as Interpol and liaison officers to cooperate across borders. At the international level, cooperation is still mainly informal and no legal framework has developed. When addressing trust between the jurisdictions and the impact on regulation, legitimacy needs to be discussed as a significant factor impacting on trust. The systems discussed here have therefore been chosen for their differences in the area of fundamental rights protection, which might impact on both trust between police and formalisation of cross-border law enforcement practices. Also relevant for the formalisation of police cooperation strategies are common approaches to fair trial rights. More broadly, the relationship between similarities and differences in human rights frameworks and the generation of transnational police regulation are likely to be interconnected.

The three systems are analysed with a view to the highest level of diversity at the international level as a benchmark. First, the EU is assessed as a region that has formed its own human rights framework applying to a number of significantly different systems and has developed a high level of formalisation through international (EU) treaties and agreements regulating police and justice cooperation. Second, the chapter addresses Greater China, which is composed of Hong Kong, Taiwan, Macao and Mainland China. The four states, while not being sovereign nation states, have distinctly different histories, legal systems and police organisations, which present challenges for cross-border law enforcement. Australia, the third system investigated, is a federal state and its states and territories are independent criminal law jurisdictions with separate police forces, making cooperation across their borders necessary. However, the cooperating states and territories adhere to very similar procedural rules and human rights requirements. Australia has been chosen as an example for the impact of greatest similarity (but not uniformity) of procedural and human rights requirements in jurisdictions on police cooperation regulation. This chapter is the first to analyse cross-border legal regulation and its relationship to trust and legitimacy in the area of police cooperation in the three different systems.[1]

II. LEGITIMACY IN A GLOBAL CONTEXT

Jürgen Habermas was one of many who foresaw a legitimacy problem in Europe stating that 'the democratic processes constituted at the level of the nation state lag hopelessly behind the economic integration taking place at the supranational level'.[2] The 1990s was a time where legitimacy was discussed in a broader context and in particular with a view to European integration. However, when focusing on legitimacy and international policing, much less literature has been produced than on legitimacy and domestic policing.[3] Habermas' fear was that the political systems of countries could not keep up with the pace of globalisation. While he was relating this to Europe, one could today ask whether this is not a problem that spans the globe rather than just one region of the world. However, we need to define legitimacy to make it applicable in a cross-border cooperation context. There is generally confusion around the definition of legitimacy and disciplines, such as law, sociology, political science and many others, have different views. To understand the concept of legitimacy better and to ultimately link it to trust in a transnational context, we therefore first need to determine which definition should be used.

The first necessary observation is that legitimacy in the transnational policing context does not apply between the state and the citizen, but between agents of the state. Between these agents, however, the same basic notions

---

[1] These findings are based on an extensive literature review in the area of transnational policing: S Hufnagel, 'Cross-Border Cooperation in Criminal Matters' in T Carty (ed), *Oxford Bibliographies in International Law* (Oxford, Oxford University Press, 2014).

[2] J Habermas, 'Citizenship and National Identity' reprinted as Appendix II in J Habermas, *Between Facts and Norms: Contributions to a Discourse Theory of Law and Democracy* (trans W Rehg, Cambridge, MA, MIT Press, 1996) 491.

[3] Of course with prominent exceptions, such as M den Boer, C Hillebrand and A Nölke, 'Legitimacy under Pressure: The European Web of Counter-Terrorism Networks' (2008) 46 *Journal of Common Market Studies* 101; B Bowling and J Sheptycki, *Global Policing* (London, Sage, 2012).

of cooperation exist as between the state and its subordinates, namely that the more legitimate the respective other authority is believed to be, the more cooperation with this authority will ensue.[4] In the context of 'inter pares' cooperation, this concept cannot be stretched to the point of there being a 'ruler' and a 'ruled', but the concept of cooperation still depends on the acknowledgement of legitimacy. Some authors would however argue that in the context of inter-agency cooperation there is an aspect of 'coercion' and 'ruler' and 'ruled' and 'power' and 'acceptance of power' and even of the loss of legitimacy of the partnership in the face of coercion.[5] However, studies on the relationship between police underlying the latter assumption were not drawn from cooperation within the systems addressed in this chapter. Evidence for coercion between police of 'stronger' states towards 'weaker' states could not be observed between the entities of the systems assessed here. The most 'coercive' relationships in the present context exist between the 'old' and 'new' Member States of the EU and between Mainland China and other administrative regions of China. Forms of coercion are nevertheless rarely mentioned as an impediment to cooperation by practitioners working in the systems addressed in this study, while the issue is frequently claimed to bar cooperation in the wider context of international police cooperation.[6]

This chapter conceives of the concept of legitimacy as linked to the implementation of international human rights, as enshrined in the International Covenant on Civil and Political Rights (ICCPR) and European Convention on Human Rights (ECHR). This is in itself a questionable way of constructing legitimacy when legitimacy is usually attributed by a society as a whole.[7] Linking it to certain standards like human rights that state agents, such as the police, have to meet is, however, a way of determining legitimacy when it is not possible to gauge whether 'society as a whole' perceives its state agents as legitimate. This is justified for the purposes of this chapter as the view of society is of limited relevance, while the view of another state's agent is paramount. Those agents, in this study of the police, have to make sure they comply with their own state's standards. This compliance could be endangered if the state they are cooperating with, for example, giving information to or getting information from, is not abiding by equivalent or similar standards.

---

[4] TR Tyler, *Why People Obey the Law: Procedural Justice, Legitimacy and Compliance* (Princeton, NJ, Princeton University Press, 2006).

[5] Bowling and Sheptycki, above n 3, 7, 17–18.

[6] Interviews for a previous study (S Hufnagel, *Police Cooperation Across Borders— Comparative Perspectives on Law Enforcement within the EU and Australia* (Farnham, Ashgate, 2013)) and a current study on international law enforcement conducted by the author, predominantly interviewing international liaison officers, police involved in peacekeeping missions, Interpol and Europol staff.

[7] See, eg, J Jackson, B Bradford, M Hough, A Myhill, P Quinton and TR Tyler,'Why Do People Comply with the Law?' (2012) 52 *British Journal of Criminology* 1051.

When recalling earlier notions of legitimacy, usually attributed to the writings of Max Weber on the social dynamics of authority,[8] it appears that legitimacy is deliberately not linked to a power dynamic (or coercion as discussed above), but to the cooperation that ensues outside this power dynamic. Legitimacy is the 'other' reason why cooperation with an authority eventuates. Legitimacy is a quality that is attributed to and results in voluntary cooperation with the authority displaying this quality. In cross-border police cooperation, as in the relationship between a state and its subordinates, authority for certain actions is delegated to another state actor. This can be rather specific in the area of police cooperation, such as the carrying out of an arrest, search or seizure, or more oblique, like the transfer of information. As such acts have to be carried out in a way that is acceptable for the commissioning party, there needs to be a similar benchmark as to what a 'legitimate' act is. This, by contrast, can be perceived very differently in the people-to-state relationship rather than in the police-to-police relationship. In the former the act has to protect the rights given to the state's subjects; in the latter the act has to be fast, efficient and leading to benefits for investigators. Human rights could therefore be the wrong benchmark when looking at international police cooperation. Legitimacy in transnational law enforcement should then rather be defined as efficiency, but this would require the complete separation of the notion of legitimacy in the police-to-police context from the people-to-state relationship. This is, however, not possible as the police are part of the state and hence part of the people-to-state relationship. If legitimacy in police-to-police cooperation were to be solely judged by efficiency, the relationship between the citizens and the state could be violated.

Furthermore, the rules binding the state and its agents function as regulators of state behaviour. If they protect the individual and are enforceable, they can prevent the interaction of law enforcement agents across borders. This strengthens legitimacy in the state-to-people relationship but can inhibit cooperation between state actors. We therefore have to choose which notion of legitimacy should apply. What is legitimate in the state-to-people relationship, and at the same time in the state-to-state relationship? Is the legitimate state actor more trusted by another state actor? Do the variants in this relationship shape the regulation developed to formalise it? These are the core questions that shall be considered in this chapter.

A. Linking Trust to Legitimacy in the Area of Police Cooperation

In the various studies the author has undertaken in the field, all practitioners interviewed have mentioned trust as a major positive impact factor on

---

[8] M Weber, *Economy and Society: An Outline of Interpretive Sociology* (eds G Roth and G Wittich, New York, Bedminster, 1968).

cooperation. Trust therefore seems to be crucial in law enforcement cooperation. Psychological research has shown that shared moral norms and
values form a basis for trust. The more we perceive others as having a similar value system, the more we consider them trustworthy.[9] Applied to an
organisation such as the police, bound by legal frameworks, this should permit a conclusion that a shared adherence to fundamental rights obligations
leads to common norms and values, which in turn leads to trust. The opposite could however equally be true. Another factor that can lead to value
commonalities is the need to produce results, to be efficient and to pursue a
common goal. On many occasions, this might complicate the maintenance
of legal values. However, it is important in the case of police to distinguish
shared legal values and shared goals. The distinction might explain why
cooperation happens not only between agencies with similar human rights
frameworks, but also with those that have very different legal restraints.

The legitimacy of an institution might rest on the legal standards they
abide by. However, research in the area of inter-agency cooperation has
shown that it also often comes down to who is known in the other organisation personally.[10] It follows that there are three broad reasons for the
establishment of a trust relationship between agencies: common norms,
common goals and personal contacts. Trust indicators hence only partly
conform to the concept of legitimacy, defined as adherence to human rights
standards. Some authors have argued that trust affects legitimacy and legitimacy affects trust, as the more legitimate agencies are, the more they are
likely to trust each other.[11] This chapter aims to look into this assertion
in the context of inter-agency cooperation. While an indicator for trust is
the troika of common norms, goals and personal contacts, the indicator
for legitimacy is the respect for human rights. Whether the two are connected shall be assessed through observations of the formation of regulation between state entities.

A question that could be asked is whether trust was the basis for cooperation mechanisms in the EU, Greater China and Australia. If it was, this
should have led to greater legitimacy. Alternatively, legitimacy could have
contributed to the establishment of the mechanism(s) and greater trust.
There could hence be two types of mechanism that need to be distinguished,
one based on trust, or the cooperation between practitioners leading to
regulation/legitimacy, the other established at the (supra-)national level with
a view to engendering trust and enabling cooperation between practitioners.
A further question is whether the creation of regulation in itself can create

---

[9] GM Breakwell, *The Psychology of Risk* (Cambridge, Cambridge University Press, 2007)
160.
[10] See, eg, Hufnagel, *Police Cooperation Across Borders*, above n 6, 86–87.
[11] M Fichera, 'Mutual Trust in European Criminal Law' Working Paper Series 2009/10
(University of Edinburgh, 2009).

legitimacy, for example, protecting suspects from informal circumvention of their rights, such as privacy. While the relationship between the agencies could be legitimised, do the agencies themselves gain legitimacy through the regulation as a manifestation that another agent trusts them to the extent that they enter into a formal relationship? Could this not be the antithesis to trust, as regulation should not be needed when there is trust? To answer the question, this chapter now examines the different relationships to shed light on the interconnection between trust, legitimacy and regulation in police cooperation.

B. EU Legal Frameworks

A significant number of bilateral and multilateral cooperation strategies exists between the Member States of the EU.[12] They shall not be outlined in detail, as there are more than 133 EU-level security provisions that highlight more impressively the level of formalisation in this region of the world.[13] However, it should be noted that bilateral and multilateral cooperation initiatives influenced EU-wide formalisation. Some of them spread throughout the Member States of the EU, leading to a de facto harmonisation of policing strategies, such as the Common Centres (or Police and Customs Cooperation Centres).[14] Others started at a multilateral level and were then taken up at EU level, such as the Schengen Convention. With regard to the trust analysis it should be noted that all mechanisms were based on a common goal: the fight against cross-border crime. Seeing that they were first established between neighbouring countries, they were very likely also fostered by personal contacts. For some cooperation mechanisms between EU Member States personal contacts were even the driving force and more crucial than the common goal, like in the Cross-Channel Intelligence Conference between the United Kingdom, France and Belgium.[15] While there was a clear need to cooperate in this region and hence a common goal, the personal and political animosities were too pronounced to lead to advanced cooperation. This changed when the head of the Kent police was replaced by a chief of police with diplomatic skills. The personal contacts thereby enabled the trust the common goals could not achieve alone.

[12] Hufnagel, *Police Cooperation Across Borders*, above n 6, ch 2.

[13] There were already 133 EU-level security provisions encompassing both substantive criminal law and procedural measures before the entry into force of the Lisbon Treaty in 2010.

[14] O Felsen, 'European Police Cooperation: The Example of the German–French Centre for Police and Customs Cooperation Kehl (GZ Kehl)' in S Hufnagel, S Bronitt and C Harfield (eds), *Cross-Border Law Enforcement Regional Law Enforcement Cooperation—European, Australian and Asia-Pacific Perspectives* (London, Routledge, 2012).

[15] F Gallagher, 'Sheer Necessity: The Kent Experience of Regional Transfrontier Police Cooperation' (2002) 12 *Regional & Federal Studies* 111, 121.

Furthermore, it could be assumed that between EU Member States a common value system is inherent through the implementation of the European Convention on Human Rights. Accession without implementation is not possible. However, the situation is more complicated than this as even the same fundamental supranational right might be implemented differently in national criminal procedure, leading to de facto incompatibilities when it comes to cross-border cooperation.

While EU-level legislation in the area of policing and security is extensive, it can be questioned whether this legislation has the power to create legitimacy. Too much and overlapping legislation might even lead to the opposite outcome: a lack of trust towards the system imposing them and a lack of coherence. The recent opt-out of some EU countries with regard to EU security provisions and, most prominently, the United Kingdom 'Brexit' decision might be indicators that extensive supranational regulation can destroy the trust in the supranational entity, which in turn might affect its legitimacy. This does, however, not mean that the trust between the nation states or their legitimacy with regard to police cooperation is affected. The question is, however, whether the implementation of the supranational regulation in the bilateral context creates more trust and legitimacy. It is unlikely that 133 instruments will do so. Studies by other authors have already concluded that most of the measures have no relevance in practice.[16] Considering that the number of instruments is vast, only a few and only those that have been considered relevant in practice shall be addressed here.

The most prominent formalised cooperation mechanism so far is the 'Europol Convention' (signed by the then 15 EU Member States on 26 July 1995), which came into effect on 1 July 1999 and has, since 2010, been replaced by a Council Decision.[17] A new Europol Regulation will enter into force on 1 May 2017. Europol can be divided into four different parts. It has a board of management, consisting of representatives of the Member States and a representative of the Commission.[18] It therefore employs an intergovernmental structure of governance. The head of Europol is its director. Europol further consists of the actual database, a liaison officer network and the national units. Europol has limited (if any) operational powers. It encompasses an EU-wide network of liaison officers, who exchange information and intelligence on transnational crime.[19] A liaison officer from

---

[16] L Block, *From Politics to Policing: The Rationality Gap in EU Council Policy-Making* (The Hague, Eleven International Publishing, 2011) 55.

[17] Council Decision of 6 April 2009 Establishing the European Police Office (Europol) [2009] OJ L121/37; also 'Europol Decision', previously Europol Convention: Council Act of 26 July 1995 Drawing up the Convention based on Article K.3 of the Treaty on European Union on the Establishment of a European Police Office (Europol Convention) [1995] OJ C316/2.

[18] See Article 37 Europol Decision.

[19] I Loader, 'Policing, Securitisation and Democratisation in Europe' (2002) 2 *Criminal Justice* 126, 128.

each of the EU Member States is situated at Europol to enable easier access to information.[20] In addition to liaison officers, there are national units of Europol established in each Member State, which are the only competent liaison bodies between Europol and the Member State authorities. Direct contacts between Europol and designated competent authorities in the Member States, governed by national law, have been allowed since 2004.[21] This indicates a growing ceding of sovereignty concerns by the Member States in relation to Europol. This is not only advantageous in relation to efficiently providing information and accessing the database, but also in relation to face-to-face contacts and informal information exchange between the officers stationed at Europol. Europol's liaison officer network is of particular importance, as the exchange of sensitive information requires a high level of trust not only between the Member States, but also between the police practitioners on the ground.[22] The liaison officers of all Member States, and even non-EU Member States, are co-located in one building to encourage the establishment of close working relationships. The liaison officers are not supervised by Europol, which gives them greater freedom to cooperate informally.[23] Practitioners accepted this network immediately and appreciate the opportunity to know their counterparts from other Member States personally, as it enhances trust.[24] In addition, the possibility to cooperate formally, as well as informally, within this network was stated to be an advantage.[25]

Another important strategy is the 2000 EU Convention on Mutual Assistance in Criminal Matters.[26] Apart from other aims, it established joint investigation teams (JITs) in the EU. JITs were included in the Convention as a new mechanism to coordinate cross-border investigations, which aims at changing the established practice of parallel investigations. While initially a resisted mechanism by practitioners, they are today a commonly used strategy to investigate cross-border crime.[27] According to Article 13 of the Convention, a JIT is an 'operational investigative team consisting of representatives of law enforcement and other authorities from different member states and possibly from other organisations like Europol and Eurojust'. The purpose of a JIT is jointly to investigate a criminal case; the

---

[20] Article 9 Europol Decision.

[21] See the Protocol Drawn up on the Basis of Article 43(1) of the Convention on the Establishment of a European Police Office (Europol Convention), Amending that Convention (Danish Protocol) [2004] OJ C2/3.

[22] V Mitsilegas, *EU Criminal Law* (Oxford, Hart Publishing, 2009) 165.

[23] ibid, 165–66.

[24] Interview with Europol Practitioner conducted for 2013 study.

[25] ibid.

[26] EU Council Act of 29 May 2000 Establishing in Accordance with Article 34 of the Treaty on European Union the Convention on Mutual Assistance in Criminal Matters between the Member States of the European Union [2005] OJ C197/3 (entered into force 23 August 2005); also '2000 Mutual Legal Assistance Convention' or simply 'Mutual Legal Assistance Convention'.

[27] Hufnagel, *Police Cooperation Across Borders*, above n 6, 221.

teams are bi-national or multinational, likely operating from one location, possibly multidisciplinary and are set up for a single investigation within an agreed time frame. An important aspect of the introduction of JITs was their advantage compared with 'traditional' cross-border investigations, the so-called 'parallel investigations'. Parallel investigations focus on cooperation through exchange of international letters of request (ILOR) in cross-border investigations, commonly based on the 1959 Council of Europe Convention, but specified in bilateral and multilateral agreements.[28] When a parallel investigation is set up between two or more Member States, investigation teams can work on the same case within their respective jurisdiction simultaneously. Information exchange and the coordination of the investigation are conducted through ILOR exchanges between the participating countries.[29] In the best case scenario, ILORs establish a legal basis for the direct and immediate exchange of intelligence and determine the preliminary measures necessary in the course of the investigation that can be taken. If particular investigative measures become necessary in one jurisdiction, such as communication interception, searches, interrogations or confiscation, additional ILORs can be issued.[30] This cumbersome back and forth of requests is not needed with JITs established under the 2000 Convention, which makes them a useful tool in cross-border cooperation. While practitioners were initially reluctant to use them, they have since become a frequent tool in EU cooperation.[31] JITs are furthermore assisted by Eurojust, which is legally based on the Eurojust Decision.[32] Eurojust national members can, for example, assist in the setting up of JITs, provide resources and help determine under which rules of procedure evidence needs to be gathered to be applicable in the relevant trial jurisdiction. Eurojust also has further competences in the area of judicial cooperation.

The question arises whether the above cooperation mechanisms have increased trust between the participating agencies or were themselves born out of trust. In the case of Europol and Eurojust, the fact that they gather together practitioners from all Member (and even non-Member) States is an important factor as it establishes personal contacts, which in turn can lead to greater trust. JITs could be said not to initiate personal contacts for further cooperation, but to enable personal interaction during an investigation that crosses borders. Another element of trust, common norms/values, is also fulfilled to a certain extent by all three mechanisms as they prescribe

---

[28] See, eg, Articles 39 and 40 of the Schengen Convention.

[29] L Block, 'Combating Organized Crime in Europe: Practicalities of Police Cooperation' (2008) 2(1) *Policing: A Journal of Policy and Practice* 76.

[30] ibid.

[31] Hufnagel, *Police Cooperation Across Borders*, above n 6, 218–19.

[32] Council Decision of 15 July 2009 on the strengthening of Eurojust and amending Council Decision 2002/187/JHA setting up Eurojust with a view to reinforcing the fight against serious crime [2009] OJ L138/14.

a certain way of engaging with each other (eg, competences and data protection regimes). All agents participating in these instruments have to adhere to the same rules even though they might come from different systems. Finally, the common goal defined for these instruments is cross-border law enforcement within the EU. While this broader goal will be inherent to all agents cooperating through these mechanisms, the more specific goals might nevertheless be different. Consideration in one country might also be given to protecting the identity of a source, or not endangering a further domestic investigation. This could then lead to conflicting goals between agencies. The interesting observation on the three above mechanisms is, however, that they provide the forum to harmonise these goals. For example, the Netherlands and the United Kingdom overcame their major differences in disclosure regimes by resorting to the Europol mechanism. Under UK law, sensitive information about police operations, such as the identity of informants or operational technique, can be exempt from disclosure to the defence (the doctrine of public interest immunity),[33] while Dutch practitioners are bound to potentially disclose all information in criminal proceedings.[34] If information is therefore classified as sensitive, it cannot be disclosed by the United Kingdom to JITs with the Netherlands. Faced with this major impediment, the UK authorities use the Europol channel to provide sensitive information to the JIT and the source of information remains protected.[35] The shortcomings of the 2000 Convention are overcome using another EU cooperation mechanism.[36] What proves to be important in carrying out the investigation is not the legal framework, but 'good personal contacts, the ability to bridge cultural differences, a shared interest and a good knowledge of the legal system of the cooperation partner'.[37]

Another initiative that is worth mentioning here is CEPOL, the European Police College, which was founded in order to create a network of police officials from all Member States and harmonise European policing standards through training.[38] CEPOL promotes training and education through seminars, workshops and the exchange of police officers at senior levels; they can work for a limited amount of time in other countries and

[33] See Criminal Procedure and Investigations Act 1996 (UK) ss 1–21; Criminal Justice Act 2003 (UK) ss 32–39.

[34] C Rijken, 'Joint Investigation Teams: Principles, Practice, and Problems. Lessons Learnt from the First Efforts to Establish a JIT' (2006) 2(2) *Utrecht Law Review* 99, 113.

[35] ibid, 114.

[36] See Hufnagel, *Police Cooperation Across Borders*, above n 6, ch 2, subsections 3.2.2.1 and 3.2.2.2.

[37] See the interview with UK–NL JIT member cited in Block, *From Politics to Policing*, above n 16.

[38] European Police College, *About CEPOL* (2016), available at www.cepol.europa.eu/who-we-are/european-police-college/about-us.

learn about another system.[39] Cooperation mechanisms with a focus on training and more generally knowledge exchange can be found in all three systems examined for this study. They are not only crucial in promoting trust between practitioners, but can also contribute to the harmonisation of practice and enhance cooperation. Practitioners participating in CEPOL seminars stressed that the major advantage of the events was getting to know practitioners from other Member States who could then be contacted directly in cross-border investigations.

The knowledge we gain by looking at the different cooperation mechanisms with regard to trust and legitimacy is rather limited. First, the fact that practitioners trust each other if they work more closely together does not prove that the jurisdictions cooperating trust each other more or are becoming more legitimate. No conclusion can be drawn from the above examples with regard to the trust between the systems more generally. What could be inferred is that the fact that practitioners are brought together in the different initiatives under a supranational framework is in itself a sign of trust as it fosters informal cooperation that should not be encouraged between systems that do not acknowledge each other's legitimacy. The fact that formalised legal frameworks exist enabling practitioner engagement and fostering cooperation could therefore be a sign of trust. This would certainly hold true if it could be observed that systems that do have a legitimacy discrepancy are not formalising their cooperation and are not fostering practitioner contact and training. The next system to be evaluated is therefore Greater China, which encompasses fewer systems, but a greater diversity of values and norms than the EU.

C. Strategies of Police Cooperation in Greater China

While Greater China only includes four distinctly different jurisdictions, the differences between them are great and the challenges to police cooperation significant. Article 2 of the Basic Law for Hong Kong[40] provides the 'one country, two systems' political settlement. However, there are more than two systems at play in the region. The Mainland Chinese system draws heavily on foreign legal models.[41] The Chinese criminal code[42] and the

---

[39] ibid.

[40] The Basic Law of the Hong Kong Special Administrative Region of the People's Republic of China (April 1990) ('Basic Law') adopted on 4 April 1990 by the Seventh National People's Congress of the People's Republic of China at its Third Session.

[41] PB Potter, 'The Chinese Legal System: Continuing Commitment to the Primacy of State Power' (1999) 159 *The China Quarterly* 673.

[42] The Chinese Code of Criminal Procedure adopted at the Second Session of the Fifth National People's Congress on 1 July 1979; revised at the Fifth Session of the Eighth National People's Congress on 14 March 1997; and promulgated by Order No 83 of the President of the People's Republic of China on 14 March 1997.

code of criminal procedure[43] in particular borrow from both the Soviet and German civil systems.[44] Hong Kong, as a former British colony is governed by the common law system, which continues even after recession to the PRC in 1997.[45] Macau, the other special administrative region (SAR) in Greater China and until 1999 under Portuguese rule, has a 'potpourri' system similar to the mainland, mainly based on Portuguese law, which in turn borrowed from German law.[46] Macau, like Hong Kong, does not apply the death penalty, which distinguishes the two administrative regions from the Mainland and has the potential to complicate police and justice cooperation between these jurisdictions.[47] Taiwan, like Mainland China and Macau, is a civil law (inquisitorial) system.[48] It contains a mixture of Imperial Chinese law, contemporary Chinese law, principles and concepts of civil law systems, such as Germany and Japan, as well as the United States. These differences in systems and legal heritage also have an impact on the regulation and structure of policing within them.

Furthermore, the international and national human rights situation in Greater China is complicated. China is a signatory to the ICCPR, but has not ratified it. For this reason, Taiwan can equally not ratify it. Hong Kong and Macao have granted adherence to the ICCPR in their Basic Laws and therefore to some extent implemented it without being able to be a party to the Convention.[49] There is hence a far greater legitimacy discrepancy between the systems in China than in the EU, at least according to the definition of legitimacy relying on common human rights requirements. If the regulation of cooperation mechanisms was a sign for trust between systems, there should be no formalised cooperation relationships between the systems adhering to the ICCPR and those not doing so within Greater China.

Unsurprisingly, a common legal framework on police cooperation does in fact not exist in Greater China. However, a number of formal agreements

---

[43] The Chinese Code of Criminal Procedure adopted at the Second Session of the Fifth National People's Congress on 1 July 1979; amended pursuant to the Decision on Amending the Criminal Procedure Law of the People's Republic of China adopted at the Fourth Session of the Eighth National People's Congress on 17 March 1996; and amended on 14 March 2012.

[44] Potter, above n 41, 674.

[45] Y Ghai, 'The Intersection of Chinese Law and Common Law in the Special Administrative Region of Hong Kong: Question of Technique or Politics?' in J Oliveira and P Cardinal (eds), *One Country, Two Systems, Three Legal Orders—Perspectives of Evolution* (Berlin, Springer, 2009)13–14.

[46] FM Luke, 'The Imminent Threat to China's Intervention in Macau's Autonomy: Using Hong Kong's Past to Secure Macau's Future' (2000) 15 *American University International Law Review* 731.

[47] ibid.

[48] H Chiu and J-P Fa, 'Taiwan's Legal System and Legal Profession' in MA Silk (ed), *Taiwan Trade and Investment Law* (Oxford, Oxford University Press, 1994).

[49] G Greenleaf, *Asian Data Privacy Laws—Trade and Human Rights Perspectives* (Oxford, Oxford University Press, 2014) 474.

were established bilaterally. An example of a bilateral cooperation framework is the 1988 Mutual Case Assistance Scheme (MCAS) between Mainland China and Hong Kong.[50] MCAS was established to investigate cross-border corruption cases. The agreement was first limited to Procurator Departments in Guangdong, but in 2000 was further extended through collaboration with the Supreme People's Procurator Department to other provinces.[51] This manifests a harmonising effect of this agreement on other regions within Mainland China. It also shows that a common goal seems to overcome the general rule that regulation is only established between systems that trust each other. The goal of fighting corruption was here stronger than the distrust created by divergent value systems.

An example for trust between systems that have similarly limited application of international human rights standards is the 2009 Cross-Strait Joint Crime-Fighting and Judicial Mutual Assistance Agreement, which was concluded between Taiwan and Mainland China. It is a formal agreement[52] and to a higher degree binding than, for example, an MOU. This agreement is the most comparable to EU mechanisms and encompasses measures similar to those available through the Schengen Convention, such as cross-border incursions and mutual legal assistance. The closeness of Taiwan and Mainland China in the area of police cooperation is very surprising as Taiwan is not recognised by the PRC as a sovereign nation state. However, under the Cross-Strait Agreement both sides had established diplomatic organisations through which cooperation, for example, in criminal matters, could be conducted.[53] A possible explanation is that the PRC and Taiwan both apply the death penalty and have a similar approach to fair trial rights. Cooperation between them, despite political discrepancies, relies on jurisdictional similarities, considering that both systems rely more on Imperial and contemporary Chinese law than Macau and Hong Kong. This stresses that a common value system can lead to closer cooperation, which could be a sign of trust. However, legitimacy is here put to the test as it could be established that both the existence, as well as the lack of legitimacy can lead to greater trust between organisations as long as they are situated within relatively similar legal systems.

However, the level of engagement between all four systems forming Greater China is more comparable to international cooperation than

---

[50] DW Choy and H Fu, 'Cross-Border Relations in Criminal Matters' in MS Gaylord, D Gittings and H Traver (eds), *Introduction to Crime, Law and Justice in Hong Kong* (Hong Kong, Hong Kong University Press, 2009) 227.

[51] ibid.

[52] Exchange Foundation and the Association for Relations Across the Taiwan Straits, Cross-Strait Joint Crime-Fighting and Judicial Mutual Assistance Agreement between the Taiwan Straits (25 July 2009).

[53] S Lo, *The Politics of Cross-Border Crime in Greater China—Case Studies of Mainland China, Hong Kong, and Macao* (New York, ME Sharpe, 2009) 173.

to the close and regulated EU cross-border law enforcement. The '1994 Agreement' established between Mainland China and Hong Kong confirmed the principle established previously, creating three different channels for mutual legal assistance. The first was Interpol, the second a direct link between Hong Kong and Guangdong province and the third were liaison officers of the Ministry of Public Security (MPS) stationed in Hong Kong.[54] Cooperation through Interpol had been the long-established practice of operational police cooperation between the two parties during the 99-year British lease on Hong Kong and the 1984 Sino–British Joint Liaison Group decided in 1989 that cooperation through Interpol should persist even after the return of Hong Kong to Chinese sovereignty in 1997.[55] The fact that the two systems chose international cooperation mechanisms (Interpol and liaison officers) rather than measures more tailored to a regional context shows that the assumption of differences is greater than in regions such as the EU with more coherent value systems.

While several bilateral regulated mechanisms exist in Greater China to enhance police cooperation across borders, cross-border law enforcement in this region is still predominantly based on informal and semi-formal cooperation mechanisms. However, between Taiwan and Mainland China a formalised framework can be observed. At the same time both of these entities have not ratified the ICCPR and still apply the death penalty. It appears that similarities in legitimacy foster the formalisation of cooperation mechanisms. More important than the legitimacy of systems seems to be the sharing of a common value base. Also, if the common goal is considered a priority in the systems, differences in the value base do not hinder cooperation as the anti-corruption cooperation between Mainland China and Hong Kong shows. China therefore provides a very good case study. Between all four systems in Greater China, formalisation did not occur, but bilateral formal cooperation exists between systems with greater similarities or with common goals. It also needs to be mentioned that despite the differences between the four systems there are common education and training initiatives, for example, between Mainland China, Macao and Hong Kong. These initiatives were described by officers to generate trust and enhance cooperation.[56] Different from the EU case study, this is here a dangerous endeavour as cooperation could lead to human rights infringements. The concept of trust seems to be therefore independent of human rights standards and a common value system in the police cooperation context.

[54] Choy and Fu, above n 50, 228.
[55] Lo, above n 53, 177.
[56] S Hufnagel, 'Strategies of Police Cooperation along the Southern Chinese Seaboard: A Comparison with the EU' (2014) 61(4) *Crime, Law and Social Change* 394.

D. Australia

Australia's nine jurisdictions (six states, two territories and federal) are not sovereign nation states, but are comparable in this context as each has distinct criminal laws and procedure as well as a separate police force. Furthermore, the Australian territory is bigger than the EU with 28 jurisdictions; hence there are unique policing problems in remote border regions that have the potential to be tackled by police cooperation mechanisms. Australia has no national human rights charter, but is a party to the ICCPR. Some states have created human rights legislation, but it is of little relevance to fair trial rights. With regard to legitimacy, the states forming the Australian federation should be more homogenous than the EU. All systems derive from the common law and more precisely the British and Irish legal systems. As Australia is a signatory to the ICCPR, it is applicable in all states. Considering the prominent similarities of the systems, trust should exist, based on common norms/values, goals and personal context (joint training). The existing similar levels of legitimacy should therefore, following the EU example, have led to cross-border legislation facilitating police cooperation.

However, while close informal cooperation between the nine jurisdictions exists in border regions, this has not generally led to the creation of bilateral and multilateral legislation facilitating cross-border police cooperation, nor has it impacted on Australian federal, or the harmonisation of state, territory and Commonwealth legislation. It has also not led to the creation of any legal cooperation frameworks. Advanced cooperation in Australian border regions, unlike in the EU, is also in turn not influenced by federal or harmonised legislation. Furthermore, federal agencies, within the limits of their competences, perform a number of cross-border tasks, which have made such developments less necessary. Australia's top-down attempts to harmonise criminal law and procedure or introduce systems of mutual recognition of laws have rarely led to harmonised implementation and cooperative practice. This lack of harmonised legal frameworks and clearly defined competences presents challenges. While the predominant informality of cooperation can have advantages, it also leads to divergent approaches between state and territory on the one hand and the more formal federal agencies on the other and makes a clear determination of competences difficult.[57]

The only 'formal' strategy that exists in Australia is limited to three jurisdictions: South Australia, Northern Territory and Western Australia. In the Ngaanyatjarra Pitjantjatjara Yankuntjatjara (NPY) lands, which is the sparsely inhabited border region in the centre of Australia, problems of domestic violence, child abuse, sexual abuse, substance abuse, and other

---

[57] Hufnagel, *Police Cooperation Across Borders*, above n 6, ch 3.

forms of offending behaviour became apparent through a women's initiative in the region. The cooperation measures created to counter these issues are probably the most advanced of all Australian border areas. The Western Australia Cross-Border Justice Act 2008, the South Australia Cross-Border Justice Act 2009 and the Northern Territory Cross-Border Justice Act 2008 allow police to exercise their powers (within certain limits) in each of the three jurisdictions under recognition of the laws of their state or territory. In other Australian border regions a police officer must be sworn into the relevant system to exercise his or her power (typically they are assigned the powers of a 'special constable' as in the Police (Special Provisions) Act 1901 New South Wales. However, while this strategy has the clear potential to grow beyond the three jurisdictions, attempts to apply this strategy to other states have not been made.[58] The cooperation mechanism is nevertheless far more advanced than anything that has been established in the EU, which shows that similarities (and presumably the underlying trust and similar levels of legitimacy due to these systemic similarities) do create close cooperation.

More important than the NPY lands cooperation is the fact that Australia is, apart from the state and territory police, also policed by federal agencies, such as the Australian Federal Police (AFP) and the Australian Crime Commission (ACC). Giving a superior entity the power to establish common agencies with enforcement powers might not show trust between the systems, but trust in the superior entity. Comparing this situation with the EU, trust between the EU Member States has led to the establishment of the common supranational agency Europol, but has fallen short of giving this agency enforcement powers. It could therefore be concluded that the higher the levels of similarity with regard to legitimacy are within an entity (Australia has different jurisdictions, but they all derived from similar systems, while the EU encompasses very diverse civil and common law systems within one human rights framework), the more likely they will be to cede power to the superior entity. This is not to say that there is not a constant quarrel between the Australian state and territory and the federal levels regarding competences.[59] However, as a system, the trust is here advanced to the point that a common representative agency can be tolerated. This seems to be an even further stage of trust than in the EU.

Furthermore, similar to both the EU and Greater China formal and informal practitioner forums and agencies or education and training initiatives have developed in Australia encompassing all systems, often initiated by

---

[58] J Fleming, 'Policing Indigenous People in the Ngaanyatjarra Pitjantjara Yankunytjatjara Lands' in S Hufnagel, S Bronitt and C Harfield (eds), *Cross-Border Law Enforcement Regional Law Enforcement Cooperation—European, Australian and Asia-Pacific Perspectives* (London, Routledge, 2012).

[59] Hufnagel, *Police Cooperation Across Borders*, above n 6, ch 3.

the federal level. This is a consequence of harmonised laws not necessarily translating into harmonised practice. Harmonised and regional laws have not been able to overcome all differences between constituent jurisdictions, which makes personal level trust building necessary. It is interesting to see that these trust building initiatives can even be identified in the Australian context, despite the pronounced similarity of legal systems and organisational structures among the states. Common training and knowledge exchange therefore seems to be necessary in all systems.

Australia could, apart from the similarity in establishing training initiatives, be seen as a system with great similarities and little formalisation at the bilateral and multilateral levels. Interviews with practitioners for a previous study,[60] indicated that formalisation would be welcomed and that the case-by-case approach can be tiring and highly dependent on single individuals. However, the systems were mostly seen as so legally similar that a real necessity for formalisation from a legal perspective did not exist. Furthermore, when cases cross borders within the Australian federation, they theoretically do fall within the competences of the AFP (at least if they are related to drug crimes, telecommunication or terrorism offences). This has also contributed to a certain reluctance to formalise cooperation frameworks at the multilateral level.

III. CONCLUSION

The interrelatedness of trust, legitimacy and regulation in the area of police cooperation has proven to be rather different from the 'traditional' views of trust and legitimacy discussed in the first part of this chapter. While the legitimacy debate was shortened by simply assuming that legitimacy levels are related to the implementation of international and regional human rights standards, this has not made the assessment of trust and its effect on legitimacy any easier.

It can be concluded that trust is established in all systems by common goals, common norms/values and personal contacts. This becomes particularly apparent through the fact that all systems foster personal contacts through education and training. However, the three trust indicators do not have to be present at the same time. A common goal can be the driver of trust and even ensuing regulation despite major differences of legitimacy levels between the cooperating systems. It also became very clear that the trust established to promote cross-border law enforcement is not necessarily related to trust between the systems or the other agencies in general. So, other than the assertion by Fichera that 'trust affects legitimacy and

---

[60] ibid.

legitimacy affects trust, as the more legitimate agencies are the more they are likely to trust each other',[61] the analysis of police cooperation strategies resulted in the view that legitimacy affects trust, but trust does not affect legitimacy in the area of police cooperation. For example, because systems with low legitimacy levels also trust each other.

While police in all three systems addressed can trust each other, even to the point of formally regulating their engagements across borders, this has absolutely no effect on the legitimacy of the other system or how police view that system with regard to legitimacy. The common goal and personal contacts can create the trust independently of the legitimacy of the system. This is likely to produce outcomes detrimental to safeguarding the rights of the defendant. Put differently, if Fichera's assertion is true, we need to redefine 'legitimacy' in the police cooperation context. If we detach legitimacy from the notion that people have to accept the state and twist it to the notion that police as a state agent need to accept the other police, we can rid the legitimacy concept of its human rights component and replace this with common (good *or* bad) values and goals. This brings to the fore the quintessential dilemma of policing.

What can be asserted is that legitimacy (applying the human rights definition) does influence trust. The common human rights frameworks in the EU have impacted on how police can cooperate and this could similarly be observed in the Australian context. Where a common norm/value basis is present, cooperation mechanisms are more likely to exist. This was also confirmed in the Chinese case study as similar systems were more likely to cooperate through a formalised legal basis. If fundamental rights were not an inherent part of legitimacy in the police cooperation context, these observations could not have been made. However, it must be concluded that similarities of legitimacy levels are just as important in the establishment of trust and cooperation as human rights.

Finally, the stages of trust within an entity comprised of different systems could be categorised as:

1. Bilateral and multilateral treaties and agreements based on situational trust (common goals, personal contacts, common norms, but not necessarily all three need to be present to create regulation) when systems show major differences in legitimacy levels.
2. Supranational frameworks as well as multilateral frameworks between all systems within an entity based on trust both between the systems and towards the supranational level (multilateral frameworks being more influenced by common goals and personal contacts, while supranational frameworks are initiated by common goals and related values/norms) when systems show differences at the criminal justice level, but not at the human rights level.

---

[61] Fichera, above n 11.

3. Superior agencies established to represent the group of systems based on both the trust between the systems, but also the superior (federal) level (trust between systems based on common goals and personal contacts, trust towards the superior level based on the common norms/values) when systems are similar both at the criminal justice as well as at the human rights level.

4

International Policing Missions: Establishing Trustworthy Policing in Low-trust Environments[1]

ANDREW GOLDSMITH AND VANDRA HARRIS

> It is one thing to walk in and everyone says, 'G'day' and shakes your hand and is all smiles, but it is another thing to have the trust of the people.[2]

> You would have to impress upon them the importance of not killing anybody especially while we were there because we would get the blame and you know if you had any respect for us, you wouldn't do it and that's where that friendship and trust and that built up.[3]

I. INTRODUCTION

In this chapter, we explore everyday understandings of trust among a group of Australian police peacekeepers and capacity-builders in international police missions. Their views provide some insight into how international police personnel approach their work in missions, including how they deal with local police counterparts and local people, and how they assess the effectiveness and relevance of what they do. Their ability to work in these environments, it will emerge, is frequently expressed in terms of trust—the need to build trust among local people, the need to establish trust with the local police to whom they are providing training or other forms of assistance. Conversely, the difficulties that these foreign police face is often

[1] This chapter is a substantially revised version of a previously published article by the authors, 'Trust, Trustworthiness and Trust-building in International Policing Missions' (2012) 45 *Australian & New Zealand Journal of Criminology* 231. This research was funded under an Australian Research Council Linkage Grant LP0560643. For correspondence, please contact the first-named author at andrew.goldsmith@flinders.edu.au.
[2] Interview, R02. To maintain confidentiality, interviewees are referred to only by interview number.
[3] Interview, R49.

seen by them as reflective of an absence of trust. Trust is arguably a more
fundamental requirement for good policing than for 'good soldiering', as
policing is premised upon ongoing, civil relationships with local people in
which mutual understanding and cooperation keeps both the use of force
or its threatened use to a tolerable minimum. Military forces, by contrast,
tend to have limited engagements with local people and to rely more upon
threat or use of overwhelming force to secure their objectives. As policing
increasingly features in international peacekeeping missions, often working
alongside military forces, how police officers can establish trust becomes an
important practical issue.

International peacekeeping was founded half a century ago upon the
principles of impartiality, consent and use of minimum force,[4] interestingly,
ideals very similar to the foundational principles of Peelian policing.[5] These
missions frequently intervene in 'low-trust' settings, in which public trust
in (domestic) authorities including police is historically low.[6] Trust deficits
facing international missions, as foreign interveners, are likely to be even
greater. According to a relatively recent report, there is 'the need to build
trust between key players in peacekeeping'.[7] The report identifies the need
to build trust 'among the Security Council, Secretariat, troop, and financial
contributing countries', and describes this need as 'fundamental, achievable,
and necessary for effective peacekeeping'.[8]

In this chapter, we take this point one step further, suggesting that the
need to build trust is not limited to 'key players' in the sense of contributing countries and UN bodies. It is also of crucial importance to achieving
strategic and tactical success in individual peace operations. We propose
to explore a number of dimensions of the place of trust in international
policing missions. The missions we consider are focused on one or both
of two functions: (1) *peacekeeping* (including executive policing), involving
the direct provision of policing services; (2) *capacity building*, the provision
of training, mentoring and other forms of assistance related to the establishment or rebuilding of local police services. The question for international policing missions is how can trust in its mission and activities be
maximised in the complex and often conflict-ridden and distrustful environments in which they are being expected to operate. As will be argued below,
international police missions are more likely to be effective and legitimate

[4] A Bellamy, P Williams and S Griffin, *Understanding Peacekeeping* (Cambridge, Polity Press, 2006) 96.
[5] R Reiner, *The Politics of Police*, 4th edn (Oxford, Oxford University Press, 2010).
[6] F Fukuyama, *Trust: The Social Virtues and the Creation of Prosperity* (New York, Free Press, 1995); A Goldsmith, 'Police Reform and the Problem of Trust' (2005) 9(4) *Theoretical Criminology* 443.
[7] JN Parker, *Robust Peacekeeping: The Politics of Force* (New York, Center on International Cooperation, New York University, 2010) 4.
[8] ibid, 6.

if they can achieve a level of trust in the settings in which they are located. In order to be trusted, we suggest, these missions need to be built upon a concept of *trustworthiness*.

In the next section (section II), we consider some features of the police role that create difficulties in terms of building and securing public trust; these features characterise policing generally but become more acute in circumstances in which international policing missions are typically involved. In section III, there is an attempt to link findings from the literature on trust to some of the conditions facing these missions. In section IV, we outline the nature of the research undertaken with Australian police personnel who served on these missions which generated interview data from more than 120 interviews. This data is drawn upon in section V to extend the analysis, and in particular identify the ways in which trust was a meaningful concept in the work undertaken by these police officers. Finally, in the concluding section (section VI), we offer some observations on how future missions might approach their tasks with a better appreciation of the centrality of trust to achieving their mission objectives.

II. STRUCTURAL OBSTACLES TO TRUSTING POLICE

Domestically, it has been noted, police work is uncertain in its aims and methods; it exhibits what has been termed *role ambiguity*.[9] If the purposes of policing are not entirely clear at home, this situation is likely to be even more challenging in international mission settings where, among other things, missions introduce different, often competing notions of what the police role is or should be. Police officers are well aware that many they deal with are resentful and in some cases at least do not accept the legitimacy of the police or of the actions taken against them by police.[10] Certain groups historically have suffered disproportionately from what are referred to, respectively, as *over-policing* and *under-policing*.[11] Being the subject of too much police attention, or failing to obtain their services in moments of need, can generate negative perceptions that work against the establishment of trust.[12] Failing to receive public endorsement for many of their actions,

---

[9] C Thomas, 'Maintaining and Restoring Public Trust in Government Agencies and Their Employees' (1998) 30 *Administration & Society* 166.

[10] S Choong, *Policing as Social Discipline* (Oxford, Clarendon Press, 1997).

[11] Open Society Justice Initiative, *Ethnic Profiling in the European Union: Pervasive, Ineffective and Discriminatory* (New York, OSJI, 2009); W Skogan, 'Asymmetry in the Impact of Encounters with Police' (2006) 16(2) *Policing and Society* 99; E Sharp and P Johnson, 'Accounting for Variation in Distrust of Local Police' (2009) 26(1) *Justice Quarterly* 157.

[12] Goldsmith, 'Police Reform and the Problem of Trust', above n 6.

police officers are frequently disposed to display suspicion and distrust.[13] As they themselves are not inclined to be trusting, this tendency contributes to the difficulties police face in building trustful relations with others.

Internationally there are also structural features that work against ready trust in police. Foreign assistance missions often must operate in settings in which previous colonial or local administrations used the police as a weapon of the regime, rather than to uphold the law and peace for the benefit of the society as a whole. The historical legacy of policing will often be of police as abusive, corrupt, or at best, indifferent to their security needs. This means the task facing international policing missions in building productive, positive relationships can be a daunting one indeed. Spin and public relations are unlikely to succeed. As Tankebe noted in relation to modern Ghana, 'utilitarian factors [will be] important in shaping public cooperation with the police'.[14] Overcoming entrenched distrust in such environments, in other words, will require tangible measures that address the perceived needs of those they are trying to assist. It also requires that foreign police strive as much as possible in their activities and behaviours in the field to distinguish themselves as much as possible from the actions and attitudes of previous police systems. If international police personnel become involved in corruption or sexual exploitation of local people, as has happened within some UN missions, this can attract negative publicity and engender local resentment.[15] Equally, if foreign police fail to restore order promptly after arrival, initial public expectations can be quickly disappointed and make subsequent relationship building with local people more difficult.

III. TOWARDS AN OPERATIONAL CONCEPT OF TRUST

In this section, we explore understandings of the concept of trust in order to identify key elements of trust for the purposes of establishing positive relationships between international police, local police and members of local communities. In teasing out relevant concepts, we shall refer to the specific challenges of policing by way of illustration and elaboration. The understandings generated set the scene for the discussion and analysis of the interview data in section V.

First, it will be seen that our data mainly addresses *interpersonal* rather than *institutional* trust. However, the relationship between the two is visible in a number of ways. Individual officer incompetence, for example,

---

[13] Reiner, above n 5, 121–22.

[14] J Tankebe, 'Public Cooperation with the Police in Ghana: Does Procedural Fairness Matter?' (2009) 47(4) *Criminology* 1265.

[15] M Odello, 'Tackling Criminal Acts in Peacekeeping Operations: The Accountability of Peacekeepers' (2010) 15(2) *Journal of Conflict & Security Law* 347.

can undermine trust in institutions[16] as well as in that individual. A police officer who abuses her power, by being identified by whatever means (her uniform, for example) with her police agency, can negatively impact upon public perceptions of that agency once her actions become publicly known. Equally, positive actions by individuals can contribute to building institutional trust on a wider basis.[17] More work is needed to establish which measures of interpersonal trust can, under different conditions, contribute to trust building in institutions.

There can be indirect as well as direct effects at work here. A recent study among young people in Queensland showed that having trust in teachers tended to increase trust not just in schools but in other institutions as well, including police, television and politicians.[18] This finding is certainly consistent with the idea that public trust, and more particularly distrust, is often generalised across a range of institutions and settings.[19] Here, 'the police', as often the most visible and tangible expression of state power, occupy a critical position in terms of their potential for building, or undermining, public attitudes to government more broadly.

Second, people and cultures differ in terms of their *willingness to trust*. Some cultures, due to intrinsic (eg, clan feuds) or extrinsic reasons (eg, long-standing repressive colonial occupation), may be less inclined to trust others (and especially outsiders).[20] Post-conflict and transitional societies are two examples where this typically is the case. It is reasonable to presume that deficits in what we can call *social trust* will impact differentially in terms of a mission's ability to build trust. Societies in which members are reluctant to trust each other are scarcely likely to trust others more readily, it seems reasonable to hypothesise, although where there are situations of abject need (eg, threat of annihilation from violence or starvation), there is likely to be at least a temporary willingness to accept help. The absence of prior familiarity or positive assistance, however, is generally likely to prove an obstacle.

Where people have little history together, or an erratic history of cooperation mixed with exploitation, or a consistent history of failure to cooperate, people will distrust one another, avoiding collaborative endeavours without guarantees on the other's behaviour.[21]

---

[16] Thomas, above n 9.

[17] B Tranter and Z Skrbis, 'Trust and Confidence: A Study of Young Queenslanders' (2009) 44(4) *Australian Journal of Political Science* 659.

[18] ibid.

[19] D Gambetta, 'Can We Trust Trust?' in D Gambetta (ed), *Trust: Making and Breaking Cooperative Relations* (Oxford, Blackwell, 1988).

[20] R Putnam, *Making Democracy Work* (Princeton, NJ, Princeton University Press, 1993); Fukuyama, above n 6.

[21] R Burt, 'Bandwith and Echo: Trust, Information, and Gossip in Social Networks' in J Rauch and A Cassella (eds), *Networks and Markets* (New York, Russell Sage Publications, 2001) 33.

Third, trust is *relational* in character. Trust will therefore be influenced in part by the position and attitude of the parties to a particular relationship. Where no previous relationship exists, establishing trust will require providing reasons for entering a collaboration or providing cooperation. Tangible actions of demonstrable goodwill will usually speak louder than words. Establishing and meeting local expectations in tangible ways is widely seen as important to taking the first steps towards establishing trust.[22] Here understanding how building trust is relevant to achieving security goals is crucial. Trust enhances feelings of security. Misztal describes trust as 'a protective mechanism relying on everyday routines, stable reputations and tacit memories, which together push out of modern life fear and uncertainty as well as moral problems'.[23] Similarly, Luhmann has described trust as a 'solution for specific problems of risk'.[24]

Fourth, in order to be trusted, an individual or institution needs to be *trustworthy*. There is considerable consensus about the qualities of an individual or organisation that facilitate trustworthiness. The three most commonly mentioned are: *competence*, *impartiality* and *beneficence*.[25] The first refers to having the relevant skills and capability to assist. Impartiality refers to a lack of bias and a willingness to follow a principled approach to providing assistance, while the third quality, beneficence, refers to acting towards the other person with a view to assisting, rather than harming, them. Where one or more of these qualities is seen to be lacking or missing in an individual or an institution, there will be a reluctance to cooperate or collaborate, making the establishment of trust difficult. Some policing scholars have pointed to *motive-based trust*. This 'turns on whether the police are seen as having the best interests of the community at heart'.[26] International missions face many difficulties under this standard. They have to be able first to know what those 'best interests' are. This may be no easy matter in the circumstances, especially since in the presence of recent conflict there may be many divisions over what this might mean.

Fifth, extending the discussion of providing reasons to trust, another potential basis for trust is through the provision of *procedural justice*. From this perspective, it is suggested that trust in legal authorities, including

---

[22] S Vangen and C Huxham, 'Nurturing Collaborative Relations: Building Trust in Interorganizational Collaboration' (2003) 39 *Journal of Applied Behavioral Science 5*.

[23] B Misztal, *Trust in Modern Societies* (Cambridge, Polity Press, 1996) 102.

[24] N Luhmann, 'Familiarity, Confidence, Trust: Problems and Alternatives' in D Gambetta (ed), *Trust: Making and Breaking Cooperative Relations* (Oxford, Blackwell, 1988) 95.

[25] K Montgomery, C Jordens and M Little, 'How Vulnerability and Trust Interact During Extreme Events: Insights for Human Service Agencies and Organizations' (1998) 40 *Administration & Society* 621.

[26] J Jackson and B Bradford, 'What is Trust and Confidence in the Police?' (2010) 4(3) *Policing: A Journal of Policy and Practice* 241, 245.

police, can emerge from fair and respectful processes, independently (under some conditions at least) of the particular substantive outcomes achieved.[27] However, in relation to policing minority communities[28] and national communities deeply distrustful of police,[29] it is far from clear that procedural justice alone can work to build trust and confidence in policing. By analogy, the challenges faced by international policing missions may mean similarly that while procedural justice offers some useful tactics, more substantive measures will sometimes be required as well.

Here the concept of *calculative trust* seems pertinent. Calculative trust is trust based upon a calculation of costs and benefits of particular courses of action. As Child notes, this form of trust is particularly apt in the context of new relationships, and to the formation of new international strategic alliances such as typify most international policing missions.[30] In this form of trust, the assumptions about 'what can be taken for granted' by all parties are likely to be different, rather than shared.[31] Given enough time (a scarce and unlikely commodity for most missions) it might be possible to work towards something akin to normative trust, which 'depends on people sharing common values, including a common concept of moral obligation'.[32] However, this is a remote and probably unrealistic goal in many, if not most, mission settings given the often very different starting points between international and local players.

A. Degrees of (Dis)trust

As trust seems likely in many situations to be in short supply, part of the response needs to be identifying variations in openness to engagement with international policing missions, and establishing the levers or drivers behind those variations. Once these are understood, there will be a better basis for planning how to reduce distrust and increase trust. In this context, it is useful to consider a number of 'motivational postures' that can be displayed towards those seeking trust or at least compliance or cooperation.[33] As the

---

[27] TR Tyler, *Why People Obey the Law: Procedural Justice, Legitimacy and Compliance* (New Haven, CT, Yale University Press, 1990); M Hough, J Jackson, B Bradford, A Myhill and P Quinton, 'Procedural Justice, Trust, and Institutional Legitimacy' (2010) 4(3) *Policing: A Journal of Policy and Practice* 203.

[28] A Cherney and K Murphy, 'Understanding the Contingency of Procedural Justice Outcomes' (2011) 5(3) *Policing: A Journal of Policy and Practice* 228.

[29] Tankebe, above n 14.

[30] J Child, 'Trust and International Strategic Alliances: The Case of Sino-Foreign Joint Ventures' in C Lane and R Bachmann (eds), *Trust Within and Between Organizations: Conceptual Issues and Empirical Applications* (Oxford, Oxford University Press, 1998) 245.

[31] ibid, 243.

[32] ibid, 245.

[33] V Braithwaite, K Murphy and M Reinhart, 'Taxation Threat, Motivational Postures, and Responsive Regulation' (2007) 29(1) *Law & Policy* 137.

prevalence of distrust or at least an absence of trust would suggest, a variety of stances short of trusting cooperation with international policing personnel must be anticipated. In addition to *defiance*, forms of *game playing*, *resistance*, *disengagement*, *cooperation* and *capitulation* can be expected among local officials, citizens and institutions dealing with international policing missions. Many of the challenges experienced by our respondents can be interpreted in terms of these different postures. Overcoming forms of resistance is likely to involve, as noted earlier, building calculative trust in the first instance; establishing normative trust is likely to be a longer-term project. As seen in other areas of international development and security sector reform, the 'quick wins' approach—in the sense of 'providing immediately tangible benefits to the population'—in order to 'impact positively upon formal and informal political dynamics at all levels'[34] suggests that calculative approaches are probably inevitable at the start of most international policing missions as well.

When dealing with distrust, it has to be remembered that distrust is not always a bad thing. It can indeed often make sense. The East Timorese who hid in the jungles from the Indonesian police and militia in mid-1999 had good reason to do so. However, the residue of distrust is typically difficult to overcome: as Gambetta has noted, 'deep distrust is very difficult to invalidate through experience, for either it prevents people from engaging in the appropriate kind of social experiment or, worse, it leads to behaviour which bolsters the validity of distrust itself'.[35] This suggests that missions that are not proactive, and that are incapable or unwilling to quickly demonstrate qualities of competent service and impartiality, will continue to struggle against what is already a steep gradient in terms of building trust. In our discussion below, we report on what our respondents have said about overcoming residual distrust and building public confidence.

IV. THE RESEARCH

In this section, we draw upon data collected from recorded interviews with more than 120 Australian police who served in peacekeeping and/or capacity-building missions in the Solomon Islands, Timor-Leste and Papua New Guinea at some time in the period between 2003 and 2007.[36] When the interview schedules were initially devised, the themes of trust and trust

---

[34] Stabilisation Unit, *Stabilisation QIPs Handbook* (London, Stabilisation Unit, 2009).
[35] Gambetta, above n 19.
[36] To maintain confidentiality, participating officers are referred to only by interview number and location of mission/s. The authors acknowledge that further information such as length of service and rank (where applicable) would be interesting to readers; however we feel that inclusion of such information would make officers too easily identifiable.

building were not explicitly addressed or indeed anticipated by the research team. However later, upon examination of the transcripts, we noted that our respondents frequently resorted to the concept of trust in relating their experiences with local police and local people during their deployment. In other words, the concept appeared integral in terms of making sense of those experiences and, in particular, the characteristics of the settings in which they had been tasked to perform peacekeeping and capacity-building roles. In what follows therefore, rather than offering an analysis of data collected with specific research objectives designed around themes relevant to trust, we use the material that emerged suggestively to illuminate some of the themes of trust and trust building as they affect international policing missions. A focus on trust, we conclude, enables us as analysts to better grasp the nature of the experiences had by police personnel in these missions. This is important not just in terms of paying respect to those experiences, but also in terms of learning from these deployments in order to better prepare future personnel. It also allows an appreciation of the fact that the realisation of mission objectives is far more complex an achievement than simply 'sending the right people properly equipped and with the right set of instructions on what to do'. A focus on trust also takes us to the relational, non-technical aspects of international policing missions that have received little systematic attention from either policymakers or researchers to date.

The three countries covered by the research are small states close to Australia with GDP per capita below $US1400[37] and low human development.[38] Approximately even numbers of personnel had served in Timor-Leste (65) and the Solomon Islands (68), with a smaller number (35) having served in Papua New Guinea (and 15 in other missions not addressed in the interviews). As will be evident from these totals, approximately half of the participants had served in more than one of these locations. At the time of our interviews, Australian police postings in one location were approximately four months before being transferred elsewhere, though often within one mission, personnel might be moved several times. As our data reveals, this represents a challenge to building trustful relationships and the Australian Federal Police (AFP) has moved to longer postings in these kinds of missions.

The missions to these three nations were diverse. For the purposes of this chapter it is useful to point out, briefly, that Papua New Guinea hosted a short-lived (8-month) bilateral mission focused on police capacity-building; the Solomon Islands continues to host a multilateral mission established in 2003 consisting of regional advisers, police and army forces working first

---

[37] World Bank, *World Development Report* (Washington DC, World Bank, 2011).
[38] United Nations, *Human Development Report 2011: Sustainability and Equity—A Better Future for All* (New York, United Nations, 2011).

to stabilise and then to build capacity in a range of fields including policing. Since 2013, the mission has been police only. Timor-Leste has been host to a series of comprehensive United Nations missions, interspersed with stabilising missions under bilateral auspices, with police performing both in-line and capacity-building functions.

As might be expected, each of the settings in which our respondents served provided challenging contexts in which to work. The missions in Timor-Leste since 1999 followed a long and violent independence struggle, and institutions such as the police carried an association with Indonesian rule and thus community perceptions of prejudice and oppression.[39] One Australian police officer we interviewed reflected that 'some people ... had a lot of anger, residual anger about the military and the police. There was a perception of corruption and that'.[40] Similarly, a key reason for the establishment of the Regional Assistance Mission to Solomon Islands (RAMSI) was the breakdown of law and order and the paralysis of the country's government during the period from 2000 to 2003. Inevitably, this had resulted in severe compromises within the Royal Solomon Islands Police (RSIP) in terms of effectiveness, impartiality and legitimacy. Many of the police were identified with one ethnic grouping (Malaitans) during this period, so that members of other groups felt threatened by the police, even if they were not victimised, which many of them were. Hence it is not surprising that the difficulty of building public trust in these environments was discussed by many of the Australian officers who served there and encountered the legacy of past policing experiences.

V. TRUST IN OPERATIONAL POLICING

This section presents some key findings on trust in relation to operational policing. This notion had resonance among many of our respondents, informing how they viewed local attitudes towards their presence and policing contributions. Inevitably, it also shaped how they assessed the effectiveness and usefulness of their operations and the overall missions in which they participated.

A. Respondents' Reflections on Trust: Local Attitudes Towards International Policing Missions

In this part we discuss the willingness of local police and people, as seen through the eyes of our respondents, to show trust towards each other as

---

[39] ibid.
[40] Interview, R23.

well as towards international policing personnel. What was clear from our data was that each of the settings considered could be regarded as low-trust settings afflicted by inter-communal (social) distrust and distrust of authorities, both local and international.

A number of officers who served in the Solomon Islands reported that the community there had little trust in the local police at the outset of the mission, and that their first job was rebuilding this trust: 'we were there to maintain a policing presence and also to help start to rebuild confidence in the police themselves'.[41] Given the prior dysfunction and partisanship of the local police, the challenge in part was working out how to capitalise upon the high standing of international personnel in the early stages of the intervention in ways that worked towards, rather than against, restoring confidence in local police, which was a core mission objective. Recognising this low willingness to trust authorities among locals, many Australian police reported a proactive approach, in which 'we encouraged people [police] to get out amongst it and regain the community's appreciation and understanding through various strategic initiatives'.[42]

Providing local people with tangible, positive experiences of policing was viewed by many respondents as important:

[W]hilst on patrol if you were going past the hospital or through the markets, we would always have our windows down and ... the kids would come up and jump on the side of the car. If we had any left over ration packs we would—again it's only community policing—give them to the kids, the lollies, or have toys sent over and try to distribute those as equally as we could. You know we did that to the orphanages as well. We would always stop and chat to people, and again, just community policing. Raising your profile, getting known, getting the trust, getting the respect of the people, and engaging them.[43]

In the Solomon Islands, as is not uncommon in such missions, Australian police encountered significant community distrust towards their local police. According to R43, in the Solomon Islands,

the communities distrusted the RSIP. If you were aligned with the RSIP, you automatically went into that basket, and they'd pull you aside and say: 'Why are you talking to Sergeant So and So? He did this, this and this. Why hasn't he been locked up?'

The potentially harmful impact upon missions from a failure to address legacy issues is a real one in situations where hiring an entirely new cadre of police personnel is not feasible on political or other grounds. The limits of vetting procedures in terms of rooting out personnel with negative

[41] Interview, R24.
[42] Interview, R29.
[43] ibid.

associations to the previous era have been apparent in the case of Timor-Leste as well. Where, as often will be the case, the international police do not control or cannot always veto those readmitted into the reconstituted local police forces, there will be consequences both for how the international police presence is regarded and the prospects for establishing a more trustworthy local police.

In terms of building relationships with local police mainly in capacity-building exercises, it might be thought that an emerging international common normative commitment to professional policing might provide a foundation for relatively trustful relationships.[44] However, our data suggests that the extent of a 'brotherhood' developing across international policing missions and with local police remains limited. Whether it can emerge at all under mission conditions remains an open question. As we have noted elsewhere, such professional 'fellow feeling' was often in short supply among participating police forces serving in multilateral peacekeeping missions in Timor-Leste, creating a difficult working environment for those police.[45]

Establishing good relationships with local police can often be marred by persistent social divisions within the local community that are also reflected in the police force. Ethnic tensions within the local police in the Solomon Islands constituted a real difficulty, described by R55:

> [Y]ou could sort of see the underlying mistrust between some of the police, you know, about the Guadis not trusting the Malaitians, but still working alongside them and having jokes with one another and—but you knew sort of deep down they probably didn't really trust them, and some of them held resent from what had happened during the tensions, during the 2000—when they had the murders and that ... Now this person hadn't been brought to justice, but they're still working with them. But I guess they knew that while the RAMSI's there ... it's not going to blow up again ... [but] they didn't really trust them, or they harboured this resentment.

In Timor-Leste in 2005 and 2006, divisions emerged between 'Easterners' and 'Westerners' within the police force as well as the military and other institutions of government. These distinctions proved to be highly destructive to mission goals of building public confidence in the local police and its ability to provide an effective, professional service to the people. In Papua New Guinea divisions were observed between those who wanted change on the one hand, and those who did not on the other, though these were not based upon ethnic lines.

It can be too easy at times for international policing missions to ignore the webs of obligation in which local police officers live their lives which from

---

[44] M Deflem, *Policing World Society. Historical Foundations of International Police Cooperation* (Oxford, Oxford University Press, 2002).

[45] A Goldsmith and V Harris, 'Out of Step: Multilateral Police Missions, Culture and Nation-building in Timor-Leste' (2009) 9(2) *Conflict, Security & Development* 189.

an outsider's perspective can stand in the way of effective capacity-building. For those local officers inclined to support mission objectives there can be risks from other local elements. Reformers commonly face personal risks when tackling the status quo, and international policing contexts prove to be no exception.

As R45 reflected on the situation in Papua New Guinea,

> probably one of my biggest concerns [was] what's going to happen with those officers who had supported us [while we were there], when it was obvious that there were other officers out there running their own race and obviously [...] didn't want us there and still continued to go about doing what they wanted to do even though we were there.

While changes in administration usually produce some casualties, the uncertainty surrounding the length and success of international policing deployments means that local police officers will be taking major risks to themselves in aligning too closely with mission personnel and objectives. Some locals will try to 'play both sides of the street' while many will practise forms of non-compliance or provide only limited cooperation.[46] The answer to this dilemma, whatever it may be, clearly lies beyond the competence of individual international police personnel in particular relationships with local police. In the complex normative environments in which these missions often operate, ways of supporting local reform-inclined police are needed that reduce the risks faced by supportive local police. Securing local high-level endorsement for mission objectives methods is likely to be crucial in the longer term for allowing trust to develop, though it cannot be guaranteed.[47]

B. Trust Building with Local Police

In this part, we consider the approaches Australian police took to building individual relationships in their work settings. Interpersonal trust, as noted earlier, is important for building institutional trust. In the development literature scholars have pointed to the critical role that relationships play in capacity building.[48] One of our respondents, R5, echoed this, stating that

> I just found myself being frustrated about [various] things and, of course, it's one thing to say that but then the other side of the equation is to actually capacity

[46] Braithwaite, Murphy and Reinhart, above n 33.

[47] On Timor-Leste in particular, see: A Goldsmith and S Dinnen, 'Transnational Police Building: Critical Lessons from Timor-Leste and Solomon Islands' (2007) 28(6) *Third World Quarterly* 1091.

[48] See M Girgis, 'The Capacity-building Paradox: Using Friendship to Build Capacity in the South' (2007) 17(3) *Development in Practice* 353; A Kaplan, 'Capacity Building: Shifting the Paradigms of Practice' (2000) 10(3–4) *Development in Practice* 517.

build people to think of those things as well, and before you can do that you have to relationship build so they'll at least work with you in doing the processes.

Australian police respondents disclosed a range of tactics to demonstrate their trustworthiness to local police. Prime among these was 'get[ting] your hands dirty'[49]—that is, showing that they were willing to do the work too. This was particularly relevant in Papua New Guinea, where 'we were supposed to be advisers. We weren't supposed to be helping them with all the paperwork', but as R24 discovered,

> we felt a bit guilty sitting on our arse doing nothing, so we helped start with some of the paperwork and that's what helps form a better bond and friendship with our counterparts. Because we were prepared to do some of the other work with them not just watch.

Of course, as an example of a familiar paradox in capacity building, by getting involved directly in police work as part of the process of building trust, the goal of building capacity at the local level risks being compromised.

Australian police held a variety of expectations around relationship building. It is noteworthy that few respondents appeared to anticipate difficulties in setting up working relationships. It seemed to surprise many of the police we interviewed that they had to build relationships from the ground up with their local colleagues, and 'show you're worthy of respect'.[50] On the other hand, several interviewees noted that they couldn't assume that they started from a point of mutual respect. As R16 reflected, 'You can't be expected to win them over in a day because they're very wary of you and the way you are'. R6 conceded that,

> there was a lot of resistance from the police at that police station in relation to the people coming in. So it was about breaking down barriers initially you know. And trying to get them all on side, the police we were working with, before we could actually start working with them ... and the way to do that was to create friendships. That is the way I saw it anyway. It certainly wasn't to go in there with a big stick and wave it around, it was to create an environment of trust.

As noted at the beginning, we had not directly sought data on what trust building meant to our respondents. However, as trust was an operative concept for many of them, some indications emerged from our interviews. The importance of showing, and getting, *respect*, was mentioned by several respondents. 'It goes back to that thing about gaining their respect, and they won't tell you things unless they respect you'.[51] Getting the respect of local police was seen by some Australian officers as a precondition to effecting institutional change. R55 noted, for example,

---

[49] Interview, R54.
[50] Interview, R53.
[51] Interview, R40 Solomon Islands (SI).

I think that when they see how you operate and like I say, if you've got their respect and their trust and they say 'Oh yeah, that's—I see why you did that' or they look up to you and they try and emulate you.

It also created a relationship in which respectful critique could be given and responded to, in that 'you go in, look, listen, learn and once you get the relationship going then you might—then you'll be able to offer some suggestions'.[52]

One of the challenges faced by international police in building good relationships is the length of time available to do so. Just as the relationships with communities were fragile and changeable, relationships with police counterparts could be interrupted or derailed. Here, the impact of short rotations was evident. As R73 pointed out, mistakes could be very costly in terms of achieving the desired capacity-building outcomes:

Anyone can ride anyone out for fifteen weeks.[53] If they don't like you, they will just, they are a bit like snails, they will crawl back into their shell, sit and ride the storm out, when you leave, they pop their head out and think, 'right I wonder if I will get on with the next guy?' Understanding that and then coping and dealing with, you know. Making an effort to develop the relationship so that they don't crawl into their shells and turn off while you are there and just ride you out, um is probably the biggest, connecting with them is probably the hardest thing.

Being able to relate *personally* to professional local colleagues was seen by a number of respondents as important. Indeed, effecting professional change was seen as dependent upon good personal relationships by some. Seeing and managing the personal/professional distinction can be difficult in a domestic environment; it can be even trickier where one is operating cross-culturally in societies where there is typically less inclination to draw or see a bright line between the two realms. Respondents spoke of the importance of building *personal* relationships with the people with whom they work most closely. In many mission environments, separating professional from personal relationships is not just difficult; it can appear to undermine mission objectives. This personal aspect included finding out about their families and communities, and acknowledging the cultural demands on them—as for example when culture would demand that an officer should not confront a community member due to personal ties, which R21 addressed by giving local colleagues the opportunity to step down from particular cases where such conflict arose. Equally important was taking a genuine personal interest in their colleagues—indeed, according to R29, 'you could not have anything but a personal relationship with the RSIP. To try and keep a strictly

---

[52] Interview, R49.

[53] At the time of the interviews (2005–07), officers were generally deployed in three-month rotations, followed by a one-month break and redeployment to a different posting.

professional arm's length would not have worked. They are a very person-alised people'.

Examples of this included the obvious approach of asking about their family members and their life outside work, as well as less obvious ones like helping a colleague to fill in bureaucratic paperwork needed to enable a family member to travel to Australia for a funeral.[54] In fact, R54 noted that you build trust in the Solomon Islands the same way 'you do it anywhere else. Guys you work with, drink with, you talk with, you socialise with ... [and] You don't speak down to them'.

Trying to deal with the blurring of the professional and the personal con-fronted some respondents with acute dilemmas. At these moments, the diver-gence between local and mission values became apparent and a real obstacle to relationship building. At times Australian officers felt forced to choose between building trusting relationships with particular officers and compro-mising foundational Australian policing values. A vivid example of this was local police wanting to use police missions to gather food, for example, by fishing from the police boat, or using police vehicles for personal purposes. R46 explained some of the aspects of this dilemma as follows:

> [T]here are a lot of pressures on the police officers to [support their families and kinship groups], and how can you say no? ... Like how do you say, no you can't bring your fish back for your starving family; you'll have to work out some other way. It's just that, those things I found a little bit confronting at times because you have to try and keep the peace I suppose because if you said no, ... they would probably just not have a good relationship with me any more, so you have to draw the line somewhere ... It's very easy for us to say, but for the local police they could never understand why you took that stance.

Learning how to juggle these circumstances was a real operational challenge for many of our respondents. While often there will be no clear or at least easy answers to these dilemmas, the prevalence and difficulty of this type of challenge suggests that more could be done to prepare international police through cultural awareness training and ethical role-plays so as to provide them with a range of tactics for managing them.

The following example points to two somewhat contradictory aspects of good relationships with local police. The first is the operational dividend that can be had from having good relationships; the second is the fragility of influence over local officers, one that can disappear with the departure or absence of the international police officer concerned. R6, who served in Papua New Guinea, explained that once trust was established, there could be quite frank discussions about behavioural change:

> [T]here was [a philosophy] to shoot first and ask questions later and we would go to a specific task where there was a possibility that there would be shootings,

---

[54] Interview, R05.

so and I would implore these guys, okay we are not to shoot unless they shoot at us, ... [so] you would have to impress upon them the importance of not killing anybody especially while we were there because we would get the blame and you know if you had any respect for us, you wouldn't do it and that's were that friendship and trust and that built up to a point and they would go okay, well we are not going to kill anyone, we won't shoot anyone because we don't want you to get into trouble. Not because they don't want to do it, because they just didn't want to get us into trouble so okay.

The sustainability of such positive influences is obviously left open to question by this example. It points to the importance of building *effective impersonal controls*, as well as relying upon personal influence, if longer-term change is to be sustained and sustainable. Despite the difficulties they encountered, respondents stressed the importance of establishing trusting peer to peer relationships, and the benefits for both sides of working to achieve this.

C. Trust Building with the Local Community

More broadly, Australian police respondents attempted to break down distrust and scepticism locally by demonstrating that Australian police were friendly and trustworthy. As noted earlier, handing out sweets and food was one means of doing so. The reasons for building trust were practical as well as noble. Achieving a measure of trust, it was viewed, 'encouraged informants, it encouraged community support, we could go to safety levels, we could get our people amongst the community safely, we could start identifying with honing down where the trouble spots were so it has a lot of strategic gains'.[55] It was well recognised that 'engendering that confidence would then start to bring people back in to report crimes that we could then use to support our mission objectives about removing these key people'.[56]

A real challenge in a country like the Solomon Islands was balancing the executive policing undertaken by the international police alongside attempts to rebuild the RSIP, a force notorious locally for its partisanship and incompetence. Establishing or re-establishing (sometimes referred to as 'standing up') local police forces requires at some point acts of confidence in them by the international police working with them in situ. This requires in part also addressing the problems that had previously led them to being distrusted. This could mean confronting local power structures and customary hierarchical relationships in the community. R15 noted that

some of the local VIPs in the village areas didn't respect the young police officers at all ... in that these guys would be ranting and raving and waving their arms at

---

[55] Interview, R29.
[56] Interview, R61.

us [but] we'd say, 'no, we're not going anywhere', and that probably helped the local police a little bit, in that we weren't intimidated whereas they might have been.

As noted earlier, when local people are more inclined to seek and trust the services of international police personnel over those of local police, putting the local police forward in order to build their capacity may, for international police, mean incurring the wrath of local people.

One area of difficulty for international missions has been the *vetting of recruits* seeking to join the local police. In many cases, those seeking to join have questionable pasts as members of the previous police force or related to their role in the internal conflict that resulted in the international intervention. How vetting is managed can shape local perceptions of the effectiveness and impartiality of international police, as well as of the local force itself. This can occur when prior vetting of new recruits has not been carried out, or has been done hastily and in an incomplete and ineffective manner.[57] Senior UN police officers interviewed by the first author in Timor-Leste in late 2006 expressed the view that the attempt by the government there to 'stand up' the Policia Nacional de Timor-Leste (PNTL) after the 2006 crisis was proceeding too quickly and that sometimes former senior PNTL officers were being 'waved through' without sufficient regard to their criminal actions during the crisis. International police officers were concerned not just that 'bad' people were being hired for the new police but also that the failure to exclude some individuals would taint public perceptions of the new police institution.

Another challenge Australian police encountered on occasion was meeting local expectations about what model of policing should be instated. The difficulty arose when locals called for approaches to policing that were inconsistent with Australian preferred models. In Timor-Leste, for example, government ministers as well as other locals indicated on more than one occasion that the Australian approach was not tough enough in terms of what local problems of disorder required. This made Australian police less trustworthy in the eyes of some locals in terms of willingness to provide a sufficiently robust form of policing. This issue was captured by an officer who had served on several missions:

> [E]specially in Papua New Guinea and I noticed it more in East Timor, the people had a fear of the police. In PNG ... they [police] had no support from up top or

---

[57] It is very difficult to find extensive treatment of the police vetting issue in post-conflict settings in the policy or academic literatures. What occurs in practice too often reflects an international desire to restore local policing responsibility quickly, alongside an influential local interest in ensuring that favoured police are returned as soon as possible to the new institution, irrespective of their past misdeeds. As has been seen in Afghanistan and elsewhere, this can have fatal consequences for international police advisers as well as significant costs for others involved.

anywhere. There was just no guidance. And they wouldn't work so the people sort of had no respect for the police anyway, but they feared them because they knew that if they did the wrong they would get an absolute flogging. What I noticed over the time was they were starting to lose their fear of the police while we were there because the people knew that while we were there the people wouldn't get a flogging and I notice in East Timor, more to the point, the Australia and New Zealanders were sort of known to be soft, where the Portuguese that were there, knew—they—the locals knew that if they mucked up in front of them there would be a scene.[58]

This description echoes Mastrofski et al's notion of a vicious cycle of recip-rocal disrespect between police and policed in marginalised communities.[59] It also highlights the reality that, especially for international police, redress-ing or breaking out of such cycles is deeply complex.

These cultural differences also affected how Australian police came to view local people. In essence, they could undermine their ability to trust local people. Such perceptions can lead international police to question their own methods as well as whether the mission goals were indeed appreciated or shared among the local population. This, in turn, could justify a stance of caution and distrust. Setbacks in the security situation perversely but somewhat understandably appeared to do significant damage to Australian police's trust in the public. R16 reflected that police had to remain on their guard and not assume that they had achieved positive relationships, stating that 'In East Timor one minute, like, they're changing your car tyre and the next minute they're [throwing rocks at] you. So ... you don't trust the peo-ple'. This unpredictability or inconsistency could contribute to a stressful environment for officers who were used to being able to judge relationships and the dynamics of policing more accurately in Australia.[60]

Similarly, in the case of the large-scale civil disturbances in both the Solomon Islands and Timor-Leste in 2006, Australian police felt betrayed by the public, in that they were not informed of the pending unrest by any of their informants. R29 discussed this clearly, saying:

The only difficulty came after the riots where you couldn't cross the personal [inaudible] the major balance of society that was rioting and causing problems by stoning you and throwing machetes at you and so on and so forth. So the problem was it was great up to the riots and a significant amount of respect and trust was lost post riots and you never knew who you trusted, therefore it took a long time to rebuild the confidence to trust locals, because during the riots you felt that everybody was against you.

[58] Interview, R17.
[59] S Mastrofski, M Reisig and J McCluskey, 'Police Disrespect Toward the Public: An Encounter-Based Analysis' (2002) 40(3) *Criminology* 519.
[60] A Goldsmith, 'It Wasn't Like Normal Policing: Australian Police Peacekeepers in Operation Serene, Timor-Leste 2006' (2009) 19 *Policing & Society* 119.

Apparent inconsistencies of attitude, and failures to provide intelligence in a timely fashion, predictably undermine feelings of being trusted by locals. Setbacks of this kind might then harden attitudes towards local people and counterparts. Rather than seeing these actions by locals as indications of distrust, it might be more productive to try to put them into context, in part by a deeper appreciation of the sometimes conflicting claims upon loyalty that can arise in ethnically divided societies emerging from periods of internal conflict. A robustness of attitude, informed by a *tragic view of the possibilities of change in particular settings*, would not seem inappropriate, and even could be seen as desirable or a necessary survival skill for overseas service. Muir describes the tragic view as

> a philosophy which holds that good and bad inhere in each of us, that self-control is an important but not exclusive determinant of man's fate, and that life is meaningful only if we give a damn about others, no matter how such concern hurts.[61]

It is, Muir indicates, an antidote to the cynicism that too readily can emerge in police officers. Meeting local distrust with distrust from members of the mission seems certain to further undermine existing relationships and the pursuit of mission objectives. Encouragingly, our respondents showed little evidence of resentment impacting on their actions. In dealing with and building trust from the public, they arguably demonstrated both commitment and forbearance. Despite setbacks, they continued to work in this way—if perhaps more warily than before.

Some respondents recognised the need for tolerance and indeed a degree of forbearance, towards local partners, attitudes consistent with a tragic frame of mind. Regarding Timor-Leste, R58 spoke of the persistent determination sometimes required to maintain this approach:

> I treat people with dignity and respect ... so I don't ever recall thinking 'I'll never get through to these people or whatever', there were—of course there were moments of frustration where I didn't understand what was going on or things that they wanted were in conflict to things that I needed to do, but that's just—you've just got to go with that. You've just got to tolerate that. That's what missions are all about. You're never going to get everything you want, it's never going to happen in the time that you expect it to, and you just have to deal with the contingencies.

Such an attitude at least leaves open the possibility of future change while crucially preserving the relationship upon which such change is likely to depend.

Finally, underlying the attitudes on all sides of these relationships are the circumstances that gave rise to the mission in the first place. It almost goes without saying that most international police entering a country such as Timor-Leste in the early 2000s would presume that the country is in dire

---

[61] WK Muir, 'Police and Politics' (1983) 2 *Criminal Justice Ethics* 3.

need of assistance in respect of (but not necessarily limited to) its policing arrangements. Thus, international police would expect, as some comments earlier indicated, that there would be recognition among locals of this situation and that consequently there would be broad public appreciation for their presence and assistance. In addition to the local political complexities that can deliver a lack of local consensus and support for such missions, there is also the fact that the provision of executive policing or capacity building strongly suggests a *deficit in local policing*. While, as in the Solomon Islands, many local people would agree with such an assessment, it cannot be consistently expected not just from those police receiving help, but also from those who saw their interests as well served by previous policing arrangements.

Many of our respondents admitted to holding a generally negative perception of local capacity, identifying their particular counterparts as exceptions to this rule.[62] The fact that some respondents were able to distinguish their immediate counterparts from a more generalised negative assessment at least leaves open ways of working constructively with local counterparts. Challenging the assumption of the relative incompetence of local police is inherently difficult given mission objectives in most instances. However, encouraging international police to focus on local officers willing to learn, but also seeking to identify and develop their existing strengths, are likely to be important in tackling this conundrum facing international missions.

VI. CONCLUSION

Rebuilding public trust in policing is fundamental to re-establishing a relatively peaceful environment in places previously afflicted with deep civil disorder and violence. This was a goal that many of our respondents understood and shared:

> [F]or us it was about re-establishing that community confidence. It is getting them to understand that it was safe again in their community. They were not going to be subject to the terrorisation that they had been subject to by the militant groups, that they could walk the street safely, that they could have confidence again in the police and engendering that confidence would then start to bring people back in to report crimes that we could then use to support our mission objectives about removing these key people.[63]

This chapter has taken for granted the general value of there being local trust in international policing missions, both from the populace as well as

---

[62] See V Harris, 'Building on Sand? Australian Police Involvement in International Capacity Building' (2010) 20(1) *Policing & Society* 79.
[63] Interview, R61.

from local police. As noted earlier, for us, it was significant and revealing that so many respondents chose to account for their experiences on mission in terms of the language of trust. Sometimes it was as an ideal that they found valuable but elusive in practice, at other times it was something that individual officers were able to build and that made their work meaningful and even effective.

Even so, the data suggests that much more needs to be done before these missions can claim to offer, or to build, resilient trustworthy police forces in these settings. Jackson and Bradford describe a trustworthy police force in the following terms:

> [It] is seen by the public to be effective, to be fair, and to have shared values, interests, and a strong commitment to the local community ... Trust extends beyond narrow public assessments that police perform their duties effectively and efficiently to include a sense that the police understand the needs of the community, that they treat people fairly and with dignity, that they give them information, and that they allow members of the community a voice to highlight local problems.[64]

It is clear that part of what is required is to recognise and take account of the different 'motivational postures' that emerge among participants in these settings. Identifying differences will enable different strategies to be developed for dealing with them. Just as we should not assume all locals will welcome these missions, we should also be alert to differences in the international policing components, both at the unit and the individual officer levels. Rather than expecting normative trust to emerge out of situations of grave necessity or emergency, we might look more to the kinds of assistance that build calculative trust. It has to be remembered that often attempts to build trust must also reckon with the negative legacy of past governance and policing arrangements. So overcoming distrust, as well as building trust, will often be required. Stronger, clearer lines of accountability for the past crimes of local police, as well as for current and future actions of international police, can contribute to this goal.

In terms of understanding trust in these settings, collecting complementary data from local people and police is vital. In our study, we did not capture the views of those local police and members of the community with whom they had contact. A more complete dataset would have sought to include their views in order to explore when trust is extended and what features of missions led to greater trustworthiness. It could also have made it possible to directly gauge the different kinds of motivational dispositions towards peacekeeping and capacity-building objectives indicated in some of the recent literature.[65]

---

[64] Jackson and Bradford, above n 26, 245.
[65] Braithwaite, Murphy and Reinhart, above n 33.

More can be done in future to prepare international police personnel to anticipate the range of difficulties reported by our respondents, and to provide them with strategies for coping with them. In preparing police personnel for future overseas deployments, efforts are needed to ensure that expectations in terms of local reception and cooperation are not unrealistically high. More emphasis should be given to local language capabilities and cultural understanding. The inability to communicate with local people remains a common obstacle to building trust as well as 'getting things done'. Mission timescales of a few months' duration or even one year will continue to work against trust building.

The future of international policing missions, as indicated by the record from the past and the present, lies in responding effectively in low-trust settings. International missions need to be planned and implemented in ways that are more cognisant of the nature of the trust-related problems facing missions on the ground and that are more successful in building cooperation, collaboration and ultimately functional and enduring forms of trust among the affected parties. They themselves need to be trustworthy institutions—competent, impartial and beneficent in providing protection and building effective local policing. Setting the parameters correctly for building institutional trust, by involving clear expectations around mission objectives and responsibilities and ensuring that other governance arrangements support these objectives, is an important contextual task that will enable the building of interpersonal trust at the ground level. Both forms of trust are so important to building mission success in their key areas of responsibility: peacekeeping and capacity building.

Part II

Trust and International Cooperation Agencies

5

Trusted Travellers: Managing Mobility in Challenging Times

MONICA DEN BOER

I. INTRODUCTION

THIS CHAPTER ADDRESSES the subject of 'trust' in the area of international (particularly European) border management practices. The objective is to scrutinise the concept of the 'trusted traveller' against the backdrop of newly arising security challenges in the fields of terrorism, organised crime and irregular migration. The concept of the trusted traveller demands the negotiation and maintenance of a variety of trust relationships. One important dimension of this trust relationship is of a vertical nature: the trusted traveller has to be trusted by a heterogeneous group of public and private actors who wield formal power on behalf of national governments. The vertical relationship also involves trust of the traveller in the professional performance and actions of these public and private authorities. Moreover, the operationalisation of the trusted traveller concept involves a horizontal trust relationship between sectors and jurisdictions. Inter-sectoral trust involves the agents of different organisations, both public and private, from border control to law enforcement, while internationally, relations and interactions will require multidisciplinary cooperation between a variety of agencies across national boundaries. I suggest that the status of 'trusted traveller' is also anything but static: it is a dynamic relationship in which the status of trusted traveller has to be tested and reconfirmed at regular intervals.

The question this chapter thus seeks to address is what makes the trusted traveller concept tick: which political, managerial, technological and professional conditions have to be met in order to meet the challenges of modern day mobility? How does the trusted traveller concept marry the contradictory need for maximum efficiency with the need for maximum security? How is trust in this context negotiated? In this chapter, the primary focus is upon the mediation of vertical and horizontal relationships of trust. First, looking closely at the evolution of the trusted traveller concept in the context of border control, before disentangling the concept of border control allows us to perceive the trusted traveller from the perspective of a dynamic semiotic interaction between sign, signifier and signified, which forms the basis of a vertical and horizontal trust relationship. Second, as risk and pre-emption are pivotal elements in the trusted traveller concept, the close connection between the precautionary principle and the management of mobility is described. In order to map the field, an inventory of existing and operational trusted traveller programmes is then detailed, with a focus on how these programmes are evolving in the context of the European Union (EU), with an emphasis on the role of Frontex, the EU Agency for the Management of External Border Controls. In order to disaggregate the machinery of international travel, the layers of mobility management are also analysed. All of these build to identify the four conditions that have to be met in order to make the trusted traveller concept tick, namely political trust, managerial trust, technological trust and professional trust. Finally, the question of whether the trusted traveller concept is the best approach to the management of modern global mobility will be reflected upon.

II. TRUSTED TRAVELLERS AND TRANSFORMATIVE BORDERS

The exercise of border control can be considered one of the ultimate powers of the nation state. Traditionally, the state is regarded as the holder of exclusive authority over the entry of non-nationals. Border controls are (still) the most important remedy at hand for the management of mobility of persons and goods across the national border. This rests on the (fictional) assumption that the borders are perfect filters against crime and irregular migration.[1] However, borders may be porous in nature: they are permeable. To 'close' the borders or vice versa to 'abolish border controls' (eg, in the context of the Schengen Agreement) evokes a fiction that all movement of people, goods and flows can be fully controlled.

This assumption about the symbiosis between state sovereignty and the borders of sovereign nations can be called into question in the context of increasing globalisation.[2] As the interdependency between states and markets is growing, states can no longer claim a 'pure' form of border governance, which is exemplified by practices in the EU, where Member States

---

[1] M den Boer, 'The Quest for International Policing: Rhetoric and Justification in a Disorderly Debate' in M Anderson and M den Boer (eds), *Police Co-operation across National Boundaries* (London, Pinter, 1994); M den Boer, 'How to Police a Porous Fortress? Evolving Practices in Policing Europe's Borders' (2013) 1(1) *European Journal of Police Studies* 2, 20.

[2] S Sassen, *Losing Control?: Sovereignty in an Age of Globalization* (New York, Columbia University Press, 1996) xv; see also M Bosworth, 'Border Control and the Limits of the Sovereign State' (2008) 17(2) *Social & Legal Studies* 199.

have developed a common regime for the management of external border controls at land, air and maritime borders.

To some extent, the management of borders has been outsourced to private entities, for instance when it concerns surveillance infrastructure, airline carriers, security controllers. Hence, the creation of the trusted traveller is not merely in the hands of government authorities,[3] but governments themselves have heavily contributed to an agenda of liberalisation, privatisation and 'responsibilisation'.[4] Given the partial privatisation of border controls, it is not just the relationship between the traveller (citizen) and the state, but also that between the traveller as consumer and the company, which needs to be accounted for. The notion of the trusted traveller itself can be considered an ambiguous notion because the granting of this status is dependent on different actors and authorities. The border is a signifier of state authority: once crossed, the sovereignty of that state declines.[5] Being granted the status of legitimate traveller involves border control and thus the determination of the authenticity of a passport.[6]

Airports for instance are 'vital and vulnerable nodes in the global mobility regime',[7] presenting different actors with a range of different dilemmas and pressures. Public and private actors pass judgements on passengers and these travellers in turn have no option but to acknowledge the rites (rights) of passage and to obey the instructions. There are 14 steps in a traveller's journey through an airport, which can be quite a stressful experience. Passengers are whisked through like cattle through a corridor. Airports themselves are nodes in networks, representing an encompassing security logic, which has been built incrementally and hence is not always coherent. Screening areas operate where travellers are distinguished between the good and the bad, the rational and the mindless, the regular and the irregular, the experienced and naive passengers. Passport reading involves the technology of identification. There, in the screening area, a lot of interpreting and discretionary decision-making takes place, based on a collage of images.[8]

---

[3] MB Salter, 'The Global Airport: Managing Space, Speed and Security' in MB Salter (ed), *Politics at the Airport* (Minneapolis, University of Minnesota Press, 2008) 2.

[4] D Garland, *The Culture of Control. Crime and Social Order in Contemporary Society* (Oxford, Oxford University Press, 2002).

[5] BJ Muller, 'Borders, Risks, Exclusions' (2009) 3(1) *Studies in Social Justice* 67.

[6] MB Salter, *Rights of Passage: The Passport in International Relations* (Boulder, CO, Lynne Riener, 2003).

[7] Salter, 'The Global Airport', above n 3, 1.

[8] M Tiessen, 'Being Watched Watching Watchers Watch: Determining the Digitized Future While Profitably Modulating Preemption (at the Airport)' (2011) 9(1–2) *Surveillance & Society* 167, 176, 177, available at library.queensu.ca/ojs/index.php/surveillance-and-society/article/viewFile/modulating/modulating.

Border controls are the subject of gradual repositioning, away from the liminal border.[9] As well as privatisation, there is a relocation of borders and border controls,[10] even to the extent that they are being 'off-shored',[11] for instance in the form of detention centres in countries with which the EU has concluded readmission agreements. Hence, we are witnessing the transformation of hard and static geographical borders to fluid, sophisticated and technological borders. Borders themselves have become more mobile (portable borders), facilitating 'border control' by means of the monitoring of devices that can be tagged and tracked. Border surveillance may consist of a chain of actors and activities subjecting persons, goods and transactions to monitoring, control and intervention. Hence, the border is also moving *within* this chain of actors and actions.[12] According to Salter,[13] the border becomes disaggregated and de-territorialised. Border control involves the politics of (inclusion and) exclusion,[14] which is particularly relevant nowadays in view of radicalised individuals who are travelling across national borders. Trusted traveller programmes encourage the 'stratification of mobility', based on the argument that:

On the one hand, 'trusted' traveller programs, through automation of the border crossing contribute to the acceleration of mobility for a group of people who have access to capital (these programs come more often than not at an extra cost), and European citizenship. Biometrics render the border crossing smoother and faster. For the group of people who however do not possess a European passport, or do not come from a country which benefits from facilitated entry procedures, the 'biometric border' becomes a site of deceleration and increased control, starting at the consulates of the EU member states, where more information and more burden of proof is put on potential migrants in order to obtain the Schengen Visa. But the differentiated relation to speed should not be mistaken for a differentiated relation to liberty.[15]

[9] MB Salter, 'At the Threshold of Security: A Theory of International Borders' in E Zureik and MB Salter (eds), *Global Surveillance and Policing. Borders, Security, Identity* (Cullompton, Willan Publishing, 2005) 38.
[10] See, eg, N Vaughan-Williams, 'Off-shore Biopolitical Border Security: The EU's Global Response to Migration' in L Bialasiewicz (ed), *Europe in the World. EU Geopolitical and the Making of European Space* (Aldershot, Ashgate, 2011); N Vaughan-Williams, *Border Politics. The Limits of Sovereign Power* (Edinburgh, Edinburgh University Press, 2009).
[11] Vaughan-Williams, 'Off-shore Biopolitical Border Security', above n 10.
[12] M den Boer, 'How to Police a Porous Fortress? Evolving Practices in Policing Europe's Borders (2013) 1(1) *European Journal of Police Studies* 2.
[13] MB Salter, *Politics at the Airport* (Minneapolis, University of Minnesota Press, 2008).
[14] Muller, above n 5, 67; see also H Van Houtum, 'Human Blacklisting: The Global Apartheid of the EU's External Border Regime' (2010) 28 *Environment and Planning D: Society and Space* 957.
[15] A Amicelle, D Bigo, J Jeandesboz and F Ragazzi, 'Catalogue of Security and Border Technologies at Use in Europe Today' (2009) INEX Deliverable D.1.2., Centre d'études sur les Conflits, FP7 Project, Converging and Conflicting Ethical Values in the Internal/External Security Continuum in Europe (INEX), available at www.prio.org/PageFiles/1520/INEX_D_1_2.pdf.

The authors observe the evolution of mobility management as 'more control with less awareness of it, and increased possibility of control at a distance'.[16] According to Amoore,[17] the bodies of travellers themselves become 'sites of multiple encoded borders'.

Border controls are also 'thickening'[18] as they evolve from pre-check to post-check, from different actors (public and private) as well as in kind (not just the person, but also his luggage and travel itinerary for instance). The scrutiny of a space (the physical border) may be intensified by a layering of technical controls that overlap or may have an interface. Moreover, the knowledge about travellers and the goods and finances they may carry is accumulative, achieved by the multiplication of data sources.[19] Border controls are also thickening in terms of telos (ie, the objective or purpose for which the control takes place): quadruple thickening (4D development). This involves the portability and mobility of borders themselves: transgressing the border happens transversally, for example, booking a ticket and subjecting to a pre-screening process already begins at home or in the office, where a ticket is being booked.[20] Hence, borders are on the move and border control is subject to the following transformations:

— From national to international, and even global.
— From static to mobile.
— From physical to virtual (from paper to biometrics).[21]
— From public to private (public–private—hybrid).
— From liminal to pre-liminal (and post-liminal).[22]
— From human-handled to automated.[23]
— From general to discriminate.
— From person-oriented to data-oriented.
— From single agency to multiple agency interaction.
— From outside to inside (from verification of identity to verification of intentions).[24]

---

[16] ibid, 15–16.
[17] L Amoore, 'Biometric Borders: Governing Mobilities in the War on Terror' (2006) *Political Geography* 336, 336.
[18] Muller, above n 5, 67.
[19] Amicelle et al, above n 15, 13.
[20] S Pickering and L Weber, 'Policing Transversal Borders' in K Franko Aas and M Bosworth (eds), *The Borders of Punishment. Migration, Citizenship, and Social Exclusion* (Oxford, Oxford University Press, 2013) 94.
[21] Commission Decision C(2006)2909 of 28 June 2006 establishing the biometric characteristics of travel documents issued by EU Member States.
[22] Salter, 'At the Threshold of Security', above n 9.
[23] By means of the introduction of Machine Readable Travel Documents (MRTD): see Amicelle et al, above n 15, 9.
[24] For instance, biometric technologies that are applied for the purpose of border control are evolving from physiological to behavioural measurement, such as emotional recognition, the computing of human gait, voice recognition, keystroke dynamics and signature: Amicelle et al, above n 15.

— From differentiated (local, regional, national) to internationally standardised (convergence).[25]
— From individual professional discretion to technologically supported advisory function.
— From focused on irregular migration to a filter against crime and terrorism (in the EU discourse).
— From government-owned to traveller-responsible.

III. UNPEELING THE LAYERS OF THE TRUSTED TRAVELLER CONCEPT

The changing management of mobility has been consciously and deliberately underpinned by an intelligence-based strategy. While all persons are nomadic (in space and in time), criminal activity, criminals and criminal goods are considered to be constantly on the move and morphing,[26] rendering static strategies of law enforcement redundant. In addition, cost-effectiveness demands a constant 'weighing of odds', so that equal resources are not applied to all passengers and all bags.[27] A balance must be struck between the importance of security versus the importance of efficiency of border controls.[28] Hence, intelligence algorithms form the basis for decision-making within border control environments. Data, surveillance and infrastructure are indispensable elements of a layered system in which the traveller is tested, tried and eventually (not) trusted.

First, border controls have an important data dimension. It is impossible to know exactly how much and what kind of data are collected on travelling individuals and how long it is retained or how far it is shared. The individual traveller becomes 'objectified' in the form of a (digital) dossier or even different dossiers, which are held by a variety of actors. Lyon calls this phenomenon the 'phenetic fix' to describe the trend whereby 'personal data triggered by human bodies' are captured and used to create abstractions of people and subject them to classification in different categories.[29] Second, the traveller is subject to a surveillance dimension: different devices that

---

[25] Mainly realised by means of common training standards, a Community code on the rules governing the movement across borders, as well as the alignment with international ICAO standards, which introduces passive radio-frequency information (RFID). However, the production of machine computable information in the form of templates is not standardised throughout the European Union.

[26] den Boer, 'How to Police a Porous Fortress?', above n 12, 5.

[27] RW Poole and G Passantino, 'A Risk-Based Airport Security Policy' Policy Study no 308 (Los Angeles, Reason Public Policy Institute, 2003), available at www.rppi.org.

[28] Salter, 'The Global Airport', above n 3.

[29] D Lyon, 'Editorial. Surveillance Studies: Understanding Visibility, Mobility and the Phenetic Fix' (2002) 1(1) *Surveillance & Society* 1, 3, available at www.surveillance-and-society.org/articles1/editorial.pdf.

place a traveller under surveillance. In addition to the data flows, there may be various ways in which the traveller, his or her goods and transfers, may be watched and filtered.[30] Third, the traveller is subject to an infrastructural dimension of borders, particularly the visual and spatial segregation between different lanes of entry, which forces people to move in discrete flows. This infrastructural dimension is not just physical, but also virtual, demonstrated for example, by no-fly lists. The latter function on the basis of programmes which are supposed to enhance the security of domestic and international commercial air travel, by means of watch-list matching and additional data collection, seen in the US Secure Flight Program.

In response to the challenges of uncontrolled mobility of persons, the EU has created numerous databases, most of which have been designed for border control and mobility management.[31] These databases include the Schengen Information System (SIS), a networked system holding numerous details relating to citizens, created to maintain public policy and public security, for instance by centralising data on third-country nationals to be refused entry to the EU; Eurodac, which is the EU database that holds fingerprints of asylum seekers; and VIS, which is the Visa Information System, the latter being designed as a multipurpose tool for the administration of visa-application and the prevention of visa-'shopping' and visa-fraud.[32] The Customs Information System (CIS) was one of the first to be created; however with a relatively small storage of active cases and only five EU Member States actively contributing to it[33] the CIS hardly plays a significant role in the data flow on mobile goods. In addition, the EU has affected a series of instruments that make it possible to store, retain, retrieve and transfer data for the purpose of security. In particular, one may think of the Passenger Name Record (PNR) instrument that has been concluded with other jurisdictions; the Terrorist Finance Tracking Programme (TFTP); the Directive on the Retention of Telecommunication, and various other measures. The rapid expansion of data systems calls into question who owns the data. When one takes the SIS as an example, numerous different authorities are responsible for procuring and using the data, varying from law enforcement to immigration officials. While it is not the prime focus of this chapter, this evokes a blurring of data ownership,[34] and with that, a blurring of privacy rights from the perspective of the traveller.

---

[30] D Lyon, 'Filtering Flows, Friends, and Foes: Global Surveillance' in M Salter (ed), *Politics at the Airport* (Minneapolis, University of Minnesota Press, 2008).

[31] F Geyer, 'Taking Stock: Databases and Systems of Information Exchange in the Area of Freedom, Security and Justice' CEPS Challenge Paper No 9/2008, available at www.liberty-security.org/IMG/pdf_Databases_and_Systems_of_Information_Exchange_in_the_Area_of_Freedom_Security_and_Justice.pdf.

[32] Amicelle et al, above n 15, 19.

[33] Geyer, above n 31, 5.

[34] Geyer, above n 31, 6.

The 'trusted traveller' can thus be deconstructed as a cluster of data that uniquely belong to a certain individual and which are trusted by a range of actors who are authorised to pass on a judgement on the veracity of these data. Hence, what we observe are the dynamics of a semiotic triangular interaction between 'trustee' (government and private authorities), 'trusted' (the travelling individual) and 'trustings' (the data which are linked to the individual). In semiotic terms, the trusted individual (or profile) is the signified, the trusting authority is the signifier and the authorisation(s) are signs of being trusted. The status of being 'trusted' changes continuously as the traveller's credibility is subject to reauthorisation with each new itinerary. This dynamic may lead to multiple interpretations.[35] Thus a 'coding' or signification process takes place every time a traveller is confronted with a new trustee. This semiotic interaction is compressed into a biometric border, which itself is capable of a performative linguistic act. The (granted) status of 'trusted traveller' can even be auto-generated on the basis of predefined risk-categories.

The traveller is not merely subject to being trusted by a range of public and private actors, but is also the subject of trusting. In fact, the trusted traveller principle relies on a reciprocal relationship of trust. In combination with the prevalence of risk-based, pre-emptive politics, the citizens have to trust that politicians, security experts and those responsible for border control, immigration and law enforcement understand the future and can even make predictions on what constitutes a real or potential threat.[36] For instance, a range of actors is involved in electronic passports (developers, manufacturers, inspectors, border officials) and a weakness in the chain of actors and actions may produce a serious security issue for the traveller, ie, the holder of the passport. Think for instance of the lack of security standards, lack of integrity or training among security officials, lack of incident reporting, lack of physical security through the transportation of the passports etc. *Ipso facto*, a similar chain of actors, actions and potential security hazards applies to the use of other security technologies, such as cameras and body scanners. Hence, the trustworthiness of actors, actions and technologies depends upon the contract with the trusted traveller. Border control demands absolute and unwavering integrity along the whole chain.

In Europe, a significant hazard from the perspective of both traveller and government authorities is actually that the process of issuing passports is not harmonised throughout the EU. Moreover, there is a lack of standardisation in data protection practices. A crucial element of the traveller's trust in the authorities is the handling of data, ie, the protection of the privacy of the traveller (data integrity and data protection). As a consequence of absent

---

[35] For a treatise on ambiguity, see Amoore, above n 17, 351.
[36] Tiessen, above n 8, 172.

or weak standardisation, several individual rights may be under pressure, including human rights and personal privacy. Border controls should not be discriminatory, degrading or humiliating. The notion of the trusted traveller rests on the logic of (un-)suspicion.

The holder of the body, identity and data—ie, the travelling individual— has no choice but to be subjected to biometric scanning. The body does not play an active but a passive role and can only be subject of signifying by a (technological and human) signifier. This subtle technique of governmentality subjects all travellers to a great deal of screening prior to being granted access.[37] Unless a traveller decides to travel across control-free passages, a traveller is mainly regarded as a passive subject of control. Moreover, the holder of the body and the identity has to be cooperative and data-ready; if not she or he may be denied the rights of passage. The traveller is forced to comply with this border control regime. This means that the conduct of the traveller is geared towards regularisation. As Button claims, security systems are about power and getting people to behave in a certain way.[38]

With the onset of virtual technology, privatisation and liberalisation, the traveller is made responsible for a good deal of self-securitisation: she or he is responsible for having the right documents, for entering it through the ticketing system, for pre-flight security clearance, for offering digital photographs and fingerprints, for passing through detection devices and for behaving appropriately at border crossing points.[39] In the domain of border management, the 'culture of control'[40] is nearly perfected, at least in terms of self-responsibilisation. The trusted travellers develop into a category of people that belong to a privileged group, which is established through the principle of inclusiveness; in fact it comes down to membership for which a submission has taken place to the regime of biopolitics.[41] In order to achieve the privileged status of the trusted traveller, the traveller has to strip down and is temporarily deprived of his or her individuality. This compares strongly with Ervin Goffman's concepts around stigmata,[42] whereby labelling and categorisation lay the basis for distinguishing the 'discredited' from the 'discreditable' and institutional control over the individual

---

[37] MA Peters, 'Neoliberal Governmentality: Foucault on the Birth of Biopolitics' in S Weber and S Maurer (eds), *Gouvernementalität und Erziehungswissenschaft* (Wiesbaden, VS Verlag für Sozialwissenschaften, 2006).

[38] M Button, *Doing Security: Critical Reflections on an Agenda for Change. Crime Prevention and Security Management* (Basingstoke, Palgrave Macmillan, 2008) 144.

[39] T Vukov and M Sheller, 'Border Work: Surveillant Sssemblages, Virtual Fences, and Tactical Counter-media' (2013) 23(2) *Social Semiotics* 225.

[40] Garland, above n 4.

[41] Amoore, above n 17, 343.

[42] E Goffman, *Stigmata: Notes on the Management of Spoiled Identity* (New York, Touchstone, 1985).

(de-individualisation through stripping).[43] The trusted traveller-to-be has to subject himself or herself to a digital stripping exercise in which invisible adjudicators categorise the stigmata of each candidate traveller.

The traveller becomes a composition or collage of different attributed characteristics, particularly facial images and fingerprints, but also iris recognition. Passports contain facial images. Facial metric systems and *eigenfaces* produce a 'template', which is processed information which becomes 'the electronic double of the facial image':[44] the template can be stored in a database and can be exchanged and matched against a picture taken at the border. Fingerprints can be turned into computable data and can be acquired through a range of sensor technologies.[45]

Membership is partially voluntary and partially compulsory[46] and hence ambiguous. One could also argue that trusted traveller schemes demand from the traveller that she or he becomes complicit to the pre-emptive inspection regime, by subjugating himself or herself to the dismembering of the inspection process.[47] The traveller has been made responsible for 'self-policing' and 'self-governance'; he or she 'establishes a low risk rating'.[48] The traveller is thus turned into a vigilant and responsible individual.[49] Core associations of the trusted traveller are: privileged, approved, documented, pre-screened, desirable, certified, checked, legitimate, entitled to rights (and rites of passage), normal (not deviant), virtuous, no-risk. The trusted traveller is also subject to a form of positive framing, which happens primarily through language: the expression of trust is a performative speech-act,[50] as it actually involves the passing of trust from one individual to another individual or entity.[51] Border control should be seen as a 'verb': bordering, ordering and othering are the three processes that constitute the act of inclusion versus exclusion.[52] The determination of the authenticity of a passport or valid(ated) travel document is crucial in that the passport has acting power towards the bearer and the interpreter.[53] In addition, the data

---

[43] E Goffman, *The Presentation of Self in Everyday Life* (Edinburgh, University of Edinburgh, 1956), available at monoskop.org/images/1/19/Goffman_Erving_The_Presentation_of_Self_in_Everyday_Life.pdf.

[44] Amicelle et al, above n 15, 10.

[45] ibid.

[46] M Leese, 'Blurring the Dimensions of Privacy? Law Enforcement and Trusted Traveler Programs' (2013) 29(5) *Computer Law & Security Review: The International Journal of Technology and Practice* 480.

[47] Tiessen, above n 8, 181.

[48] Amoore, above n 17, 343.

[49] ibid, 346.

[50] Compare the Copenhagen School of Barry Buzan et al who regard 'securitisation' as a performative speech-act, which is a concept derived from the linguistic philosopher JL Austin for words that actually change things; hence which transform one situation into another.

[51] See also Muller, above n 5, 69.

[52] Van Houtum, above n 14, 959.

[53] Salter, *Rights of Passage*, above n 6.

that are in the chip on the passport have to be authenticated in the sense that it should be verified whether the data stem from the official issuing authority.[54]

Once the traveller has been granted the status of 'trusted' individual, she or he may enjoy a variety of privileges of the trusted traveller which may include fast-track boarding (no waiting lines), a less intrusive kind of questioning or no questioning at all, and identification on the basis of a few pre-screened characteristics. Having been given the status of 'trusted traveller' means that one may receive expedited processing at airports.[55] Enjoying the status of a trusted traveller rests on a contractual agreement between the holder of that status and the granting authority, for instance that the traveller declares that she or he has submitted 'true data' about himself or herself. The determination of the veracity of the trusted traveller is thus subject to a so-called 'pre-clearance process'. The emphasis is increasingly on 'happy', 'relaxed' or 'comfortable' travelling, which involves the redesign of security control locations at airports such as Schiphol Airport Amsterdam,[56] where travellers step through only one 'security filter'. Security checks are made to feel as a service towards the traveller. This development should however be analysed in conjunction with the increased importance of information, risk management and biometrics in the process of border control, which—as mentioned before—happens long before, during as well as after the physical passage of travellers across the border.

IV. MOBILITY MANAGEMENT AS A PRECAUTIONARY PRACTICE

The trusted traveller concept buttresses the rationalisation of mobility management: though control and surveillance may be ubiquitous, interventions are more selective and targeted when abnormalities emerge, for instance in the context of risk-profiling. Risk is a pivotal notion in the trusted traveller concept.[57] 'Risk' is now a concept, which is virtually omnipresent as a tool for security governance,[58] departing from the overall notion that we live in a 'risk society',[59] and the risks we are presented with include terrorism

---

[54] For more details on this authentication process, see for instance: Frontex, *Operational and Technical Security of Electronic Passports* (Frontex, Warsaw, July 2011), available at frontex.europa.eu/assets/Publications/Research/Operational_and_Technical_Security_of_Electronic_Pasports.pdf.

[55] Poole and Passantino, above n 27.

[56] 'Schiphol heeft centrale security' *De Volkskrant*, newspaper advertisement (9 June 2015).

[57] D Lyon, 'The Border is Everywhere: ID Cards, Surveillance and the Other' in E Zureik and MB Salter (eds), *Global Surveillance and Policing. Borders, Security, Identity* (Cullompton, Willan Publishing, 2005) 66.

[58] Leese, above n 46.

[59] U Beck, *Risk Society. Towards a New Modernity* (London, Sage, 1992).

and organised crime. Risks can also be defined as a way in which the world is being ordered through the management of social problems and surveying populations.[60] The management of mobility is now largely risk-based and is based on a preventative and prognostic framework. Prevention goes together with proactivity and profiling and is oriented towards a worst case scenario. For instance, the EU external border controls focus on filtering 'abnormal' and risk-posing individuals from 'normal' or regular travellers, based on prognostic technology.

The management of risk may involve the application of rationalities and technologies. The trusted traveller programme is coined on data-based passenger risk assessment. Muller characterises the application of risk management by border security in the border area between Canada and the United States as 'near obsessive'.[61] The assessment of risk is pushed far beyond the border and has become a pervasive practice in society.[62] Risk is a core concept in the politics of pre-emption.[63] The future is made predictable through a set of risk indicators, and is based on the precautionary principle.[64]

Risk management is paralleled by ubiquitous surveillance: precautionary risk-management involves the whole population and technologies of surveillance are indiscriminately targeted at the whole population.[65] This involves an upsurge of profiling practices, which are based on typifications, categories, risk-assessment profiles that are predetermined on the basis of low versus high risk, a history of claims and frequent traveller patterns. Kroker regards the Trusted Traveller Programme as a form of 'preventative certification'.[66]

V. TRUSTED TRAVELLER PROGRAMMES IN ACTION

The discourse on counterterrorism provided a policy window for the development of trusted traveller programmes. Trusted traveller programmes enhance the streamlining and effectiveness of border control authorities

---

[60] C Aradau and R Van Munster, 'Governing Terrorism Through Risk: Taking Precautions, (Un)knowing the Future' (2007) 13(1) *European Journal of International Relations* 89.

[61] Muller, above n 5, 67.

[62] ibid, 68.

[63] Aradau and Van Munster, above n 60.

[64] M de Goede and S Randall, 'Precaution, Preemption: Arts and Technologies of the Actionable Future' (2009) 27(5) *Environment and Planning D: Society and Space* 859; M den Boer, 'Preventive Empires: Security Dynamics at Multiple Levels of Governance' (2011) 3(3) *Amsterdam Law Forum* 102; L Zedner, 'Pre-crime and Post-criminology?' (2007) 11(2) *Theoretical Criminology* 261.

[65] Aradau and Van Munster, above n 60, 27.

[66] A Kroker, 'Born Again Ideology. Religion, Technology and Terrorism' in *The New Biometric State* (2006), available at www.ctheory.net/articles.aspx?id=549.

as they allow them to focus more on higher-risk passengers while trusted passengers are or may be considered as low-risk passengers. Not only the United States, but several other jurisdictions are known to run similar programmes (see below), such as the Trusted Traveller Program in Israel, which is footed on a risk-based approach. Other programmes include the Transport Security Administration (TSA) Program (US), in which the US Customs and Border Protection (CBP) has partnered with TSA on this Department of Homeland Security initiative, designed to help TSA focus resources on passengers we know less about while expediting the process for lower-risk passengers whenever possible. Another example is SmartGate (Australia), which has been designed for eligible travellers arriving at Australia's international airports to self-process through passport control. Viajero Confiable Mexico is a trusted traveller programme operated by the Government of Mexico. The programme provides expedited processing for pre-approved, low-risk travellers at designated airports in Mexico via the use of automated kiosks. US Customs and Border Protection has partnered with the Instituto Nacional de Imigracion to link Viajero Confiable with the Global Entry Program. This arrangement is open to both US and Mexican citizens. The Smart Entry Service (SES) is a trusted traveller programme operated by the Government of Korea. The SES Program provides expedited processing for pre-approved, low-risk travellers at designated airports in Korea via the use of e-gates. US Customs and Border Protection has partnered with the Korean Immigration Service to link the SES Program with the Global Entry Program. This arrangement is open to both US and Korean citizens. US citizens must first become a Global Entry member, and may then apply for the Korean SES Program. US citizens with Global Entry membership travelling to New Zealand may use a dedicated lane arriving at Auckland, Wellington and Christchurch airports. The lanes are supposed to streamline border processing for US Global Entry members. Lanes will be clearly marked with signs that say 'US Global Entry'. To be eligible to use the lanes, US Global Entry members simply present their membership (Trusted Traveler) card, their US passport and arrival documentation. FLUX is a programme in the Netherlands, which stands for Fast Low Risk Universal Crossing. FLUX expedites and secures international travel with an automated border passage programme. This programme is open to both US and Dutch citizens. Only US citizens with a valid US machine-readable passport can participate in FLUX through the United States. Their citizens must first become Global Entry members and then be approved for the Dutch Privium Programme.

The Dutch Privium Programme applies iris recognition technology. In October 2001, the commercially-oriented Amsterdam Schiphol airport launched a one-year trial of a more limited biometrically based system for speeding up one element of passenger processing. One year later, the system had close to 5000 paid-up members. Privium uses iris scans instead of hand geometry measurements for its biometric identifier. Potential members (who must hold EU passports) go through a 15-minute enrolment process, which includes a check of the validity of their passport, a check against a European police database and an iris scan. Membership costs €99 per year. Members in Privium Basic are allowed to use special automated lanes at border control and separate and faster passenger security screening lines. Privium Plus, in cooperation with participating airlines, provides separate check-in counters and priority parking at Schiphol airport. The system was developed by Schiphol Group and Dutch security technology company Joh.Enschede Security Solutions. The technology is also being tested at several Canadian airports, at Frankfurt and at New York's JFK International Terminal 4, which is run by Schiphol Group. In April 2002 IBM announced a joint venture with Schiphol Group to sell and install the technology worldwide.[67]

The United States introduced the CAPPS system, which stands for Computer Assisted Passenger Prescreening System. The system makes use of information that is actually provided by passengers and uses algorithms to determine patterns believed to be associated with terrorism.[68] The concept is used by the US authorities and forms the basis of different border inspection programmes. One of these programmes is the NEXUS inspection programme, which allows its members to have 'crossing privileges' at air, land and marine ports of entry.

Under the Western Hemisphere Travel Initiative (WHTI), the NEXUS card has been approved as an alternative to the passport for air, land and sea travel into the United States for US and Canadian citizens. The NEXUS Program allows pre-screened travellers expedited processing by US and Canadian officials at dedicated processing lanes at designated northern border ports of entry, at NEXUS (CA Entry) and Global Entry (US Entry) kiosks at Canadian Preclearance airports, and at marine reporting locations. Approved applicants are issued a photo-identification, proximity Radio Frequency Identification (RFID) card. Participants use the three modes of passage where they present their NEXUS card, or have their iris scanned, or present a WHTI and make a declaration. The US Customs and Border Protection (CBP) and Canada Border Services Agency (CBSA) are cooperating in this venture to simplify passage for pre-approved travellers. The privileges include 'expedited passage' at specially dedicated lanes, but also crossing the border with a minimum of questioning by immigration and customs authorities.[69]

---

[67] Poole and Passantino, above n 27.
[68] ibid.
[69] See www.cbp.gov/travel/trusted-traveler-programs/nexus.

A practical application is the so-called ABC gates. For instance, in the Schengen area, there were 700 million border crossings to and from the Schengen area, which has 1800 border crossings at the external border. There are around 288 operating ABC gates in 13 EU Member States, which is regarded as 'just the beginning'.[70] The ABC gates can lead to a two-tier traveller experience, with

> on the one hand the frequent flyer, flying business class with convenient processing through border controls thanks to RTP programs, arriving at the airport 30 minutes before their flight, and on the other the infrequent traveller only flying twice a year, often increasingly elderly due to demographic changes, who must be at the airport three hours before their flight.[71]

ABC technologies are primarily introduced to make it possible to risk assess more passengers at a quicker rate without the need to appoint more border control guards or security personnel.[72] Inherently, legitimate and illegitimate activities are segregated.[73] There is a double movement between normalising and regularising on the one hand, and criminalising on the other.[74] A sifting is performed in which a sorting process takes place between the 'bona fide' and the 'bogus' traveller. For these bona fide travellers the border passage is smooth and unhindered.[75]

Currently there are also ideas for trusted traveller's programmes at EU-level, but under a different title, such as the Automated Border Control (ABC) systems.[76] Germany and the United States introduced a reciprocal agreement on trusted traveller programmes, which provide 'expedited clearance for pre-approved' travellers through dedicated lanes and kiosks.[77]

In the view of Neal the EU Agency for the Management of External Border Controls, Frontex, plays many roles.[78] While its operational role heavily hinges on the concept of risk, the agency also functions as a tool to which the Member States can take recourse in the event of migratory emergencies. When it concerns its role in risk analysis, the logic revolves

---

[70] Frontex Conference Report, available at frontex.europa.eu/assets/Images_News/ABC_Conference_Report.pdf, 16 (Frontex, Warsaw, 2013).

[71] ibid.

[72] D Stevens and N Vaughan-Williams, 'Border Security: Public Perceptions and Experiences' paper (Frontex Conference, Warsaw, 2013).

[73] Amoore, above n 17, 351.

[74] Kroker, above n 66.

[75] Amicelle et al, above n 15.

[76] See frontex.europa.eu/assets/Publications/Research/Best_Practice_Technical_Guidelines_for_Automated_Border_Control_Systems.pdf.

[77] See www.expatbriefing.com/expat-news/Germany-And-US-Agree-On-Trusted-Traveler-Programs-66885.html.

[78] AN Neal, 'Security and Risk at the EU Border: The Origins of Frontex' (2009) 47(2) *Journal of Common Market Studies* 333.

around anticipation and management rather than 'response'.[79] The way Frontex evolves is through a proliferation of 'diversified technological governmentalities',[80] which means that the agency primarily seeks to develop through the application of state of the art technology, for instance on facial recognition.

VI. DISENTANGLING THE LAYERS OF MOBILITY MANAGEMENT

Border management has political, managerial, technological and professional aspects. The political level is essential because it is there where political choices are made to build a free movement area, in which global access to Europe is provided and vice versa. The economic effects of free travel are vast. On the technological level, the assumption is that smart borders and biometric technologies help to control terrorism, organised crime and irregular migration. The development of trusted traveller programmes is also closely connected with technological innovation and with the concept of the 'smart border'.[81] 'Bordering increasingly relies in technological forms of mediation that are embedded within hi-tech, military and private corporate logics'.[82] Several technologies are now in play including the use of biometric identification systems such as facial recognition, fingerprint recognition or iris recognition, as well as smart ID systems, coupled with CCTV etc. The IT industry has a major (and growing) foothold in the arena of border management.[83]

Of particular significance is the rapidly growing application of biometric technologies for the identification and authentication of travellers. Authentication is to make sure that the person who crosses the border is the person she or he claims to be and for this purpose, the data that are captured by 'biometric instruments is checked against information either contained in a database the individual has previously enrolled in ..., or in a "token", a card or a document held by the person willing to cross the border'.[84] Identification involves the process of identifying an individual whose identity is unknown: the individual 'has not previously consented to record biometric information in a specific program, nor to hold this information in a travel document'.[85]

One can distinguish the following dimensions in the trusted traveller programmes:

---

[79] ibid, 349.
[80] ibid.
[81] Amicelle et al, above n 15.
[82] Vukov and Sheller, above n 39, 225.
[83] Amicelle et al, above n 15, 13.
[84] ibid, 7.
[85] ibid.

Table 1: Dimensions in trusted traveller programmes

	Political	Managerial	Technological	Professional
Master narrative	Political master narrative is that the European borders coincide with the controls of a common physical space; it involves the stretching of sovereignty beyond national borders.[86]			Professionals are educated according to standardised formulae and hence can be entrusted with professional 'disposition'.[87]
Policing of mobility	Political balance between economic benefits of free market and free movement of persons and safety risks as a consequence of open borders. Biopolitics regarded as a neo-liberal technique of governmentality.	Logistic management: streamlining of travellers.	Fingerprint or iris scan, coupled with for instance air mile databases.	Potential use of deterrence and the use of force. Distinguishing the legitimate from the illegitimate. Matching people with their biometric records; human interface (professional judgement) reduced to a minimum. However, manual, human checks still performed on top of pre-screening and automated border control.

(continued)

---

[86] den Boer, 'How to Police a Porous Fortress?', above n 12, 7.
[87] D Bigo, 'The (In)securitization Practices of the Three Universes of EU Border Control: Military/Navy—border guards/police—database analysts' (2014) 45(3) *Security Dialogue* 209, 225.

Table 1: (*Continued*)

	Political	Managerial	Technological	Professional
Self-policing	The neo-liberal agenda demands subjugation in combination with self-responsibilisation.	Self-policing, self-governance: traveller governs his or her own mobility particularly in terms of trails, queues and lanes.		Through a regime of pre-screening and pre-entry warnings, the travelling individual is made aware of risks and prompted to strip him/herself from potential security risks.
Public–private policing	Technique of governmentality and control: permission/authority versus denial/refusal of entry.	Segregation: traveller's categories.	Data-veillance: data input, data screening, data-mining, data-matrixing. Biometrics are related and linked to international information systems.	

VII. MAKING THE TRUSTED TRAVELLER CONCEPT TICK

Principal conditions for making the trusted traveller concept 'tick' are the negotiation and maintenance of trust and reciprocity, both 'vertically' as well as 'horizontally'. The trust of the traveller in all four dimensions is a necessary condition to make the trusted traveller concept effective.

The first dimension is the *political trust* that different governments may have in each other's capacity to manage their border controls effectively, efficiently and legitimately. In the history of Schengen, which is the common external border control regime between the Schengen signatories, there have been a lot of misgivings about this, and even nowadays there is a lack of trust as epitomised in the controversy about the migrants from North Africa who travel to Europe by boat. An essential ingredient of political trust is reciprocity, which is also clearly expressed in a number of agreements, such as the recent bilateral Trusted Traveller Programme between Germany and the United States. Moreover, on the level of international politics, the EU can be seen a global transporter of border management practices, which are in part technologically-driven and in part buttressed by the multi-agency. In order to be seen as a reliable exporter, the EU as a polity has to be accredited/assigned with integrity by the recipient jurisdictions.

Second, trusted traveller programmes have to be built on a layer of *managerial trust*, which can be regarded as inter-sectoral trust, interagency trust. A good example is the case concerning access by law enforcement authorities to the Eurodac system. This has been controversial, but the German Government pushed to officially grant police and security services access to Eurodac as a general investigation tool against terrorism and other crimes.[88] With regard to the Schengen Information System, it should be noted that the Member States are free to designate their competent authorities, which means on the one hand that many national authorities have access to the SIS in practice,[89] and on the other that there is a wide discrepancy between the Member States who they regard as 'competent authorities'.[90] Moreover, common position 2005/69 requires information on stolen and lost passports to be shared between Interpol and the countries that operate the SIS. Europol has access to the system and may be able to communicate data from the SIS to third countries and third parties. Access to the SIS by security and intelligence agencies has been requested but remains controversial and ambiguous.[91] With regard to VIS, it should be noted that designated authorities of the EU Member States and Europol may have access to the system for the prevention, detection or investigation of terrorist offences and other serious criminal offences. Moreover, the Stockholm Programme has advocated increased interoperability between the data systems.

Third, there has to be *technological trust*, which involves trust in the unfailing capacity of technology. However, studies 'consistently show that none of the biometric technologies is fully accurate'.[92] The European system which registers asylum seekers, Eurodac, is the only pan-European database that contains biometric identifiers, namely fingerprints.

Finally, there has to be *professional trust*, which involves trust in the integrity, judgement and discretion of the individual professionals who are involved along the chain of mobility management. Given the increase in multi-agency partnerships and public–private cooperation, this trust among

[88] Geyer, above n 31.
[89] Amicelle et al, above n 15, 18.
[90] Geyer, above n 31, 8.
[91] See List of competent authorities which are authorised to search directly the data contained in the second generation Schengen Information System, [2014] OJ C278/1, available at eur-lex.europa.eu/legal-content/EN/TXT/PDF/?uri=OJ:C:2014:278:FULL&from=EN.
[92] Amicelle et al, above n 15, 15.

professionals who work in entirely different organisations clearly has to transcend national and organisational borders, which cannot be considered self-evident.

VIII. CONCLUDING THOUGHTS

The analysis of the mechanisms behind the trusted traveller concept has unravelled a complex interaction between actors, rules and expectations with a lot of inbuilt interdependencies and potential vulnerabilities. Trusted traveller programmes as such benefit from international stability, in which governments, organisations and professionals trust each other on a sustained basis. The status of trusted traveller depends on the success of these programmes. The operation of the trusted traveller programme involves multiple lines of entry and permission as well as a good deal of governmentality, subjugation and self-policing. The impact of internationalisation, technologisation, informatisation and privatisation is that individual human rights, such as privacy and personal dignity, are becoming more hybrid.

Citizens would benefit if trusted traveller programmes evolve into a rights-based direction in which the free movement of persons principle is the rule, rather than the exception. As explained by the EU Fundamental Rights Agency, the Charter of Fundamental Rights of the European Union sets out rights that are relevant during border checks, which include human dignity, the prohibition of torture and degrading treatment, the right to liberty and security, and the protection of personal data, the right to a good administration and the right to an effective remedy.[93] In practice, however, the operationalisation of these core principles may be rather slippery because border controls become invisible and transversal. Moreover, the passage of trust involves several layers of trust, including political, technological, professional and managerial trust. Whether the absence of a human interface at the border will enhance the trust of travellers remains to be tested in due course.

---

[93] Fundamental Rights Agency, *Fundamental Rights at Airports: border checks at five international airports in the European Union* (2014), available at fra.europa.eu/sites/default/files/fra-2014-third-country-nationals-airport-border-checks_summary_en.pdf.

6

Brand Interpol

JAMES SHEPTYCKI

I. INTRODUCTION: WHAT'S IN A BRAND?

I N AN EARLIER paper I made the casual claim that Interpol was the most widely recognised brand name in transnational policing.[1] In this chapter I wish to unpack the concept of Interpol as a brand in order to think again about the (lack of) accountability of the institution and the high degree of trust that its image has accrued. Transnational policing is an abstraction which scarcely features in popular discourse and so it is difficult to engage in discussions about its place in the institutions of global cosmopolitan democracy. Interpol is a brand which has global recognition and yet the institution is poorly understood. The Interpol logo combines images of the globe, pierced through by the sword of justice, framed by olive branches, suspended from which are the scales of justice. Along with the Interpol name itself, this logo stands for transnational policing and so it is important to think about what lies behind the image of Brand Interpol. Its logo is a registered trademark in the European Union (EU) and the United States and the organisation rigorously polices its intellectual property. The meaning of the image is important in the justification of actually existing transnational policing—it is an emblem of global social order which signals, among other things, the rule of law and the power of police to ensure social peace. The Interpol brand is supposed to be an assurance of trust in transnational policing.

The sociology of 'the brand' and of 'branding' has, in the main, emerged from the sociology of consumption, where dyadic relations between consumers and the objects of their consumption have been problematised chiefly in terms of 'brand loyalty' and the social meanings and political

---

[1] J Sheptycki, 'The Accountability of Transnational Policing Institutions: The Strange Case of Interpol' (2004) 19 *Canadian Journal of Law & Society* 107.

economy of advertising, trademarks and intellectual property.[2] There are good reasons for this. Historically, branding of commodities began in the late nineteenth-century when a few goods began to be marketed on the basis of the product name rather than the commodity itself. In the later years of that century thousands of branded products replaced previously unbranded commodities as the consumer capitalist order was consolidated. By the end of the twentieth century a variety of other types of institutions, including religious sects, public universities and even cities and national parks were consciously 'branded' as the tide of neo-liberalism normalised the logic of consumerism globally.[3] Colin Campbell has argued that the sociology of consumption and of advertising needs to emphasise the irrational belief structures underpinning the social order of consumption. Reviving some of the ideas of Karl Mannheim, Campbell sought to show how the guiding presumptions of rationality and reason in the constitution of the capitalist social order were girded by Romanticism and that irrational thought processes were just as important in the manufacture of consent in consumerism as was the supposed rationality of '*homo economicus*'. Campbell was not referring to 'romance' in some narrow sense, but in a wider understanding as being exotic, imaginative and idealised.[4] In what follows, I wish to depart from the literature on the sociology of the brand and branding, which has almost exclusively been the bedfellow of the sociology of consumerism, to consider the mystique of Interpol as an institution. Interpol is the marque of transnational policing par excellence, but it has not been sold in the normal sense of the word, nor has marketing expertise been an evident facilitator of this brand recognition.

II. BRANDS AND TRUST

Frequently talk about brands and branding seems to be little more than 'management babble' concerning brand awareness in the maximisation of shareholder value. In the sociology of consumerism, the mainstay of thought about branding is that selling commodities is not so much about

---

[2] S Fox, *The Mirror Makers: A History of American Advertising and its Creators* (New York, Vintage, 1984); T Frank, *The Conquest of Cool: Business Culture, Counterculture, and the Rise of Hip Consumerism* (Chicago, University of Chicago Press, 1997); CL Hays, *The Real Thing: Truth and Power at the Coca Cola Company* (New York, Random House, 2004); N Klein, *No Logo Taking Aim at the Brand Bullies* (Toronto, Vintage Canada, 2000).

[3] C Campbell, *The Romantic Ethic and the Spirit of Modern Consumerism* (Oxford, Blackwell, 1987); JB Twitchell, *Branded Nation: The Marketing of Megachurch, College Inc and Museumworld* (New York, Simon & Schuster, 2004).

[4] Campbell, *The Romantic Ethic*, above n 3.

the commodities themselves—the shoes, cosmetics, watches, handbags and other paraphernalia of 'consumer lifestyle'—it is about the production of meaning around the image of the brand.[5] In this literature, 'brand identity' and the visual imagery of 'the brand' are important elements for sustaining one's consumer identity close to its narcissistically preferred social positioning in a universe of shared meaning. Intrinsic to this is 'brand trust'. This is the 'believability' that the brand symbol invokes. In the jargon, brand trust impacts the behaviour and performance of stakeholders, converting awareness into commitment. The power of brand images to communicate complex ideas, mix emotional impact with presumptions of rational understanding and to demonstrate continuity establishes the foundation of trust that aims at ensuring that the meanings associated with any given brand are broadly positive.

The importance of trust cannot be over-emphasised.[6] Trust is an essential element of social order because 'the social' is constituted in the margins between what is known from direct everyday experience and contingency in new possibilities that derive from social action. In particular, trust is essential in the social actions concerning control, risk and power. This is precisely the point at which an understanding of 'Brand Interpol' presents an interesting departure from the usual confines of the literature concerning brands and branding. Interpol does not market normal consumer services or products. Indeed, it is probably safe to say that Interpol does not market anything in the usual sense of the word. And yet, the image of the 'Man from Interpol' is pervasive. Almost *revered* as one of the oldest, largest and most famous police agencies in the world, it has inspired two television series and played a role in countless novels and movies—its globetrotting agents travelling the world to snare criminals, terrorists and spies. The issue with this is that what most people think about Interpol is untrue. Its agents are not allowed to carry firearms or make arrests and, in fact, rarely leave the office. In this fictive world where 'crime is international, but so is the law' people can trust that, 'in constant touch with all the police forces of the world is the Man from Interpol!'.[7] Apart from noting its place in the romance of crime fiction, it is interesting to chart the establishment of Interpol, not only as an institution, but also as a brand, since the universe of meaning that has sprung up around the name has come to signal a kind of trust in the international order.

---

[5] D Chaney, *Lifestyles* (London, Routledge, 1996).

[6] A Giddens, *The Constitution of Society: Outline of a Theory of Structuration* (Cambridge, Polity Press, 1984).

[7] From the voice-over of the original British television series made in 1958, starring Richard Wyler as Interpol agent Anthony Smith.

III. COKE HAS PEPSI, MICROSOFT HAS APPLE: WHY INTERPOL HAS NO BRAND COMPETITION

Back in 1997 Apple co-founder Steve Jobs made a surprising announcement at the Macworld tradeshow in Boston: that Bill Gates and Microsoft would be supplying the company with a $150 million cash infusion. The funds were a financial life-saver for the struggling company. Famously, Jobs soothed the tempers of hostile members of the Apple crowd by saying: 'We have to let go of a few notions here. We have to let go of the notion that for Apple to win, Microsoft needs to lose'.[8] A number of reasons were touted at the time to explain this behaviour. Microsoft needed a shield from the 'trust busters' and, if Apple went out of business, its rival would be in possession of 100 per cent of the personal computer market leaving it vulnerable to antitrust actions that could break up the company. It made Gates look noble and therefore offered a public relations victory to him, while Jobs, who had only recently returned to the struggling company, could pose as something of a saviour for brokering the deal. Both companies stood to gain through sharing of software and hardware innovations. But at a more basic level, the brand rivalry functioned to normalise the presence of both marques in the fabric of the newly emerging networked society of informational capitalism. Possibly both Gates and Jobs were not aware, or only dimly aware at an unconscious level, of this functionality. But a closer look at other iconic brands shows that brand rivalry is a very common component in the attainment of hegemonic presence. The so-called Cola wars are the classic example. Beneath the façade of deep brand rivalry, where Pepsi and Coke seem forever locked in an advertising fight-to-the-death over market share, is a kind of partnership which allows the two dominant brands to command an impressive 75 per cent of the market in soft drinks in the United States. In other words, by appearing to be locked in fierce competition for customers, these 'Brand Bullies' all but corner the market between them. Deep within the social psychology of capitalist consumerism are buried notions about consumer choice and market competition. Brands, perhaps especially super-brands, need the presumption of rivalry in order to foster consumers' perceptions of choice. Brand rivalry creates an important conversation essential to a romantic pretence of consumer capitalism, a conversation about choice. Very few brands, Disney is one, successfully create a conversation that amounts to autopoiesis, that is: a self-referential discourse that is autonomous and operationally closed, self-organising and self-writing.[9] Disney is not selling a product. They are selling an idea of selfhood, of

---

[8] MM Flores and TW Haines, 'Microsoft, Apple Join Forces—Disbelief, Boos Greet Today's Stunning Announcement at Macworld Expo' *Seattle Times* (6 August 1997).
[9] JF Keane, AW Truman and GH Wright, 'Autopoiesis in Disneyland; Reassuring Consumers Via Autopoietic Brand Management' (1999) 18 *International Journal of Advertising* 519.

family, of individuality of a lifestyle inscribed in the American Dream—the ultimate romantic essence of consumer capitalism.

Brand Interpol is rather different. Because the image of Interpol is the marque that exemplifies transnational policing there is a sociological reason why it remains alone as a symbol. This is not because of any deliberate marketing strategy. The fact is that transnational policing is an emergent phenomenon that has evolved within the broader processes of globalisation without coordinated policy planning and, indeed, in the context of inter-institutional conflict.[10] Really existing transnational policing is riven by complex conflicts concerning state sovereignty and institutional rivalry between many policing and control agencies both within and across states' boundaries. But policing is a concept that transcends this messy reality. The policing idea promises to impart peace, order and good governance.[11] It is, however, an idea that is always already in precarious balance because the sword of justice forever implies notions about the use of force in the maintenance of social order.[12] Despite any deliberate planning, indeed despite any demonstrable efforts to project the brand, Interpol has succeeded as the transnational policing marque *par excellence* because the natural assumption surrounding the policing idea draws upon images of 'the Sovereign' in Hobbes' *Leviathan*. The book, as is well known, concerns the structure of society and legitimate government and is the earliest and, some would argue, most influential example of social contract theory. Hobbes argues, in essence, that the command of sovereign secures the social contract that binds society into one coherent whole: Leviathan. Abraham Bosse's etching, which forms the book's famous frontispiece, dramatically captures the idea of Leviathan: a crowned giant, whose body is actually composed of many human figures, rising up from the landscape clutching a sword and a staff of office beneath a quote from the Book of Job (41:25—*Non est potestas Super Terran quae Comparetue ei*—There is no power on earth but him). That picture presents a theory of the state and it is echoed in Max Weber who defined the institution as an entity that successfully claims a monopoly on the use of coercive force in the maintenance of social order. The policing idea exemplifies this thought. The global system is not under the command of any one sovereign.[13] However, at a deeper level there is probably a widely held albeit unconscious understanding or expectation that, insofar as that system is 'policed', there is, or ought to be (behind a green curtain somewhere) a sovereign in charge; hence the symbolism surrounding

---

[10] B Bowling and J Sheptycki, *Global Policing* (London, Sage, 2012).

[11] A Goldsmith and J Sheptycki, *Crafting Transnational Policing* (Oxford, Hart Publishing, 2007).

[12] JP Brodeur, 'An Encounter with Egon Bittner' (2007) 48 *Crime, Law and Social Change* 105.

[13] See Bowling and Sheptycki, above n 10.

global policing ought to somehow reflect conventions originally depicted in Bosse's dreamlike image.

An important aspect of the Interpol brand is that, perhaps unwittingly, its symbolisation—the globe, sword and scales of justice, olive branches— accomplishes something at the symbolic level that does not exist at the practical level of political reality. The Interpol flag is another iteration of the theme. The flag is light blue and has at its centre the logo, which is surrounded by four lightning bolts arranged symmetrically around the emblem. These are meant to symbolise telecommunications and the speed of policing action in securing the world. Manuel Castells has explained that a late twentieth-century revolution in information and communications technology consolidated the global networked society, and the Interpol flag neatly encapsulates both this notion and that of policing. It is a brand placement that can, in fact, allow no competition because the notion it projects—the police idea—is one which assumes a monopoly. Deeply buried in our understanding of social order is its opposite—Hobbes' 'man in a state of nature' a condition of 'war of all against all'. Policing is an opposing idea to that image and it is one, again perhaps only unconsciously, inspired by the anxieties and fears that Hobbes detailed in *Leviathan*. The high degree of trust assigned to the brand is dependent on this underlying psychology of anxious fear. This psychology helps to consolidate and naturalise an impulsive search for meaning. The symbolic unity required in order for us to begin imagining transnational policing explains why other global policing brands do not find it easy to rise up in challenge of Brand Interpol.

IV. INTERPOL: ESTABLISHING A BRAND

The history of Interpol is already quite long, and at certain transitional moments, the story is complicated.[14] It is very difficult to do justice to the complexities of this institutional history, especially in a short book chapter. Here a chronology of the institution focusing on brand building, maintenance and re-branding is presented. Since the Interpol brand is very nearly a century old, appreciating the historical evolution of the brand is useful for understanding the trust, acceptance and legitimacy Interpol enjoys in the present day.

In the long list of international organisations Interpol occupies a very unusual position. It lacks a treaty basis and yet, ultimately, it is funded with taxpayers' money. Over time it has come to achieve legally recognised roles in transnational police and judicial cooperation and has acquired something

---

[14] J Sheptycki, 'Transnational Policing and the Makings of a Postmodern State' (1995) 35 *British Journal of Criminology* 613.

like customary recognition in international law as an intergovernmental organisation (IGO). The idea for the organisation was first mooted in 1914—just prior to the First World War—a point emphasised in most, if not all, historical commentary regarding Interpol. Since the lineage can be traced back to the 'progressive era' and very nearly to the Victorian period, the brand has accrued the same kind of epoch transcendence that Remington rifles, Levi jeans and Tiffany silver have. The reasons for brand longevity are complex and depend on the industry in which the brand is present. Most brands that do well over such long periods are well regarded by consumers. Remington rifles are among the best made in the world. Tiffany silver is considered the 'gold standard' for products in its category. With Interpol, the status of the 'consumer' is rather different and the nature of the product differs as well. Clues as to the product and how it is consumed are intrinsic to the history of the brand.

The idea for Interpol was articulated prior to the First World War, but its actual genesis did not come until 1923. Much has been written about Interpol since then, but little is of scholarly value. The following account draws on the best of these contributions.[15] The idea was first put forward by Prince Albert of Monaco who sponsored the First International Police Congress in Monaco in 1914. Another attempt was made in 1922, when an International Police Conference was held in New York. At these meetings an assortment of police officers, lawyers and magistrates met to discuss extradition and arrest procedures, centralised records management and scientific policing techniques, but 'police science' and 'professional policing' were in their infancy and the efforts failed to gather momentum.

It was a scheme designed and pursued by Dr Johan Schober the head of the Austrian state police (and a three-times Chancellor of Austria) that gave the idea of the International Criminal Police Commission (ICPC) 'launch velocity'. Schober's motive was chiefly to extend the influence and reach of his police agency beyond his country's borders. Austria was then a recently established country set up by the terms of the peace treaties that drew the First World War to a close. It was the vestigial rump of the Austro–Hungarian Empire that preceded it. The ICPC police network certainly

---

[15] M Anderson, *Policing the World: Interpol and the Politics of International Police Co-operation* (Oxford, Clarendon, 1989); M Barnett and L Coleman, 'Designing Police: Interpol and the Study of Change in International Organizations' (2005) 49 *International Studies Quarterly* 593; M Deflem, 'Bureaucratization and Social Control: Historical Foundations of International Police Cooperation' (2000) 34 *Law & Society Review* 601; M Deflem, 'The Logic of Nazification: The Case of the International Criminal Police Commission ("Interpol")' (2002) 43 *International Journal of Comparative Sociology* 21; M Deflem, *Policing World Society. Historical Foundations of International Police Cooperation* (Oxford, Oxford University Press, 2002); M Fooner, *Interpol: Issues in World Crime and International Criminal Justice* (New York, Plenum Press, 1989); RS J Martha, *The Legal Foundations of Interpol* (Oxford, Hart Publishing, 2010).

provided functionality in terms of facilitating international police cooperation for ordinary criminal behaviour. At least as important, it provided a
way to maintain police surveillance with respect to more overtly political
matters as well.[16] Schober's obituary recorded that his success as president
of the police 'made him a symbol of law and order and a bulwark against
outbursts of political violence in the eyes of the nervous bourgeoisie'.[17]
Liang recorded that Schober was a master political policeman who actively
coordinated the work of the police central intelligence bureau. According
to him, Schober 'laid down that every political activity in Austria should
be under police surveillance, including the behaviour of police officials'.[18]
Under Schober's influence, the original Interpol—then referred to by its full
name: the International Criminal Police Commission—was developed as a
vehicle for scientific policing and objective intelligence gathering without
directly seeking to apply executive police powers against individuals. By
these means, Interpol became a key component in a continuing geo-strategic
game. Schober was remembered in his obituaries as a bulwark against com-
munism that, after the success of the Bolshevik revolution in Russia, was
considered a threat in many countries in Western and Central Europe. The
ICPC was a masterful institutional development. It allowed Austria (by then
a minor geo-strategic power) to continue to play a role in European power
politics. It did so by developing a brand image that emphasised scientific and
professional policing with respect to ordinary crime (and de-emphasising
political policing). Something new and historically unique was created: an
independent forum for cross-national police cooperation in intelligence and
information exchange. The ICPC was, in fact, the first *supra* national brand
in professional policing.

The influence of the ICPC in those early days should not be overstated.
The febrile politics of interwar Europe made international police cooperation, even in areas of mutual interest such as cross-border currency counterfeiting and train-travelling petty criminals, a delicate matter. Nevertheless,
the practical incarnation of the ICPC, managed to create a brand presence
as the International Criminal Police Commission. From that time, and up
to the present, the organisation has essentially been a network of police
officials facilitating police-to-police contact across international boundaries,
for the purposes of information and intelligence exchange and the circulation of ideas relating to the scientification and professionalisation of police

[16] C Fijnaut, 'The International Criminal Police Commission and the Fight Against Com-
munism, 1923–1945' in M Mazower (ed), *Policing of Politics in the 20th Century* (Oxford,
Berghahn Books, 1997) 107; RB Jensen, 'The International Anti-Anarchist Conference of 1898
and the Origins of Interpol' (1981) 16 *Journal of Contemporary History* 323.

[17] See 'Former Austrian Chancellor Dies; Dr Johan Schober' *Lewiston Daily Sun* (20 August
1932).

[18] H-H Liang, *The Rise of Modern Police and the European State System* (Cambridge,
Cambridge University Press, 2002) 222.

work. Publically the major emphasis has been on ordinary criminal policing. Political policing was assuredly not to be part of the Interpol image. Perhaps unsurprisingly then, the brand emerged as that of an independent entity because, institutionally speaking, the ICPC was able to maintain some degree of bureaucratic semi-autonomy from central governments.[19] It gained consultative status as a non-governmental organisation (NGO) upon the founding of the United Nations in 1949. It is well accepted that in the interwar period the organisation acted partly as an arm of the Austrian state police. To paraphrase Anderson, the old habits of the Habsburg police of maintaining international contact to keep track of political radicals and subversives were the 'hidden motives' behind Schober's moves.[20] The norms underlying the hidden politics of policing—anti-communism and anti-anarchism in those days—were, with rather few notable exceptions, shared by professional police internationally.

Upon the capture of Vienna in 1938 the headquarters was moved to Berlin and the organisation entered its period of 'Nazification'.[21] During the Second World War period, the ICPC network was most certainly used in the fulfilment of Nazi aims, but it was not wholly subjugated to them. Interpol was not under a 'command relationship' to the Nazi Party. This chapter of Interpol history had complicated implications for the brand. According to Deflem:

> Nazification of the International Criminal Police Commission [Interpol] involved strategies of influence through participation and command through controlling the fulfilment of a police ideology that was only partly new. Additionally, it is revealed that there was a continued portrayal of diplomacy and semi-legality, a case of institutional *impression-management* that is attributed to the Commission's international character ... in view of the relative ease with which the ICPC was subjected to nazification, the ironic consequence is that the ICPC became amenable to be politicized by whoever had control of the organization and wanted to use it to advance a particular ideology (precisely because the organization was established as an international institution independent from international political considerations). Hence, it was the very independence of the ICPC as an expert bureaucracy of criminal policing that paved the way for its nazification and attempted use for political and nationalist purposes (emphasis added).[22]

In other words, the brand image remained one of an independent international policing cooperation body. Nazi sympathisers within it used diplomacy, semi-legality and impression management to play on the institution's reputation as an international and professional police organisation.

---

[19] See Deflem, 'Bureaucratization and Social Control', above n 15.
[20] See Anderson, above n 15, 40.
[21] Deflem, 'Bureaucratization and Social Control', above n 15; Deflem, *Policing World Society*, above n 15.
[22] Deflem, 'The Logic of Nazification', above n 15.

The paradox is that, as long as these reputational issues were accorded due consideration, continued surreptitious politicisation was possible. The nefariousness of this politicisation inevitably had negative consequences for the brand.

The blemished brand was gradually polished up in the post-war years, from the 1940s until 1986, during which time the organisation was under almost total French influence.[23] This polishing was a delicate operation, made more difficult due to the evident desire to keep the network of police information exchange away from matters having to do with war crimes. Collaboration, either active or passive, by police officials was a shameful secret, and lack of Interpol action in this regard helped to ensure this manifestation of the 'collaboration issue' languished in historical obscurity. Lack of significant action, rather than bold action, was requisite. It is therefore unsurprising that during this time Brand Interpol presence faded somewhat, seemingly unimportant in a Cold War world where John Le Carré's anti-hero and Ian Flemming's action-hero were more resonant.[24] The refusal of decision-makers in the organisation to use Interpol facilities in the search for alleged Nazi war criminals was a significant act of omission.[25] German historian Daniel Stahl's work has uncovered how, up to at least 1962, French police officials in senior decision-making positions within Interpol were active in preventing the use of Interpol communication channels with regard to war criminals, calling such work 'victor's justice'. Since investigation of war crimes was potentially the most high profile task for international police cooperation in those years, such action would have inevitably impacted on the brand, calling attention to both the organisation and the role of French police collaborators during the war years. The brand languished, because Interpol had been co-opted into what Stahl called 'the coalition of the unwilling'.[26] A notable feature of this period was a studious steering away from police work of a demonstrably 'political nature'.

In 1956 the brand began its phoenix-like rise from the ashes of the Second World War. In that year the organisation adopted telegraphic exchange of

---

[23] See Fooner, above n 15, 91.

[24] This period continued well into the 1960s and for some time after that. It is therefore not surprising that the television series *The Man from Interpol* sunk into obscurity after only one season, whereas the wholly fictional *Man from UNCLE* ran for four successful seasons and has enjoyed continued viewership for decades. UNCLE stands for United Network Command for Law Enforcement, and can be read as a disguised version of INTERPOL. As revealed in one episode ('The Shark Affair') UNCLE was a fictional organisation consisting of agents of all nationalities responsible for maintaining political and legal order anywhere in the world; its principal sponsoring countries being the United States, Russia, England, Italy, Greece, Yugoslavia and Spain.

[25] See Barnett and Coleman, above n 15, 593.

[26] D Stahl, *Nazi Hunt: South America's Dictatorships and the Avenging of Nazi Crimes* (Göttingen, Wallstein Verlag, 2013).

information and intelligence. Its brand presence as 'Interpol' derives from this technological advance, INTERPOL being the telegraphic address of the organisation's headquarters in St Cloud, a suburb of Paris. Another important aspect of the organisation's modernisation was the adoption of a new constitution. The avoidance of 'political policing' was embedded into the Interpol constitution, also adopted in 1956, and 'political neutrality' consequently became an integral element in the brand image. Detailed analysis of Interpol's constitutional history can be found elsewhere.[27] The point to emphasise here is Article 2 and its interpretation. Article 2 of the original 1956 Interpol constitution states the aims of the organisation:

(A) to ensure and promote the widest possible mutual assistance between all criminal police authorities within the limits of the laws existing in the different countries and in the spirit of the Universal Declaration of Human Rights;

(B) to establish and develop all institutions likely to contribute effectively to the prevention and suppression of ordinary law crimes.

The concept of 'ordinary law crime' is important, but its meaning is complicated. In French the term is *criminalité de droit commun*, but the term is not common parlance in either language. The focus on 'ordinary law crime' is intended to bracket off illegalities that are 'political'. This point is further emphasised in Article 3, which stipulates that 'it is strictly forbidden for the Organisation to undertake any intervention or activities of a political, military, religious or racial character'. Historically, this Article has been interpreted to mean that the organisation should refrain from all matters that might be deemed 'political'. The 'ordinary law crime'—'political crime' distinction meant that the Interpol brand evolved to connote professional police activity. International professional policing avoided infringements of states' sovereignty by remaining fixated on the law enforcement mission.

There are several notable chapters in the history of Brand Interpol where this became very important. Three instances in particular illustrate what was at stake. The first of these concerns the simultaneous hijacking of three Czechoslovak planes in March 1950. The Czechoslovak Government, then under communist rule, requested that the hijackers be repatriated from whence they had sought refuge, which happened to be an American airbase in West Germany. The Czechoslovakian NCB issued red notices requesting extradition and, in so doing, argued that the offences of kidnapping and hijacking were 'ordinary law crimes'. Indignant that the organisation should be used to further the ends of a communist government, J Edgar Hoover opined that the offence was 'political' in the sense laid down in the Interpol

---

[27] See Martha, above n 15; Sheptycki, 'The Accountability of Transnational Policing Institutions', above n 1.

constitution, but this view was not shared by the Interpol General Secretariat and the red notices were issued. The red notices proved to be a dead letter and extradition never happened. Perhaps with half-an-eye to his own institution's brand, Hoover severed FBI relations with Interpol, citing this incident as one of the principal reasons for doing so.[28] The second instance was the refusal of a request made by the Cuban NCB to the General Secretariat in 1959 to issue a red notice pertaining to senior police officers of the Batista regime that formerly ruled Cuba. In arguing the case, the head of the Cuban NCB stated that Batista's police, notorious for their violence and corruption, were 'really thieves and criminals pretending to be police' and that they were 'offenders against ordinary criminal law'.[29] Various members of the Secretariat spoke out in a General Assembly, arguing that the request had 'a political motive', and a red notice was never issued. The third instance emerged after the attack by Black September at the Munich Olympics on 5 September 1972. To most observers at the time this was clearly a terrorist attack and the Interpol Secretariat refused to involve the organisation in the matter on the grounds that terrorism is politically motivated and therefore, under Article 3, could not properly be considered part of the organisation's mission.[30]

In each of these instances the 'ordinary law crime'–'political crime' distinction was contested and raised difficulties for brand-image maintenance. Limiting the scope of Interpol's mission to 'ordinary law crimes' was essential to maintaining an image of political neutrality in a world increasingly divided by north–south cleavages as well as the Cold War imposed by an east–west axis. As the Cold War wound down the world system evolved and on the new global stage, new expectations of Brand Interpol arose. By the beginning of the 1980s the distinction between 'ordinary law crime' and 'political crime' was breaking down.[31] The inaction subsequent to Munich tarnished the Interpol brand in the eyes of a few members who stalked the corridors of professional police institutions around the world acting as 'liaison agents'. By the early years of the 1980s a new Headquarters Agreement

[28] Interpol continued to liaise with US authorities through the offices of the US Treasury, despite the fact that at the time US law designated the FBI as the only official conduit for international police transactions.

[29] F Bresler, *Interpol* (London, Mandarine, 1992) 127.

[30] For more details on these incidents consult Bresler, above n 29. On the case of the Czech hijacking, see ibid 110–12 and 120–21; on the case of the request of the Cuban NCB for a red notice against former members of the Cuban police establishment, see ibid 127–28; and on the Black September attacks at Munich, see ibid 149–55. Incidentally, the Cuban instance throws up another possible deficiency of the Interpol constitution, since there is no provision within it to withdraw membership. This is why Cuba remains a member of the organisation despite the fact that, as of this writing, it has not paid any membership dues since 1959.

[31] M Deflem and LC Maybi, 'Interpol and the Policing of International Terrorism: Developments and Dynamics since September 11' in LL Snowden and B Whitsel (eds), *Terrorism: Research, Readings, & Realities* (Upper Saddle River, NJ, Pearson Prentice Hall, 2005) 175.

with the Government of France had been signed and the customary legal status of Interpol as an independent intergovernmental organisation (IGO) was recognised. The Interpol marque was projected in a variety of institutional contexts both across the UN system itself and in other transnational contexts independent of it.[32] The basis of brand independence was firmly consolidated. The organisation began to reorient Brand Interpol with regard to the terrorism trope by modifying certain policies. The 1983 Interpol General Assembly in Cannes resolved to look again at acts committed by organised groups with multiple victims and 'which are usually covered by the general term "terrorism"'. The following year, two Resolutions were passed in the Interpol General Assembly meeting held in Luxemburg. The Resolutions, AGN/53/RES/6 and AGN/53/RES/7, changed the interpretation of Article 3 in crucial respects.[33] The former Resolution, on Violent Crime Commonly Referred to as Terrorism, used the term 'terrorism' for the first time and concerned organised groups engaging in violent criminal activities that are designed, by spreading terror or fear, to attain 'allegedly political objectives'. Resolution AGN/53/RES/7 set out a list of offences that could be considered 'political' in nature, while also stating that it was not possible to give a precise general definition of 'political, military, religious or racial matters' and that each case had to be examined separately. These Resolutions broke new ground by setting out the 'doctrine of the conflict area'. With this new doctrine in hand, Brand Interpol began to involve itself in international police matters concerning terrorism. As Raymond Kendal, Interpol Secretary General from 1985 to 1999 explained it,

> what goes on in a particular conflict area would not be of interest to us for international police co-operation while it remains in that conflict area. On the other hand, if a Jordanian comes to Paris and shoots the Israeli Ambassador, then it does become our concern because it is outside of the strict conflict area.[34]

Inevitably, this political and legal shift required some re-branding as the organisation reoriented, transformed and upgraded its functional basis. In 1985 the Interpol General Assembly passed a resolution creating the 'Public Safety and Terrorism' (PST) sub-directorate to coordinate and enhance cooperation in 'combating international terrorism'. This effectively ended any discussions concerning terrorism and the political prohibitions of Article 3. It also made international terrorism a standing agenda item for all future Interpol General Assembly and Executive Committee

---

[32] See Sheptycki, 'The Accountability of Transnational Policing Institutions', above n 1.

[33] Resolution No AGN/53/RES6, 1984 Subject: Violent Crime Commonly Referred to as Terrorism; subject heading Constitution, Application of Article 3; Resolution No AGN/53/RES/7, 1984 Subject: Application of Article 3 of the Constitution, sub-heading: Constitution, Application of Article 3.

[34] See Bresler, above n 29, 184.

meetings and led to the development of training based on the 1986 *Guide for Combating International Terrorism*.

But the independence of Brand Interpol was important and a delicate balance had to be struck because policing matters so often seemed to impinge on the jurisdictional sovereignty of states. Harkening back to the earlier observation that most branding is thought of in the context of purely market-based relations, these manoeuvres show how transnational police branding responds with specific strategies in order to successfully project a police marque in the global system of states. The difficulties of doing so are exemplified in the occasional 'conspiracy outrage' about the legal status of Interpol in the United States where the use of what are presumed to be the organisation's intrusive powers have been taken to be an affront to national sovereignty on more than one occasion.[35]

The 'doctrine of the conflict area', coincident with national sovereignty issues, gave rise to a balanced view by which the organisation could maintain its image of political neutrality. This 'balance' and notions of brand-neutrality changed with the times. At the Interpol General Assembly meeting in Cairo in 1998, held not long after a series of bomb attacks on US embassies in Dar es Salaam and Nairobi, a Declaration Against Terrorism, was issued. Brand Interpol was inextricably linked with the global fight against terrorism. In condemning the threat posed 'not only with regard to security and stability, but also to the State of Law, to democracy and to human rights', the Interpol brand was adapted to a world in which both the 'end of history' and the 'clash of civilizations' were said to be taking place. It is well known, but nevertheless worth repeating, that Francis Fukuyama's *The End of History and the Last Man*[36] claimed that the end of the Cold War brought an end-point in human ideological evolution with the universalisation of Western values of liberal democracy and human rights. At more or less at the same time, Samuel P Huntington's book *The Clash of Civilizations and the Remaking of World Order*[37] pointed at the 'bloody borders' between Islam and 'the West' in what was said to be a fundamental and inevitably violent conflict between civilizations. Brand Interpol did not want to lose its historically won rights as a marque—a guarantee of trust—that encapsulated the image of a professional, scientific policing institution respected the world over regardless of jurisdiction. And this was significantly before the attacks of September 11. At the Interpol General Assembly in Budapest that year a resolution was passed condemning 'murderous attacks perpetrated

---

[35] M Stalcup, 'Interpol and the Emergence of Global Policing' in W Garriot (ed), *Policing and Contemporary Governance* (New York, Palgrave Macmillan, 2013) 231, 246–47.

[36] F Fukuyama, *The End of History and the Last Man* (New York, Free Press, 1992).

[37] SP Huntington, *The Clash of Civilizations and the Remaking of World Order* (New York, Simon & Schuster, 1996).

against the world's citizens in the United States of America' as 'an abhorrent violation of law and of the standards of human decency' that constitute 'cold-blooded mass murder [and] a crime against humanity'. The brand could now surpass its long forgotten concepts distinguishing 'political' and 'ordinary' crime and draw on the universalising language of crimes against humanity. The Interpol brand was visible in the 'war on terror'.

In closing this section, it is worth noting that by this time, there were a host of emerging transnational police brands. An impressive array of acronyms proliferated. One of my personal favourites is an early European effort: the Police Working Group on Terrorism; its acronym PWGOT, transposes phonetically in my mind to be pronounced 'pug-wat'. The TREVI Group was a more successful brand, perhaps partly because it was a witty in-joke among high-level security bureaucrats and police officials that combined an association with Rome's Trevi fountain, a historic fixture then in the process of an expensive restoration and its chairman AR Fonteijn, from the Dutch Ministry of Justice, while TREVI itself was said to stand for 'terrorism, violence, extremism, international'. This brand, although only really relevant to relatively few people 'in the know' about high policing and security matters at the time, was a success because the witticism took the apparent sting out of what was being attempted, which was to cast a Europe-wide security net. In the 1990s and later Europe was crowded with different transnational policing efforts and in the subcultural world of liaison policing scores of local networks produced a veritable alphabet soup of acronyms, each an attempt to establish a brand that would suffice to ensure trust among the technocratic elite who made up the transnational subculture of European policing, but none could surpass Brand Interpol. Not even the much-touted Europol could successfully establish the same degree of trust. It could not challenge Interpol for brand recognition outside European territory and, even within the territory of the union there was still a substantial preference for using its functional network and thereby benefiting from its brand. Europe was a field crowded with transnational policing agents[38] and it could afford the plethora of emerging brands, but at the same time the global cops had arrived[39] and Brand Interpol had an edge. In its early history the brand was mostly a European marque with world bragging rights. At the dawn of the twenty-first century the Interpol brand was vying with Coca Cola for bragging rights as to whose trademark was visible in the most legal jurisdictions around the globe. In 2008 a new kind of brand presence was established when Vladimir Putin spoke before the Interpol General

[38] D Bigo, 'Liaison Officers in Europe: New Officers in the European security Field' in J Sheptycki (ed), *Issues in Transnational Policing* (London, Routledge, 2000) 67.
[39] J Sheptycki, 'The Global Cops Cometh; Reflections on Transnationalisation, Knowledge Work and Police Subculture' (1998) 49 *British Journal of Sociology* 57.

Assembly, welcoming the 160-officer Vatican gendarmerie, represented by Bishop Renato Boccardo, as the 187th Interpol member.[40] Brand Interpol was a transnational marque of inestimable value that could be displayed whenever its image merited the occasion in places as diverse as Washington and Moscow, Vatican City, Tel Aviv, Tehran and 182 other countries.

V. BEHIND THE INTERPOL BRAND

People on the outside in the 'world community' see little beyond the marque itself. Interpol uses its mystique and a certain dose of ostentatious security as a tool of publicity; because Interpol holds secrets, it must be important.[41] In the world of transnational policing, the ability of a brand to attract the trust of its users—police practitioners around the world—is never ending. Not unlike the early fictional characters of international policing, Interpol's branding has always depended on cultivating its image as a place where cutting-edge technology is involved and this was instrumental in globally selling Brand Interpol to users. For example, during the latter half of the 1980s Interpol was given a 'radical overhaul' of its information and communications systems, moving directly from Morse code to e-mail 'almost overnight'. With the election of former Undersecretary for Law Enforcement in the US Treasury Department Ron K Noble as Interpol Secretary General in 2000 (twice renewed, in 2005 and again in 2010), the organisation consolidated its technologies around another clever trope in policing discourse: intelligence-led policing. In the contemporary period, Interpol functions as part of the complex web of global policing communications. It facilitates the transnational police mission by providing channels of communication between police agencies in its many member countries. The list of places where you can't find the Interpol marque is notably short, including North Korea (the last frontier of the Cold War) and Vanuatu, Tuvalu and the Solomon Islands (all known for offshore banking). While the man from Interpol never arrested anyone and Interpol is strictly non-operational (it cannot initiate investigations or undertake judicial enquiries on its own behalf), its cutting-edge communications technologies make the network an important information broker in a worldwide web of police knowledge exchange.

Interpol's backstage role is facilitating the exchange of information and intelligence between member police authorities. The organisation uses a system of coloured 'notices' to facilitate police-to-police communication.

---

[40] Resolution No AGN-2008-RES-01, 2008 Subject: Membership of the Vatican City State; M Moore, 'Pope Benedict XVI sets up anti-terrorist squad' *The Daily Telegraph* (11 June 2008).
[41] See Stalcup, above n 35, 234.

Red notices amount to a worldwide diffusion of national arrest warrants and can therefore be confused as a semi-official international arrest warrant. Blue notices request information on named persons. Green notices circulate information on suspected criminals and their activities. Yellow notices relate to missing persons and black notices relate to unidentified dead bodies. Additionally, there is the circulation of information about stolen goods and other materials and things of interest, and about the modus operandi of criminals. In 2005 the UN–Interpol 'Special Notice' was introduced. These notices, issued jointly by the UN Security Council and Interpol, pertain to a list of groups and individuals associated with international terrorism.

From the mid-1980s onwards Interpol developed and maintained large electronic databanks based on information created by these exchanges. Interpol has begun to mine this accumulated data for the purposes of crime analysis, but there is no way of knowing with precision what this has resulted in. It cultivates a low public profile in respect of its operation, but displays of the marque aim to show it has high impact. Stories emerge in the press in various jurisdictions, which indicate that Interpol has played a role in a police operation, but it is seldom clear from the press accounts precisely what Interpol contributed. For example, in 2002 a member of the Greek terrorist group 'November 17' was apprehended after an accidental explosion. This turned out to be the first step in bringing to an end an almost 30-year-long history of terrorism which claimed the lives of many people, including the CIA station chief in Athens (in 1975) and a British brigadier general who was a military attaché there (in 2002). Following interrogation of the detainee, Interpol was said to be involved in intelligence exchange, but because officials from the United Kingdom and the United States had been assassinated, British and American police were equally involved. On 7 July 2002 the *Daily Telegraph* led on the story announcing that 'Greece has credited Scotland Yard with the success of an operation against November 17, a terrorist group that has [had] the attention of agencies such as Interpol and the FBI for 30 years'. The *Telegraph* quoted a spokesperson for the Greek Government explaining that their police strategy had been directed by British detectives: 'We sealed off the area and conducted the search according to Scotland Yard methods ... we have worked with the FBI but Scotland Yard are better because of their experience with the IRA'. Here we see Interpol competing with major national policing brands for a chance to be seen on the world stage.

Interpol is also active in the organisation of conferences on a multitude of criminal matters, including the sexual exploitation of children, counterfeiting, drugs markets, money laundering and terrorism, attaching its brand image to these vital sources of global insecurity. Although there are many participants in transnational policing, few are in as powerful position as Interpol to shape it, both symbolically and practically. The network of policing communications of which it is a part is productive of information (data), which practically shapes expectations of what policing consists in, from the local to the transnational level. The Interpol marque, along with the symbols of a handful of other policing-type agencies, is recognised worldwide and therefore the image of the policing mission it projects has important consequences for the nature of policing globally. Interpol's communications nodes are an important part of the global policing network. As such it plays an important role not only in helping to orchestrate policing operations, but also in the symbolic representation of policing and it does so both globally and locally.

In the early years of the twenty-first century Interpol continued to enhance its brand image through continuous technological innovation and police scientification. In 2002 communications via the internet were established with the I-24/7 communication system. As the name suggests, this system offers information constantly 24 hours a day, seven days a week through Interpol databases. This communications network has been expanded and, in some countries, Interpol computer terminals are located in airports and border crossings offering transnational direct access to police Big Data. In 2009 Interpol Secretary General Ronald K Noble announced, in conjunction with representatives of the United Nations, a new 'visionary model' of a 'global policing doctrine' reaffirming Brand Interpol as central to the worldwide web of networked policing.[42] According to Nobel: 'We have a visionary model ... the police will be trained and equipped differently with resources ... when they stop someone, they will be consulting global databases to determine who they are stopping'.

In 2011, in advance of a series of mega sporting events, including the World Cup of Soccer and the Olympics scheduled for 2014 and 2016 respectively, Interpol established another major hub for the I-24/7 system in Buenos Aires. At the time, Interpol's brand benefited from being seen in the context of high-profile global sports, helping it look as indispensible to global governance as FIFA is to the global governance of sport (brand associations are not always necessarily good ones). A third hub opened in Singapore in 2014—the Interpol Global Complex for Innovation (ICIG).[43] This facility warehouses data and acts as a research and development centre for exploiting it. The location in Singapore associates the marque with a stable, strong, successful capitalist city state in South East Asia with a reputation for law and order. Furthermore, since Singapore is known as a cutting-edge twenty-first century technopolis, it helps to further project the image of Interpol as equally technologically sophisticated and forward looking. Growing technical proficiency in such areas as database management, victim and

---

[42] D Carvajal, 'Interpol and UN Back "Global Policing Doctrine"' *New York Times* (11 October 2009).
[43] See Interpol Global Complex for Innovation, *Newsletter* (11 October 2014) 2.

suspect identification, command, coordination and logistics brings Interpol ever closer to worldwide operational policing. According to its annual report in 2011,[44] in the event of an international happening, such as a natural disaster or terrorist attack, the organisation can dispatch an international response team offering a range of expertise. The brand image stands for a seamless global web of policing communications. In promoting the brand, Interpol shapes perceptions thereby helping to naturalise the policing we have as an inevitable part of the global system. There is nothing natural about it. All policing is political. The ubiquity of Brand Interpol ought to raise questions about the basis of its legitimacy.

VI. BRAND INTERPOL, GLOBAL GOVERNANCE INSTITUTIONS AND ACCOUNTABILITY

'Interpol is a dubious legal object'.[45] It is often simply stated that Interpol is an intergovernmental organisation (IGO).[46] According to the UN Economic and Social Council, '[e]very international organisation which is not created by means of inter-governmental agreements shall be considered as a non-governmental organization'.[47] Since, strictly speaking, Interpol was never created by such an agreement (it was an agreement between police agencies, not their governments), the unproblematic view that it is an IGO is not accurate. One way to think about the system of global governance would be to place the UN at its centre with three concentric rings wrapped around it.[48] At the centre of this model are the core bodies of the UN, including the Security Council, ECOSOC, the International Court of Justice, the office of the Secretary General, and the General Assembly. In the first concentric ring are the UN programmes themselves, for example, the UN Drug Control Programme (UNDCP), the UN High Commissioner for Refugees (UNHCR) and the Office of the High Commissioner for Human Rights (OHCHR). There are more of these in different policy domains. Obviously, Interpol is not in this class of agencies, because it is not a programme of the UN. In the second concentric ring are specialised agencies, as defined by Article 57 of the UN Charter, which states that such agencies are 'established by inter-governmental agreement, and having wide international responsibilities, as

---

[44] See Interpol, *Annual Report* (2011) 14.

[45] M Savino, 'Global Administrative Law Meets "Soft" Powers: The Uncomfortable Case of Interpol Red Notices' (2011) 43 *International Law and Politics* 263.

[46] See, eg, Anderson, above n 15, 71; Bresler, above n 29, 131; Fooner, above 15, 45; Martha, above n 15, 135.

[47] See Economic and Social Council, Resolution 288 (X) (27 February 1950).

[48] D Held and A McGrew, *Globalisation/Anti-Globalisation* (Cambridge, Polity, 2002).

defined in their basic instruments ... [they] shall be brought into relationship with the United Nations'.[49] These are the IGOs.

Interpol was not initially constituted by treaty or any other similar legal agreement, so it is difficult to see how it would have IGO status. The problematic nature of this claim was voiced in the UK Parliament. In 1977 the MP for Southampton (Brian Gould, Labour) asked the UK Home Office by way of a written question 'whether there is any formal signed agreement under which the United Kingdom is a member of Interpol'.[50] The reply was: 'Membership of the International Criminal Police Organisation (Interpol) is not obtained by an intergovernmental treaty or agreement. The question of a formal signed agreement by the United Kingdom does not therefore arise'.[51] In point of fact, precisely who or what is a member of the organisation is a somewhat ambiguous matter. The precise wording of Article 4 of the Interpol constitution states that '[a]ny country may delegate as a Member to the Organisation any official police body whose functions come within the framework of activities of the Organization'. Further, '[t]he request for membership shall be submitted to the Secretary General by the appropriate governmental authority',[52] but what is an 'appropriate governmental authority' is not defined.[53] The use of the word 'country' and not 'state' is not standard nomenclature in documents of this type and that it is police agencies and not 'countries' that constitute the membership is clear. Ultimately, it is police agencies that constitute Interpol membership, not governments. This might place Interpol in the third ring of the model, the zone inhabited by organisations described as non-profit citizen's voluntary organisations, or non-governmental organisations (NGOs), which is where Held and McGrew place it.[54] Examples of other agencies that inhabit this space include Greenpeace, FIFA and the International Olympic Committee, none of which are formally externally accountable to any other institution. Despite wide acceptance of the brand around the world, there is considerable room for ambiguity about the legal status of the institution it represents.

During the second half of the twentieth century Interpol gradually acquired customary (legal?) status as an IGO. In 1947 the organisation applied to ECOSOC for recognition as a NGO. This was in fact initially turned down because UN officials could not understand how an organisation of police officials (who are usually thought of as an essential arm of the

---

[49] ibid, 61.
[50] House of Commons, 1977.
[51] Quoted in Sheptycki, 'The Accountability of Transnational Policing Institutions', above n 1, 51.
[52] ibid.
[53] Quotations from Interpol website, *Home*, available at www.interpol.int/Public/ICPO/ LegalMaterials/constitution/constitutionGenReg/constitution.asp#constitution.
[54] See Held and McGrew, above n 48, 60.

state and firmly integrated into states' administrations) could be considered 'non-governmental'. Later that year NGO status was granted, but this was awkward partly because the agents of the organisation were police officials and also because the organisation was given consultancy status as part of the UN drug control strategy.[55] Interpol's NGO status was reviewed in 1954 and again in 1969, but it was not until 1971 that changes were made. It was at this time, and after what Fenton Bresler[56] described as some 'de Gaulle-like posturing' by the then Interpol Secretary General Jean Nepote, that a new 'special relationship' was constituted between the UN and Interpol. This was done by means of a Special Arrangement in which Interpol would, under certain circumstances, be treated *as if* it were an intergovernmental organisation.[57]

This resolution approved cooperation between the two organisations for the purposes of the prevention and repression of commonly recognised crimes. It allowed for the exchange of information, documentation and other types of collaboration. In a legal opinion, written at the behest of the organisation and concerning the legal problems of Interpol's constitution, the distinguished international lawyer Paul Reuter regarded this resolution as, in effect, a treaty between the two organisations.[58] Professor Reuter's legal opinion states, in part, that Interpol could 'apparently be rightly called an international intergovernmental organisation, and indeed has been recognised as such by the United Nations Secretary General after some degree of understandable hesitation'.[59] He went on to say that, while it is true that nearly all IGOs have been set up thorough formal treaties, under the principles of international law 'it is even possible to conceive of an intergovernmental organisation being set up without a single written instrument, merely as the result of a series of precedents created by governments'.[60] Professor Reuter conceded that this was not a complete answer to the question of Interpol's status because it did not consider the terms of constitutional law in all of the (very numerous) participating countries. However, his view was that because the various parties to the Interpol organisation had 'been applying its provisions for many years without ever having claimed that their commitment thereunder was unconstitutional', and because Interpol was 'a centre of voluntary cooperation, exercising no powers which would conflict with national sovereignty' it would therefore 'ill become a State to claim after so many years of successful activity that its commitment was

---

[55] See Anderson, above n 15, 69–70.
[56] See Bresler, above n 29, 131.
[57] See the UN Economic and Social Council, Resolution 1579 (L) 288 (3 June 1971).
[58] P Reuter, 'Legal Problems Concerning the ICPO-INTERPOL Constitution: Preliminary Observations' (undated, unpublished legal opinion, English Translation).
[59] ibid, 1–2.
[60] ibid, 3–4.

unconstitutional and therefore invalid'.[61] Were such questions to be raised, it 'would be more legal and more seemly for it [the objecting state] to withdraw from the agreement'.[62] Professor Reuter drew his legal opinion to a close by asking if there would be any benefit in raising Interpol's status to that of a fully-fledged and bona fide UN Specialized Agency. His answer was that, although the organisation might accrue a greater measure of prestige as a result, this had to be weighed against the loss of independence that this would bring, since any such agreement would require full coordination with the administrative practices of the United Nations. He averred that participating states 'would probably not adopt a unanimous position on such a transformation'.[63]

Speaking about the topic of the special arrangement between Interpol and the UN, Andre Bossard, who followed Nepote in the office of Interpol Secretary General, said that '[i]t is true that this arrangement did not officially modify Interpol's status, but it did constitute recognition of the fact that Interpol differed from the other non-governmental organisations having consultative status with ECOSOC'.[64] Since by this time the Interpol brand had become associated with organisations such as the Customs Co-operation Council and the International Civil Aviation Organization, residual questions about its lack of a treaty basis gradually disappeared. Over time, Brand Interpol accrued customary status and the police association it represented was therefore treated as an IGO.

As Savino[65] outlines, Interpol functions as a police network. Interpol decisions are taken by police bureaucrats, not diplomats or government representatives. Interpol's General Assembly meetings are between police officials who make decisions governing the organisation. The Interpol network of National Central Bureaux (NCBs) is regulated by their respective domestic laws, but act as extensions of Interpol, not of their governments. NCBs implement Interpol decisions, feed Interpol databases and engage in permanent dialogue with other member agencies and with Interpol communications hubs. Clearly, Interpol functions as an administration based on the collective transnational action of police officials (sub-state actors), who have considerable room for independent action. While the brand has been confirmed as a warranted feature of global governance, the activities it symbolises take place in a transnational space that falls outside the international system.[66] It is the double ability for Brand Interpol to manufacture belief in

[61] ibid, 5–6.
[62] ibid, 6.
[63] ibid, 19.
[64] Quoted in C Valleix, 'Interpol' (1984) 3 *Revue générale de droit internationale public* 90 reprinted in (1985) 97 *International Criminal Police Review* 90.
[65] See Savino, above n 45, 274.
[66] See Bowling and Sheptycki, above n 10, 52–56; AM Slaughter, *A New World Order* (Princeton, NJ, Princeton University Press, 2004) 13–14.

its users and simultaneously trust among the more general global public that makes it a powerful marque.

Interpol signed its first Headquarters Agreement with the Government of France in 1972. While France was the country in which Interpol headquarters had been based for over 25 years, previous governments had not officially recognised the organisation. The 1972 agreement gave Interpol official legal status in France. This was later enhanced in the second Headquarters Agreement in 1982 which established the Interpol HQ as substantively free of external accountability to interested states or, by way of private court action, to private individuals. The legal immunities granted in the 1982 Agreement are extensive. Personnel working for the organisation have effective full diplomatic immunity, as does the organisation itself. Even after they have ceased to work for the organisation, Interpol people continue to enjoy such immunities.[67] The Interpol *Annual Report* for 2011 announced the 'travel document initiative'—an e-passport allowing personnel to travel without fulfilling visa requirements which, reportedly, was recognised by 'around 35 countries' with 'a further 70 … considering the proper way to support the initiative within their national visa regulations'.[68] The police elite who share these privileges, for that is what legal immunities are, depend on the strength of the Interpol brand in order to maintain their institutional positions.

Historically, financial accounts were kept totally secret, and it was not until 1990 that Interpol changed its practice in this regard. According to the 2011 *Annual Report* the organisation's financial reporting is 'where possible, in compliance with the International Public Sector Accounting Standards (IPSAS)'.[69] Listed companies routinely issue annual reports, putting awareness of the firm's financial solvency as a way of further securing trust in the brand. Interpol has become no different. In 2010 the Office of the Auditor General of Norway became Interpol's external auditor, for a period of three years, which was extended to 2015. In 2014 the Association of Certified Fraud Examiners issued a report suggesting that external audits are an ineffective way to prevent fraud; fudged documents are not difficult to conceal from outsiders. Not long after, the US Department of Justice's, Office of the Inspector General issued a report regarding nepotism in the Washington Interpol office that concluded in part that managers there had 'used their leadership positions to benefit their friends and acquaintances'.[70] Preserving brand trust in a globalised context, for Interpol at least, has meant providing

---

[67] See Anderson, above n 15, 64; Fooner, above n 15, 61.

[68] See Interpol, *Annual Report* (2011) 7.

[69] See International Public Sector Accounting Standards (IPSAS) (2011) 51.

[70] See Department of Justice, 'Investigation of Allegations of Improper Hiring Practices at INTERPOL Washington' (Washington DC, Office of the Inspector General, Oversight and Review Division, February 2015) 15-04, iv.

some financial transparency, but even trusted brands on Wall Street can go amiss and still present to the world an image of financial propriety.

In the United States, four federal court cases mounted by private parties during the 1970s and early 1980s challenged Interpol's working relationship with US law enforcement agencies. These legal challenges suggested that Interpol was a world police agency and that, insofar as it might act with respect to US citizens, US cooperation was a constitutional infringement. Anderson observed of these cases that they exemplified a 'mythology which appeals to imaginations prone to conspiracy theories'. The court cases nevertheless represented a serious threat to US participation in Interpol.[71] On 16 June 1983, US President Ronald Reagan signed Executive Order 12425 designating Interpol 'a public international organization entitled to enjoy the privileges, exemptions and immunities of the International Organizations Immunities Act'.[72] While such immunity can be withdrawn, Executive Order 12425 was another loosening of external accountability. Here the independence of the brand from the symbolism necessary to satisfy American nativism and WASP (White Anglo Saxon Protestant) identity led to legal challenges about the propriety of allowing display of the brand on American soil, that were overridden by executive order.

The main acid test concerning Interpol's external accountability is with respect to data protection and information and intelligence cooperation.[73] Information flow is the lifeblood of police organisations, and this is especially the case with Interpol. However, 'it was not until 1982 that information dissemination became subject to rules and supervision originating outside of the organization'.[74] The impetus for this came after the passage of new data protection legislation in France in 1978—legislation that was intended to protect individuals from abuse of privacy and civil rights and to prohibit unwarranted disclosure of personal information. This law would have imposed the scrutiny of the French Government on Interpol's use and exchange of information and was viewed by many inside the organisation as antithetical to its operations. Eventually, a compromise was devised and a supervisory board was constituted by an exchange of letters included in an appendix to the 1982 Headquarters Agreement. The board thus created was comprised of five members, three selected on the basis of their expertise in data protection. Of these three, one is appointed by the French Government and one by Interpol, and these two choose the third who serves as the chair of the Supervisory Board. The fourth member is from Interpol's Executive Committee and the fifth is selected by the chair from a list of five

---

[71] See Anderson, above n 15, 63.
[72] See Fooner, above n 15, 184.
[73] See Martha, above n 15.
[74] ibid, 77.

data protection/computer security experts submitted by Interpol. Initially, the French Government chose the then head of the French data protection agency the Commission Nationale de l'Informatique et des Libertés (CNIL). What cannot escape notice is that only one member of the board is not directly appointed by Interpol or chosen from a list pre-selected by that organisation. Anderson observed that 'both in the composition of the Board and its terms of reference, the compromise seemed to lean towards the Interpol rather than the French government's position'.[75] In other words, these arrangements should be understood to be a superficial mechanism of external accountability. This issue remained a continuing problem, perhaps only 'definitively settled by formal treaty provisions'.[76] Continuing pressure and scrutiny from outside bodies[77] to strengthen the Commission for the Control of Interpol's Files as an independent, remedial body, led to some changes being implemented in the early years of the new millennium.[78] Although some steps towards improving external purview and redress have been made, shortcomings remain. The trade-offs between legitimacy and continuing autonomy remain and Interpol information and data handling continues to be significantly autonomous and lacking in external account-ability.[79] Brand Interpol is likely to continue to be stuck in this bind for some time to come, because the demands for greater external control over police Big Data held by Interpol run directly counter to the need to satisfy internal users regarding the integrity of police data.

In terms of external accountability then, the legal position of Interpol as an organisation functioning worldwide is one that grants it a consider-able degree of latitude and the brand thereby sends a powerful signal of police independence in a globalising world. The organisation was ranked the lowest of all the IGOs evaluated in the *2007 Global Accountability Report*.[80] Interpol's 1956 constitution, supplemented by some subsequent resolutions of the annual General Assembly, sets out the organisation's internal lines of accountability. The General Assembly, which consists of police officials from member institutions, is the organisation's controlling body. It admits new members and may sanction existing members if they fail to comply with the rules set out in the organisation's statutes, although this is extremely rare. The General Assembly elects the executive committee,

---

[75] See Anderson, above n 15, 66.

[76] M Anderson, M den Boer and M Cullen et al, *Policing the European Union* (Oxford, Clarendon Press, 1996) 52.

[77] R Lloyd, J Oatham and M Hammer, *The 2007 Global Accountability Report* (London, One World Trust, 2007).

[78] Cheah Wu Ling, 'Policing Interpol: The Commission for the Control of Interpol's Files and the Right to a Remedy' (2010) 7 *International Organizations Law Review* 375.

[79] See Barnett and Coleman, above n 15.

[80] See Lloyd et al, above n 76.

which consists of 13 members: a president, three vice-presidents and nine delegates—all chosen from among the membership itself. This committee draws up the agenda for the General Assembly, plans Interpol's activities and oversees the work of the General Secretariat. The latter is responsible for daily management and is not formally held to account by any government of any member country. This suggests that the Secretary General of Interpol is independent, 'rather like the UN Secretary General'.[81] Except, of course, that the UN Secretary General is almost entirely beholden to the Security Council. As Kofi Annan explained it, the office of UN Secretary General is 'invested only with the power that a united Security Council may wish to bestow'.[82] Brand Interpol is much less fettered by formal lines of accountability than is the UN marque. Further to this point, Anderson notes that Articles 29 and 30 of the Interpol constitution establish the independence of the Secretary General;[83] that the Secretary General should represent the organisation, not a particular country; and that the Interpol Secretary General should neither solicit nor accept instructions from any government or authority outside the organisation and should abstain from any action which might be prejudicial to its international role. Also, under Article 30, each member country is expected to undertake to respect the exclusively international character of the duties of the Secretary General and the staff, and abstain from influencing them in the discharge of their duties. Constitutionally speaking, Interpol functions as an autonomous transnational organisation, subject only to its own internal accountability regime, making the Interpol brand a rather unique marque in the panoply of accepted acronyms symbolising global governance.

VII. CONCLUSION: BRAND IMAGE IS NO SUBSTITUTE FOR DEMOCRATIC LEGITIMACY

Interpol, as an organisation, does not receive much in the way of public attention and scrutiny.[84] Brand Interpol has significant global visibility, however. The media presence of the brand is seldom other than positive and the Interpol marque can be read as emblematic of transnational policing more generally. Brand Interpol provides an assurance of trust, especially to its members, and is an important image in the public legitimation of global policing. The power of Brand Interpol to communicate a complex

---

[81] See Anderson et al, above n 76, 51.
[82] Quoted in W Shawcross, *Deliver Us From Evil: Warlords and Peacekeepers in a World of Endless Conflict* (London, Bloomsbury, 2000) 19.
[83] See Anderson et al, above n 76, 61.
[84] See Lloyd et al, above n 77, 43.

reality that underlines the legitimacy of transnational policing practice is seldom remarked upon. And yet, when the basic facts that concern the legal and political accountability of the organisation are laid out, it becomes evident that it is the persuasive capacity of the brand itself that has put world order under the influence of a policing power with no democratic basis. Brand Interpol accomplishes something at the symbolic level that does not exist at the practical level of political reality. The marque symbolises speedy policing action in the securitisation of the world, but there is more to it than that. The mirror opposite of the high degree of trust and reassurance now assigned to Brand Interpol, and upon which the value of the marque depends, is the pervasive psychology of anxious fear that permeates the project of globalisation. This comforting imagining of transnational policing as the project of tech-savvy, globetrotting, crime-fighting, security experts with little more than law and order on their minds explains why Brand Interpol has so much influence. It is disconcerting to think that concerns about the democratic deficit in global policing is allayed by little more than the olive branches that form part of the Interpol logo.

7

The Evolving Role of Europol in the Fight Against Serious Crime: Current Challenges and Future Prospects

CELINE COCQ AND FRANCESCA GALLI*

I. INTRODUCTION

R EINFORCING LAW ENFORCEMENT cooperation within the European Union (EU) has been one of the priorities of the Area of Freedom, Security and Justice (AFSJ), especially since the adoption of the Tampere Programme in 1999.[1] The exchange of information in order to improve shared knowledge of common threats[2] between competent national authorities constitutes a core element in the fight against serious crime.[3]

In this context, Europol—a key actor in the fight against serious crime in the EU[4]—aims at collecting and analysing information and intelligence[5]

* The authors wish to thank Professor Anne Weyembergh and Dr Jan Ellermann for their valuable comments and inputs on an earlier draft of this contribution. The authors wish to specify that this contribution was finalised in August 2015. Any changes that happened after this date have not been taken into account.

[1] It was also mentioned in The Hague Programme (2004); the Stockholm Programme (2010); and recently reaffirmed in the Strategic Guidelines (2014). See European Council Conclusions, EUCO 79/14 (Brussels, 27 June 2014).

[2] As required in the Preamble of Council Decision 2005/671/JHA of 20 September 2005 on the exchange of information and cooperation concerning terrorist offences [2005] OJ L253/22; European Council Conclusions, EUCO 79/14, para 3; see F Boehm, *Information Sharing and Data Protection in the Area of Freedom, Security and Justice. Towards Harmonised Data Protection Principles for Information Exchange at EU-level* (Heidelberg, Springer, 2012) 8.

[3] European Council Conclusions, EUCO 79/14, paras 10–11.

[4] Article 88(1) TFEU; and Article 3, Council Decision 2009/371/JHA of 6 April 2009 establishing the European Police Office (Europol) [2009] OJ L121/37 (Europol Council Decision).

[5] Article 3(1) Convention based on Article K 3 of the Treaty on European Union, on the establishment of a European Police Office (Europol Convention) [1995] OJ C316/1, 2. Now based on Article 5 Europol Council Decision.

in order to prevent and investigate serious crime[6] and to use its limited, but increasing, operational competences in order to foster this fight within the EU.

Europol's status, legal basis, competence and powers have evolved very quickly since its establishment in 1995.[7] The current Europol Council Decision was adopted in haste before the entry into force of the Lisbon Treaty in order to avoid the mandatory involvement of the European Parliament in the legislative process as required by the Treaty's new provisions.[8] This has delayed the legal effects of the Treaty on the European Union (TEU) and Treaty on the Functioning of the European Union (TFEU) giving the European Court of Justice (ECJ) full competence over Europol's decisions after the entry into force of the Lisbon Treaty on 1 December 2014.[9]

The Proposal for a Regulation of the European Parliament and of the Council on the European Union Agency for Law Enforcement Cooperation and Training (Europol) of 27 March 2013[10] is of particular importance, because it aims at making Europol more effective in collecting and analysing information, then sharing such analyses with Member States. The new legal framework would in fact allow Europol to provide more comprehensive support to competent national authorities involved in cross-border investigations. Europol is maintained in a strict supporting position regarding Member States' action.[11] Yet, the European Parliament and the Council reaffirmed the necessary democratic controls over Europol actions. For instance, during the first reading[12] the need to enhance the role of national parliaments and data protection authorities has been highlighted, thus improving the democratic legitimacy and accountability of Europol.

---

[6] Europol has no control over the definition of the term 'information'. It may receive intelligence considered as such in some states and not in others. The expression 'exchange of information' by Europol must therefore be understood broadly.

[7] Council Act of 26 July 1995 drawing up the Europol Convention.

[8] European Union Committee, *Europol: coordinating the fight against serious and organised crime* (29th report) (2007–08, HL 183) 15.

[9] Article 10 Protocol 36 on transitional provisions [2008] OJ C115/1.

[10] Commission, 'Proposal for a Regulation of the European Parliament and of the Council on the European Union Agency for Law Enforcement Cooperation and Training (Europol) and repealing Decision 2009/371/JHA and 2005/681/JHA' COM (2013) 173 final.

[11] Council of the European Union, Proposal for a Regulation of the European Parliament and of the Council on the European Union Agency for Law Enforcement Cooperation and Training (Europol); European Parliament's amendments, eg, amendments 76 and 87. By contrast, both the Council and the European Parliament rejected the project of reinforcing the link between training and operational cooperation support by merging the European Police College (Cepol) with Europol.

[12] Draft European Parliament legislative resolution on the proposal for a regulation of the European Parliament and of the Council on the European Union Agency for Law Enforcement Cooperation and Training (Europol) and repealing Decisions 2009/371/JHA and 2005/681/JHA (Europol Regulation Proposal) (First reading), A7-0096/2014 (Brussels, 25 February 2014); Council of the European Union, Europol Regulation Proposal (First reading), General Approach, doc 10033/14 (Brussels, 28 May 2014).

Europol has developed from a hub of information to an increasingly (pro)active agency. In particular, the agency has had a growing impact on the exchange and analysis of information.[13] Its supporting and operational capacity has evolved. This can be explained by two factors. On the one hand, the agency acquired maturity and experience over time and its data-bases evolved to enhance the added value of the agency in cross-border cooperation. On the other hand, Europol benefits from major changes of the AFSJ with the improvement of cooperation mechanisms and the harmonisa-tion of Member States' legislation.[14]

In addition, following the Amsterdam Treaty, Europol can facilitate and support the preparation—and encourage the coordination and enforcement—of specific investigative actions by the competent national authorities. These could include operational actions of joint investigation teams (JITs). Europol staff 'participate in supporting capacity'[15] on the basis of information gathered and analysed by Europol[16] and assist in all activi-ties of the JITs.[17] It is, however, noteworthy that Europol has no coercive power. Until recently, Member States were quite reluctant to share informa-tion with Europol and this is probably still true for some Member States and/or for some competent national authorities. Europol's legitimacy is still sometimes questioned by Member States, and this may hinder effec-tive action of the agency both in the EU and abroad. However, because its legitimacy and effectiveness has developed over time, and especially over the past few years, Europol has become a very useful forum to trigger and foster cooperation.

Furthermore, a proven track record of adding value to national investigations would increase EU Member States' trust in Europol. Fast and effective cooperation would be based on personal contact and mutual trust. Although EU Member States have often made little information avail-able, showing little trust in each other and in Europol until very recently,[18] Europol receives a significant amount of information and now needs to focus on how to transform information shared with Europol and Europol's channel into a useful tool for Member States and other partners.

The question is whether Europol may today be considered the most effec-tive means for information exchange and analysis and coordination of

---

[13] Council Decision 2005/671/JHA of 20 September 2005 on the exchange of information and cooperation concerning terrorist offences [2006] OJ 253/22.

[14] See, eg, *Anniversary Publication: 10 Years of Europol 1999–2009* (The Hague, Europol Publications, 2009); V Mitsilegas, *EU Criminal Law* (Oxford, Hart Publishing, 2009) 165.

[15] A JIT is a group of national competent authorities who cooperate for a specific purpose and a limited time period to carry out criminal investigations. See Article 1 Council Decision 2002/465/JHA on joint investigation teams [2002] OJ L162/1.

[16] Article K.2(2) Treaty of Amsterdam; now Article 5(1) Europol Council Decision.

[17] Article 6 Europol Council Decision.

[18] See, eg, JI Walsh, 'Intelligence-sharing in the European Union: Institutions Are Not Enough' (2006) 44(3) *Journal of Common Market Studies* 625.

Member States' common action in the prevention and investigation of serious crime while respecting fundamental rights. The respect of fundamental rights would also foster EU Member States' trust in Europol.[19]

This contribution examines challenges that Europol still encounters and assesses whether, and to what extent, EU institutions and Member States are addressing them. In particular, the authors will focus on the improvement of its means and legitimacy in gathering, analysing and sharing information and on the development of its operational capacity. Europol has certainly developed over the years in coordinating the Member States' efforts (II), but also vis-a-vis strategic partners such as Eurojust and external actors (III).

II. STRENGTHENING EUROPOL'S CAPACITIES: A HUMAN RIGHTS-BASED APPROACH

Europol is one of the strongest manifestations of the European strategy to exchange information. However, it still has to overcome a number of obstacles both for gathering and exchange purposes and to enhance its operational means in order to establish itself as a major EU actor in the prevention and investigation of serious crime in cross-border investigations. In parallel with the gathering and exchange of information, Europol is acquiring more operational means (A). Discussions are, however, ongoing as to whether Europol's data protection standards are appropriate (B).

A. Europol's Purposes: From a Hub of Information to Operational Capacities

At first, Europol was developed to be a hub of information for EU Member States. The agency gathers information from competent authorities and shares it with EU Member States and third parties in compliance with 'the principle of ownership'.[20,21] It also offers strategic[22] and operational analysis.[23]

---

[19] D Drewer and J Ellermann, 'Europol's Data Protection Framework as an Asset in the Fight Against Cybercrime' (2012) 13(3) *ERA Forum* 381.

[20] The 'principle of ownership' implies that information sharing can only go as far as Member States allow it to go.

[21] A Weyembergh, I Armada and C Brière, *The inter-agency cooperation and future architecture of the EU criminal justice and law enforcement area*, Study for the LIBE Committee, PE 510.000 (Brussels, 2014) 24 ff, available at www.europarl.europa.eu/RegData/etudes/STUD/2014/510000/IPOL_STU%282014%29510000_EN.pdf.

[22] Article 1(g) Council Decision 2009/934/JHA of 30 November 2009 adopting the implementing rules governing Europol's relations with partners, including the exchange of personal and classified information [2009] OJ L325/6.

[23] Ibid, Article 1(h).

i. Hub of Information

States must have the most up-to-date and detailed information possible for an effective fight against serious crime, including terrorism. National units hence supply Europol 'on their own initiative with the information and intelligence necessary for it to carry out its tasks'[24]—and with reference to this, trust is crucial for Europol to carry out its activities. The European Commission proposal reinforced such obligation amending the existing provision, adding that this 'includes providing Europol without delay with information relating to crime areas that are considered a priority by the Union'.[25] However, the proposed amendment, which stressed Member States' obligations to provide information without delay, was replaced by the Council and the European Parliament with the wording 'on their own initiative'.

Since Council Decision 2003/48/JHA of 19 December 2002, each Member State is required to ensure that at least the following information, necessary for Europol to fulfil its tasks, is communicated to the agency:

a. Data which identify the person, group or entity.
b. Acts under investigation and their specific circumstances.
c. Links with other relevant cases of terrorist offences.
d. The use of communications technologies.
e. The threat posed by the possession of weapons of mass destruction.[26]

Going further, following the terrorist attacks of September 11 (and the introduction of an EU definition of terrorist offences),[27] the Council enacted Council Decision 2005/671/JHA on the exchange of information and cooperation concerning terrorist offences. By contrast to Council Decision 2009/371/JHA, Council Decision 2005/671/JHA obliges Member States to designate a specialised service within its police agencies that collects relevant information.[28] Yet, the Council Decision seems to emphasise policy priorities in this field rather than increasing the amount of data stored at Europol.[29]

---

[24] Article 8(4) Europol Council Decision.

[25] Article 7 Europol Regulation Proposal.

[26] Council Decision 2003/48/JHA of 19 December 2002 on the Implementation of Specific Measures for Police and Judicial Cooperation to Combat Terrorism in Accordance with Article 4 of Common Position 2001/931/CFSP [2003] OJ L16/68.

[27] Council Framework Decision 2002/475/JHA of 13 June 2002 on combating terrorism [2002] OJ L164/3.

[28] Council Decision 2005/671/JHA; see also Statewatch, '"Scoreboard" on Post-Madrid Counter-Terrorism Plans' (Statewatch, 2004), available at www.statewatch.org/news/2004/mar/swscoreboard.pdf.

[29] Article 2(4) Council Decision 2005/671/JHA; Boehm, above n 2, 192.

Information is transmitted by the European National Units (ENU)—the liaison body between Europol and each competent national authority—to Europol SIENA (Secure Information Exchange Network Application). The information is then stored for operational and strategic analysis purposes. The Europol Information System (EIS) and the Analysis Work Files (AWFs) are the two databases containing personal data at the moment, with the AWFs containing the same data as in the EIS, namely suspects, convicted criminals or persons on whom there are factual indications or reasonable grounds to believe that they will commit crimes that fall within Europol's competence, and adding contacts, associates, witnesses, victims and informants.[30] AWFs are divided into two categories: terrorism and organised crime. In addition to these databases, the Europol Platform for Experts provides specialists in a variety of law enforcement areas, private industry and academics with opportunities to discuss matters of interest to law enforcement; to share unclassified non-personal data; and to share unclassified information and best practices on combating crime and to support training events.

A clear overlap between EIS and AWFs exists and Europol is currently discussing the best approach to make information more accessible to authorised actors for investigation purposes as well as for analysis purposes. However, AWFs are more specific as they contain several analysis groups dedicated to tackle, for example, Islamist terrorism and trafficking in human beings.

The feeding of the Europol databases is still controversial. To address this issue, the proposal for a Regulation does not target any specific database, which gives more flexibility to Europol to make its internal system of analysis and information exchange evolve without having to renegotiate and modify national and European norms targeting a specific database. In fact, while the original proposal removed the safeguard clause which allows Member States not to share information with Europol when this may endanger public order and internal security,[31] the European Parliament reintroduced Member States' discretion when sharing information would entail 'harming essential national security interests; jeopardising the success of a current investigation or the safety of individuals; or disclosing information relating to organisations or specific intelligence activities in the field of State security'.[32] In any case, no Member State should be forced to supply information, especially if it is considered contrary to national security interests.[33] Highlighting the shared threats and the need for effective cooperation and common analysis of these threats would foster trust between Member States.

---

[30] Articles 8(4), 12 and 14 Europol Council Decision.
[31] See Article 8(5) Europol Council Decision.
[32] Amendment 80, European Parliament legislative resolution, 25 February 2014.
[33] Articles 72 and 346(1)a TFEU and, eg, Article 2 Council Decision 2005/671/JHA.

Yet, Member States have long remained reluctant to exchange information with each other and with Europol.[34] This could be explained by several reasons. First, information tends to be compartmentalised at both organisational and legal levels. It is often dispersed between several ministries, services and authorities thus involving different degrees of secrecy. In the area of counterterrorism, coordination has proven a particularly difficult task.[35] Second, the lack of a clear policy on information channels and on the protection of sensitive and confidential information has hampered for a long time effective cooperation with Europol.[36] However, this is less true today. Third, a concern arises from the fact that in Europol's analysis work files personal data of victims and witnesses are not separated from personal data of criminals.[37] This would not be in compliance with the European Court of Human Rights (ECtHR) judgment in *S and Marper v UK* where the Court maintained that data related to suspects must be treated differently from those of convicted individuals.[38] However, the AWF rules stipulate that a review on the continued storage of data is regularly carried out and a specific regime is prescribed by Article 20(1) of the Europol Council Decision and Article 7(4) of the AWF rules.[39] As the situation was not considered very clear the Regulation Proposal prohibits the processing of personal data related to victims, witnesses or other persons who can provide information on criminal offences, or persons under 18 years of age, unless it proves necessary for preventing and combating crime that falls under Europol's objectives.[40]

---

[34] International Centre for Migration Policy Development, *Study on the status of information exchange amongst law enforcement authorities in the context of existing EU instruments*, JLS/2009/ISEC/PR/0001-F3, 9; E Disley, B Irving, W Hughes and B Patruni, *Evaluation of the implementation of the Europol Council Decision and of Europol's activities* (2012), available at www.europol.europa.eu/sites/default/files/publications/rand_evaluation_report.pdf; see also O Bures, 'Europol's Counter-Terrorism Role: A Chicken–Egg Dilemma' in C Kaunert and S Léonard (eds), *European Security, Terrorism and Intelligence: Tackling New Security Challenges in Europe* (New York, Palgrave Macmillan, 2013) 504. The issue emerged after the Madrid terrorist bombings, when Spanish police refused to share information on the types of explosives that had been used with its French counterparts.

[35] France, for example, has a centralised system, whereas Germany works at a more fragmented federal level. France has robust laws for detaining terrorist suspects and judges specifically trained to deal with the cases; other Member States do not.

[36] Council of the European Union, Third round of Mutual Evaluations 'Exchange of information and intelligence between Europol and the Member States and among the Member States respectively' Final Report, 13321/07 (Brussels, 16 October 2007) 29.

[37] Boehm, above n 2, 187 ff and 213.

[38] *S and Marper v UK* (2009) 48 EHRR 50, para 122.

[39] Council Decision 2009/936/JHA of 30 November 2009 adopting the implementing rules for Europol analysis work files, OJ L325/14.

[40] Article 36 Europol Regulation Proposal, amendment 149 of the European Parliament and Article 36 as modified by the Council of the European Union.

Information may still be exchanged directly between Member States without formally going through Europol channels and thus being stored in Europol databases, despite the existence of SIENA.[41] If exchanged directly, Member States keep control over the information they share[42] and can decide which Member State they trust to the point of sharing information. These bilateral exchanges escape Europol data protection standards.

Europol has developed increasing operational powers that facilitate the fight against serious crime, especially terrorism. However, the previous sections highlight the need to further improve Member States' trust in Europol and most importantly among each other, so that the agency can become more effective.

ii. Towards a supranational Agency with decisional powers binding EU Member States?

At the time of its establishment the plans for Europol's development were rather ambitious: it should have been a 'European FBI' as German Chancellor Helmut Kohl repeatedly suggested in the 1980s and 1990s.[43] Yet, the transfer of competences and powers to a common EU security agency that would not only coordinate national efforts, but also take action in delicate domains such as national security and terrorism seemed impossible.[44] National experiences are profoundly different in terms of threat (past and present) experiences. And trust in each others' criminal justice systems varies.

Over time Europol was attributed an increasing number of tasks, such as the possibility to analyse and exchange information as well as to propose, support and assist JITs to investigate serious crime falling within the remit of its competences. However, the European Parliament firmly opposes any transfer of coercive powers to Europol.[45] Such transfer was always considered inconceivable.[46]

Europol participates in the JITs in a supporting capacity, mainly by exchanging information.[47] In addition, Europol can request the initiation,

---

[41] Article 9(3) (d) Europol Council Decision.

[42] A Jonsson Cornell, 'EU Police Cooperation Post-Lisbon' in M Bergström and A Jonsson Cornell (eds), *European Police and Criminal Law Co-operation*, Swedish Studies in European Law, vol 5 (Oxford, Hart Publishing, 2014) 158.

[43] C Kaunert, 'Europol and EU Counterterrorism: International Security Actorness in the External Dimension' (2010) 33 *Studies in Conflict & Terrorism* 652, 654.

[44] Article 9 Europol Regulation Proposal.

[45] Amendment 65 concerning Article 5 Europol Regulation Proposal.

[46] Mitsilegas, above n 14, 163.

[47] Article 6 Europol Council Decision and Article 5 Europol Regulation Proposal.

conduct or coordination of criminal investigations in specific cases, based on its own analysis,[48] ie, on the analysis of data gathered. National authorities are free not to investigate.[49] Yet, the current proposal limits such discretion: 'National Units shall inform Europol without delay of the initiation of the investigation'. Europol can ask Member States to give specific reasons for not complying with the request. Currently, after amendments from the European Parliament, Member States are required to give such requests due consideration and, through their National Units, to inform Europol without delay whether an investigation will be initiated.[50] By contrast, it is interesting to note that cooperating with Eurojust, the competent national authorities that decide not to comply with a request regarding the setting up of an investigation or prosecution shall inform Eurojust of their decision and underlying motives without delay.[51]

Some necessary safeguards associated with the agency aim at fostering trust in order to make the cooperation more effective. First, the European Parliament and national parliaments have control over Europol's activities. Second, the absence of enforcement powers combined with the participation of Member States on a voluntary basis limits Europol's freedom of action. Europol's role and action are rigorously framed, which should reassure Member States that information shared is only to be used for strictly limited purposes.

B. Europol: A Very Active EU Agency Equipped with a Strong(er) Data Protection Regime

The agency is competent to deal with a certain number of serious offences (ie, 'organised crime, terrorism and other forms of serious crime'[52] affecting two or more Member States).[53] Given the seriousness of the offences and the high risk of infringements of fundamental rights in sharing data related to

---

[48] Articles 5(1) (d) and 7 Europol Council Decision and Article 6 Europol Regulation Proposal.

[49] Article 7 Europol Council Decision.

[50] Amendment 75 of the European Parliament on the Europol Regulation Proposal.

[51] Article 8 Council Decision 2009/426/JHA of 16 December 2008 on the strengthening of Eurojust and amending Council Decision 2002/187/JHA setting up Eurojust with a view to reinforcing the fight against serious crime [2009] OJ L138/14 (Eurojust Council Decision (2009)).

[52] Article 4 Europol Council Decision.

[53] Previously, the scope of its action was limited to 'terrorism, unlawful drug trafficking and other serious forms of international crime where there are factual indications that an organised criminal structure is involved and two or more Member States are affected'. See Article 2 Europol Convention.

these offences, strict data protection rules are the basis for maintaining trust among the parties that share information and intelligence with Europol and via Europol's SIENA system.

Europol data protection provisions cover a very high volume of personal data processed in the context of cooperation in criminal matters. The agency is empowered to use such data 'only for the performance of its tasks'.[54]

The flexibility of Europol databases and tasks more generally may be seen as an improvement from an efficiency perspective, but it must be effectively associated with strong data protection standards in compliance with the principle of proportionality.

In this regard, it is important to mention the 2008 Data Protection Framework Decision[55] adopted before the Europol Council Decision. This Framework Decision does not affect the set of data protection provisions applying to Europol[56] as framework decisions are meant to harmonise national laws. However, the Preamble of the Europol Council Decision highlights that a Council Framework Decision on the protection of personal data processed in the framework of police and judicial cooperation in criminal matters will be applicable to the transfer of personal data by Member States to Europol. The missing link between the two instruments is therefore rather confusing.

Europol is known to have a strong data protection policy.[57] An internal control mechanism has been put in place 'to allow the verification of the legality of retrievals from any of its automated data files'. Such requests can be audited, upon request, by Europol, the National Supervisory Bodies and the Joint Supervisory Body (JSB).[58] An important point is also the appointment of a Data Protection Officer who, while being a member of Europol staff, acts independently.[59]

Some qualify Europol as 'the most controlled police agency in Europe'.[60] However, the involvement of independent bodies in Europol's data protection regime is not a solution in itself.[61] It is crucial to ensure the protection

---

[54] Article 19 Europol Council Decision.

[55] Council Framework Decision 2008/977/JHA of 27 November 2008 on the protection of personal data processed in the framework of police and judicial cooperation in criminal matters [2008] OJ L350/60.

[56] Preamble, Council Framework Decision 2008/977/JHA, para 19.

[57] A De Moor and G Vermeulen, 'The Europol Council Decision: Transforming Europol into an Agency of the European Union' (2010) *Common Market Law Review* 47.

[58] Article 34 Europol Council Decision; Article 33(2) of this same Council Decision provides the right for people to access their personal data.

[59] Article 28 Europol Council Decision.

[60] C Fijnaut, 'Police Co-operation and the Area of Freedom, Security and Justice' in N Walker (ed) *Europe's Area of Freedom, Security and Justice* (Oxford, Oxford University Press, 2004) 255; see also A De Moor, *Europol, Quo Vadis? Critical Analysis and Evaluation of the Development of the European Police Office* (Antwerp, Maklu, 2012) 35.

[61] See P de Hert and V Papakonstantinou, *The data protection regime applying to the inter-agency cooperation and future architecture of the EU criminal justice and law enforcement area*, Study for the LIBE Committee, PE 510.001 (Brussels, 2014) available at www.europarl.europa.eu/RegData/etudes/STUD/2014/510001/IPOL_STU(2014)510001_EN.pdf.

and promotion of fundamental rights, while addressing security concerns and, for this purpose, adopting a strong(er) EU data protection framework.[62] This task is a difficult one. Member States still have different data protection legislation, especially with reference to data sharing.[63] The development of common principles on data protection is also crucial to foster the necessary trust required for an in-depth exchange of information.

In addition, the oversight of the intelligence services' work in many Member States is far too rudimentary given the means of mass surveillance currently employed for national security purposes or the fight against terrorism.[64] The prevention of crime is mainly entrusted to the executive, which can conduct secret investigations to gather information and/or intelligence. And it will be the executive that decides on the disclosure of information to other States,[65] on the basis of both political and legal factors.

As discussed earlier, Europol's data oversight remains a source of concern for academics, civil society, public officials and practitioners. In particular, the European Data Protection Supervisor (EDPS) has recommended more safeguards regarding the access to data involving people who have not yet been convicted.[66] In this respect, the Europol Regulation under discussion adds that processing of personal data on victims, witnesses or other persons who can provide information on criminal offences, or on persons under the age of 18 'shall be prohibited unless it is strictly necessary for preventing or combating crime that falls under Europol's objectives'.[67] Such provision would ensure the differentiation between criminal and non-criminal personal data, as required by the ECtHR.[68]

Paradoxically, Europol already has a very strong data protection framework. The issue is not really that of the relationship between Member States and Europol but rather of Member States among themselves. Exchange of information will not improve unless there is more approximation of national

---

[62] This is the aim of the European Council for 2015: European Council Conclusions, EUCO 79/14, para 4.

[63] The respect for personal data is emphasised under Articles 7 and 8 of the Charter of Fundamental Rights of the EU and Article 16 TFEU.

[64] European Parliament, Committee on Civil Liberties (LIBE Committee), Justice and Home Affairs, '*Draft Report on the US NSA surveillance programme, surveillance bodies in various Member States and their impact on EU citizens' fundamental rights and on transatlantic cooperation in Justice and Home Affairs*' 2013/2188 (INI) (8 January 2014).

[65] S Braum, 'Are We Heading Towards a European Form of "Enemy Criminal Law"? On the Compatibility of Jakob's Conception of "an Enemy Criminal Law" and European Criminal Law' in F Galli and A Weyembergh, *EU Counter-terorrism Offences. What Impact on National Legislation and Case-law?* (Bruxelles, Editions de l'Université de Bruxelles, 2011) 241.

[66] Opinion of the European Data Protection Supervisor (EDPS) on the Proposal for a Council Decision establishing the European Police Office (Europol), COM(2006) 817 final (2007/C 255/02) [2007] OJ C255/13.

[67] Article 36 Europol Regulation Proposal.

[68] *S and Marper v UK*, para 122.

data protection regimes and rules are developed so that the information gathered may only be used for certain purposes in all Member States.

III. HOW TO BECOME THE IDEAL PARTNER IN THE COOPERATION AGAINST SERIOUS CRIME

In the aftermath of September 11, Europol became competent to share information with the Federal Bureau of Investigation (FBI),[69] as well as with other third states and organisations. However, sharing information with external actors is even more challenging than within the EU. The level of trust of EU Member States may be even lower towards external partners. For this reason, Europol has to develop its internal governance in order to improve its cooperation and potentially become the most effective means for information exchange with other EU actors, such as Eurojust (A) as well external actors (B).

A. Europol's Relations with Other Agencies: The Case of Eurojust

Europol and Eurojust are two 'sister agencies'.[70] The former is said to be a 'mega-search engine'[71]—without being a European FBI—and the latter a 'control tower'[72]—without being a European prosecutor. While Europol provides support and coordination to law enforcement authorities, Eurojust supports and coordinates national investigating and prosecuting authorities.[73] It does so by exchanging information between the interested parties, facilitating and strengthening cooperation between competent national authorities and establishing relations with other partners, including third states.[74]

---

[69] The FBI has liaison officers based at Europol and Europol maintains a liaison office in Washington DC. This agreement was first adopted a few weeks after 9/11 and renewed after the March 2004 terrorist bombings in Madrid. Council of the European Union, 'Declaration on Combating Terrorism', available at www.consilium.europa.eu/uedocs/cmsUpload/DECL-25.3.pdf. See also M-P Ratzel, 'Europol—das Europäische Polizeiamt. Teil 1: Geschichte, Organization, Aufgaben, Zuständigkeitenund Rechtsgrundlage' (2007) 5 *Kriminalistik* 284.

[70] Weyembergh, Armada and Brière, above n 21, 11.

[71] French Senate, *Europol et Eurojust: perspectives d'avenir*, Rapport d'information no 477 (17 April 2014) 10.

[72] Ibid, 39.

[73] Article 85 (1) TFEU.

[74] Eurojust, *News*—'Eurojust 10th Anniversary' Issue 6 (February 2012) 1–2.

i. Rising Levels of Cooperation between Two Sister Agencies

Europol and Eurojust are working closely to share both information and best practices.[75] This cooperation is essential to assist national authorities from the preliminary police investigation phase up to the trial phase. In fact, the two agencies pursue the same purpose at different phases of the criminal justice process.[76] Judicial coordination and cooperation activities are complementary to the criminal analysis and police cooperation tasks, as illustrated by the *Skanderberg, Koala* and *Baghdad* operations.[77]

Yet, the practical relationship between the two agencies has at times been complicated, to the extent that some wondered whether there was rivalry rather than cooperation. In particular, Europol's strict data protection regime proved initially to be a major obstacle for information exchange, including in the domain of counterterrorism.[78]

A first cooperation agreement between Europol and Eurojust was signed in 2004; bilateral meetings were organised from 2006. Several provisions now make specific reference to the other agency. For instance, the 2008 Eurojust Council Decision invites parties to give assistance to improve cooperation between competent national authorities 'on the basis of Europol's analysis'[79] and to assist Europol, 'by providing it with opinions based on analyses carried out by Europol'.[80] A special task is entrusted to the Eurojust National Coordination System, which maintains 'close relations with the Europol National Unit' within each Member State.[81] Similarly, Europol shall inform Eurojust when making a request for the initiation of criminal investigations.[82] The two instruments illustrate the EU legislator's intention to strengthen the interactions between the two agencies.

A new cooperation agreement between Europol and Eurojust was concluded in 2010. It aims at establishing and maintaining close cooperation to

[75] Speeches of B De Buck (Europol) and V Jamin (Eurojust) at 'The Relationship between Europol and Eurojust: State of the Art and Future Prospects' (ECLAN Conference, Brussels, 12 February 2014).

[76] M Busuloc and M Groenleer, 'Beyond Design: The Evolution of Europol and Eurojust' (2013) 14(3) *Perspectives on European Politics and Society, Special Issue: Agency's Governance in the EU's AFTJ* 285.

[77] HL European Union Committee, *Europol: coordinating the fight against serious and organised crime*, above n 8, 126.

[78] O Bures, 'Euroust's Fledgling Counter-terrorism Role' (2010) 6(2) *Journal of Contemporary European Research* 236, 243–46.

[79] Article 7(1)(b) Eurojust Council Decision (2009).

[80] Ibid, Article 7(1)(f).

[81] See ibid, Article 12(5)(d). Europol National Units are organised by Article 8 2009 Europol Council Decision.

[82] Article 7(2) Europol Council Decision.

increase their effectiveness in combating serious crime through the exchange of operational, strategic and technical information as well as coordination of their activities.[83] Europol must inform Eurojust by its own actions of its findings and strategic analyses. On its own initiative or upon request, Europol will give Eurojust its analysis when information provided by the agency matches information stored in its databases.[84] Eurojust has a parallel obligation.[85] Both agencies may be associated with the activities of the other: Eurojust to Europol's AWFs[86] and Europol to Eurojust's strategic and coordination meetings.[87]

The Commission drafted a proposal for two Regulations based respectively on Article 85 TFEU (Eurojust) and Article 88 TFEU (Europol).[88] The purpose is to foster an enhanced cooperation between the two agencies,[89] although some overlaps remain, especially regarding the investigation phase. Both, Article 2 Eurojust Regulation, which is based on Article 85, and Article 3 Europol Regulation, which is based on Article 88, provide that the two agencies shall support and strengthen the cooperation between Member States in investigating serious crime.

While the two agencies increasingly cooperate,[90] several problems have been acknowledged,[91] namely: the identification of their respective roles on

---

[83] Article 2 Agreement between Eurojust and Europol (2010), available at www.eurojust.europa.eu/doclibrary/Eurojustframework/agreements/Agreement%20between%20Eurojust%20and%20Europol%20%282010%29/Eurojust-Europol-2010-01-01-EN.pdf.

[84] Ibid, Article 7.

[85] Ibid, Article 8(2).

[86] Ibid, Article 11. Article 9 gives Eurojust a right to request Europol to open a new AWF; Europol must reply and state its reasons if it refuses to follow the request.

[87] Ibid, Article 12. Article 10 gives Europol the right to request Eurojust to offer national authorities its assistance; Eurojust must also reply and state its reasons if it refuses to follow the request.

[88] According to Article 85(1) Eurojust coordinates investigations and prosecutions. Article 88(2) provides that Europol will coordinate, organise and implement investigative and operational action carried out jointly with Member States' competent national authorities.

[89] Discussions are still ongoing to improve their collaboration. See Article 27 Europol Regulation Proposal and Article 40 Eurojust Regulation Proposal. The Council's General Approach on Europol's proposal amended this Article mirroring further the provision in the Eurojust Regulation Proposal. Council, 'General Approach on the Proposal for a Regulation of the European Parliament and of the Council on the European Union Agency for Law Enforcement Cooperation and Training (Europol)' doc 10033/14 (Brussels, 28 May 2014).

[90] See, eg, Europol, *2013 Europol Review* 26 available at www.europol.europa.eu/sites/default/files/publications/europol_review13_web_complete.pdf; *2012 Europol Review* 70 available at www.europol.europa.eu/content/europol-review-2012; *2011 Europol Review* 70–71 available at www.europol.europa.eu/sites/default/files/publications/europolreview2011.pdf; and Eurojust, *2012 Annual Report* 42–43 available at www.eurojust.europa.eu/doclibrary/corporate/eurojust%20Annual%20Reports/Annual%20Report%202012/Annual-Report-2012-EN.pdf; Eurojust, *2013 Annual Report* 43 available at www.eurojust.europa.eu/doclibrary/corporate/eurojust%20Annual%20Reports/Annual%20Report%202013/Annual-Report-2013-EN.pdf.

[91] See Weyembergh, Armada and Brière, above n 21, 17–26.

the coordination of criminal investigations;[92] the funding of JITs; and the exchange and analysis of information. The question of trust is not a particular issue between the two agencies. The dialogue between the two agencies focuses more on the division of tasks and on the working methods.

ii. Towards an Effective Mutual Exchange and Enhanced Analysis of Information

Information exchange between the agencies takes place for operational purposes and for policymaking purposes.

Information exchange for operational purposes may take different forms. First, in order to ensure reciprocity, it may take place during inter-agency meetings. Second, information exchange may occur in the context of coordination/operational meetings in which both agencies participate,[93] as well as during joint operational activities such as JITs.[94] Third, AWFs are a means of information analysis offering to states involved the most accurate and updated intelligence.[95] By virtue of Article 11 of the Europol–Eurojust Cooperation Agreement, Europol may invite experts from Eurojust to participate in a specific analysis group, upon the conclusion of a working arrangement.[96] Eurojust can also request to be involved. This is a particularly effective cooperation mechanism, which fosters the interplay between the two agencies.[97] As mentioned above, since 2013 most of Eurojust's National Desks and the Case Analysis Unit have access to SIENA, allowing them to communicate safely, including with Europol National Units and with Europol itself.[98]

Concerns arise as the closer relationship between the two agencies allows for more information exchange. Article 13 of the Europol–Eurojust Cooperation Agreement only states that the use of transmitted data shall be limited to the purposes for which they were communicated.[99] In this respect, the

---

[92] C Rijken, 'Joint Investigation Teams: Principles, Practice, and Problems. Lessons Learnt from the First Efforts to Establish a JIT' (2006) 2(2) *Utrecht Law Review* 99; JL Lopes de Mota, 'Eurojust and its Role in JIT' (2009) 3 *Eurim* 88; L Horvatis and B de Buck, 'The Europol and Eurojust Project on Joint Investigation Teams' (2007) 8 *ERA Forum* 239.

[93] See, eg, Article 12 Agreement between Eurojust and Europol (2010).

[94] For further information see Boehm, above n 2, 322 ff; C Rijken and G Vermeulen, *Joint Investigation Teams in the EU* (The Hague, Hasser, 2006).

[95] Article 11 Agreement between Eurojust and Europol (2010); Boehm, above n 2, 322 ff.

[96] Article 14(8) Europol Council Decision.

[97] On the rights of associated third parties, see Europol, *New AWF Concept, Guide for Member State and Third Parties* (31 May 2012) 40–41.

[98] Ibid.

[99] However, this does not imply that the use is limited to the purpose for which they were gathered. See the conditions of transfer of data to other authorities in *Weber and Saravia v Germany* App no 54934/00 (ECtHR, admissibility decision, 29 June 2006).

EDPS correctly wondered who would be in charge of sharing the information and who would be the supervisor.[100]

Both agencies have a Data Protection Officer[101] and a Joint Supervisory Body—an external supervisor.[102] They are in charge of ensuring that the data processing is in compliance with data protection standards incorporated in Europol and Eurojust Council Decisions.

The two proposals under discussion provide different rules for processing personal data. The draft Regulation on Eurojust proposes the application of Regulation (EC) 45/2001[103] to the processing of personal data by Eurojust subject to *lex specialis* rules included in the draft Eurojust Regulation. By contrast, the draft Regulation on Europol introduces a specific and comprehensive set of rules on data protection based on the principles of Regulation (EC) 45/2001. Yet, it does not provide for its direct application to the processing of data by Europol.[104] The Regulation Proposals also introduce EDPS oversight over personal data processing.

In addition to the exchange of information for operational purposes, Eurojust and Europol collaborate in sharing information for analysis purposes. Eurojust contributes to Europol's Serious and Organised Crime Threat Assessment (SOCTA) and to the EU Terrorism Situation and Trend Report (TE-SAT) by providing information and analysis with a policymaking purpose.[105] Eurojust also provides an overview of the legislative amendments to counterterrorism provisions in the Member States.[106]

In the field of information exchange, inter-agency relations have not always been smooth.[107] As mentioned, the 'principle of ownership' remains

---

[100] Opinion of the European Data Protection Supervisor (EDPS) on the Council Decision concerning the strengthening of Eurojust and amending Decision 2002/187/JHA, [2008] OJ L310/6, para 34.

[101] Article 28 Europol Council Decision and Article 17 Eurojust Council Decision (2009).

[102] Article 34 Europol Council Decision and Article 23 Eurojust Council Decision (2009).

[103] Council Regulation (EC) 45/2001 of the European Parliament and the Council on the protection of individuals with regard to the processing of personal data by the Community institutions and bodies and on the free movement of such data [2001] OJ L8/1.

[104] Council of the European Union, Proposal for a Regulation on the European Union Agency for Criminal Justice Cooperation (Eurojust), Strategic Discussion on Data Protection, 2013/0256 (COD), 8772/14, 16 April 2014, 1.

[105] Eurojust's contribution consists of quantitative and qualitative analysis of terrorism-related national court judgments, which reflect the number of convictions and penalties over the last 12 months. See Europol, *TE-SAT 2014, EU Terrorism Situation and Trend Report 2014*, 16–19. See also M Busuioc and D Curtin, *The EU Internal Security Strategy, the EU Policy Cycle and the Role of (AFSJ) Agencies*, Study for the LIBE Committee, PE.453.185 (Brussels, 2011) 60, available at www.europarl.europa.eu/meetdocs/2009_2014/documents/libe/dv/01_study_eu_iss_/01_study_eu_iss_en.pdf.

[106] Eurojust, *2012 Annual Report*, 25.

[107] In 2008, the extent to which sensitive data in AWFs could be passed from Europol to Eurojust still caused problems (HL European Union Committee, *Europol: Coordinating the fight against serious and organised crime*, above n 8, 49).

one of the fundamental principles:[108] the information supplier remains the owner of the information and is entitled to refuse any further distribution, which should foster cooperation. States always have their say regarding the use of the information by another competent authority. This principle may explain why Eurojust only receives the version of the SOCTA available to any third party, thus preserving the confidentiality of Member States' information.[109] It also partially explains why the agency is not yet involved in some potentially more sensitive issues dealt with in particular focal points subdividing the two AWFs. Competent national authorities are in fact reluctant to share sensitive information with the judiciary.[110]

Over the years the inter-agency relationship has gradually improved.[111] For instance, Eurojust is increasingly participating in Europol's AWFs. Enhancing operational cooperation between the two agencies has been crucial for establishing mutual trust. In addition, we can expect information exchange to improve following the adoption of the new Regulation currently under discussion. The two proposals in fact include mirroring provisions whereby a new cooperation framework is established:[112] on the basis of a hit/no hit system, each agency must provide its counterpart, within its mandate, with indirect access to information, yet without prejudice to any restriction indicated by the 'owner'. In case of a hit, the agency initiates the procedure so that the information may be shared in accordance with the owner's decision. Two restrictions apply: searches can be made only for the purpose of identifying a hit and only staff members specifically authorised may perform searches. If, in the course of information-processing activities, Eurojust identifies a need for Europol to intervene, it shall immediately notify the sister agency and begin the procedure for information sharing.[113]

The new system will not overturn the 'principle of ownership'. Member States, or any other information suppliers, retain the right to oppose information sharing under specific circumstances.[114] However, the mechanism is likely to improve the information exchange between the two agencies. First, the provision on information exchange is not simply included in the cooperation agreement but in the Regulation itself. This is a crucial change in terms of visibility and enforceability. Second, a request is no longer needed to discover whether the other agency is in possession of information or not.

---

[108] Weyembergh, Armada and Brière, above n 21, 24 ff.

[109] Busuioc and Curtin, above n 106, 9.

[110] Ibid.

[111] See Weyembergh, Armada and Brière, above n 21, 24.

[112] Article 27 Europol Regulation Proposal and Article 40 Eurojust Regulation Proposal. The Council's General Approach on Europol's proposal amended this article, but its amendments seek to mirror further the content of the Eurojust Regulation Proposal.

[113] This provision is reciprocal; Weyembergh, Armada and Brière, above n 21, 24.

[114] Article 25(2) Europol Regulation Proposal and Article 40(5) Eurojust Regulation Proposal.

Finally, the new mechanism reflects the change of mentality and enhanced trust of national authorities with regard to information sharing.[115]

Information shared by Member States and exchanged through Europol and Eurojust is analysed by the agencies.[116] Europol's expertise is well established[117] and the existence of specific devices enabling national authorities to upload data automatically enhances its analytical capacity/capabilities.[118] By contrast, Eurojust's information analyses have only been introduced recently. Even though the transfer of data from national authorities to Eurojust is not fully ensured,[119] the agency now receives a sufficient amount of information[120] and gradually establishes its own analytical capacities.[121]

Some have wondered whether Eurojust's information analysis would not duplicate Europol's effort without the resources or expertise.[122] It is noteworthy that the first Cooperation Agreement repeatedly highlights that one of the purposes of the document is to avoid duplication of efforts between the two agencies.[123] It is true that they both pursue operational and

---

[115] See Weyembergh, Armada and Brière, above n 21, 24.

[116] About Europol's intelligence-led rationale, see D Bigo, L Bonelli, D Chi and C Olsson 'Mapping the Field of the EU Internal Security Agencies' in D Bigo (ed), *The Field of the EU Internal Security Agencies* (Paris, l'Harmattan, 2007) 39.

[117] French Senate, above n 71, 12.

[118] See www.europol.europa.eu.

[119] Article 13 of the Eurojust Council Decision (2009) has not yet been transposed by some Member States, such as Italy (Report on Italy, doc 15858/1/13, 29). Moreover, in countries where it is transposed, difficulties arise in its concrete implementation by national authorities (French Senate, above n 71, 24).

[120] See the numerous evaluation reports: *Report on Estonia*, doc 17899/2/12, 19 available at www. eurojust.europa.eu/doclibrary/Eurojust-framework/6thRME/6th%20RME%20Report%20 on%20ESTONIA%20-%20Declassified%20(26%20April%202013)/6RME-Estonia-2013-04-26-Declassified_EN.pdf; *Report on Finland*, doc 7989/2/13, 24 f available at www. eurojust.europa.eu/doclibrary/Eurojust-framework/6thRME/6th%20RME%20Report%20 on%20FINLAND%20-%20Declassified%20(11%20July%202013)/6RME-Finland-2013-07-11-Declassified_EN.pdf; or *Report on Poland*, doc 13682/1/13, 34 f available at www. eurojust.europa.eu/doclibrary/Eurojust-framework/6thRME/6th%20RME%20Report% 20on%20POLAND%20-%20Declassified%20(3%20December%202013)/6RME-Poland-2013-12-03-Declassified_EN.pdf.

[121] P Jeney, *The Future of Eurojust*, Study for the LIBE Committee, PE 462.451 (Brussels, 2012) 85, available at www.europarl.europa.eu/RegData/etudes/etudes/join/2012/462451/ IPOL-LIBE_ET%282012%29462451_EN.pdf.

[122] See Weyembergh, Armada and Brière, above n 21, 25–26. See also G de Kerchove, Evidence to HL European Union Committee in *Europol: coordinating the fight against serious and organised crime: evidence* (2007–08, HL 183) (London, 25 June 2008) 153; and earlier, on the same issue, M Felgenhauer, Evidence to HL European Union Committee: 'Eurojust: evidence' in *Judicial Cooperation in the EU: the role of Eurojust* (23rd report) (2003–04, HL 138) (London, 18 May 2004) 61.

[123] See 'Preamble' and Article 2 Agreement between Europol and Eurojust (2004), available at eurojust.europa.eu/doclibrary/Eurojust-framework/agreements/Agreement%20Eurojust-Europol%20(2004)/Eurojust-Europol-2004-EN.pdf. See also Joint Eurojust–Europol *Annual Report to the Council 2009* pursuant to Point III 2.3 of the Hague Programme on the cooperation between Eurojust and Europol 2009, doc 5843/2011 (Brussels, 18 February 2011).

strategic analyses; yet, the content and purpose of the activities are distinct.[124] First, Europol's operational analyses[125] address an individual operation as short-term analyses providing the investigative team with information and leads.[126] Eurojust's operational analysis is case related and prepares coordination meetings by identifying links between judicial investigations and prosecutions. Second, Europol's strategic analyses address long-term goals of law enforcement authorities by reviewing current and emerging trends in order to identify concrete opportunities to take actions, as well as possible policy developments, programmes and legislative changes,[127] while Eurojust's strategic analyses aim at identifying recurring judicial cooperation issues and possible solutions in the prosecution of criminal networks operating across borders.[128]

Europol and Eurojust increasingly share information with each other and with EU Member States and other partners. They also analyse this information. In order to improve the cooperation between agencies the question arises whether it would be desirable to associate this cooperation with a common data protection regime.

Given the routine exchange of personal information between the agencies and with third states and international organisations, the lack of a common data protection regime is in fact a significant legal gap. The question is whether it would be sufficient to apply the EU common data protection package currently under negotiation or if agency-specific data protection should be stipulated for this purpose. The agency-specific approach—which is also the current approach—risks fostering a continuous fragmentation, which is harmful for a comprehensive data protection scheme. The creation of a common data protection framework for Europol and Eurojust, or even a transversal EU data protection framework, would facilitate data exchanges between the two agencies, while fostering transparency and a higher degree of legal certainty for individuals and thus mutual trust.[129]

---

[124] Weyembergh, Armada and Brière, above n 21, 37.

[125] *2013 Europol Review*, 14.

[126] A Smith (ed), *Intelligence-Led Policing: A European Union View*, IALEIA, Intelligence Led Policing, International perspectives on policing in the 21st century, 1997, available at www.oss.net/dynamaster/file_archive/040319/bb333cd178e0921c85076e8fb9532424/OSS1999-E1-15.pdf, 12; Horvatis and de Buck, above n 92, 258.

[127] Smith, above n 127, 12; Council, *Conclusions on the creation and implementation of a EU policy cycle for organised crime and serious international crime*, doc 15358/10 (8–9 November 2010); L Paoli, 'How to Tackle (Organised) Crime in Europe? The EU Policy Cycle on Serious and Organised Crime and the New Emphasis on Harm' (2014) 22(1) *European Journal of Crime, Criminal Law and Criminal Justice* 1, 5.

[128] Eurojust, Strategic project on Eurojust's action against trafficking in human beings, 2012, available at www.eurojust.europa.eu/doclibrary/corporate/Casework%20publications/Eurojust%20action%20against%20trafficking%20in%20human%20beings%20%28 October%202012%29/THB-report-2012-10-18-EN.pdf; Eurojust, *Annual Report 2012*, 25.

[129] M McGinley and R Parkes, 'Data protection at the EU level: a stocktaking of the current state of affairs' SWP Working Paper FG1, 2007/03 (Berlin, May 2007).

B. Europol's Relations with External Actors including States and Organisations

Europol is becoming a star in popular movies and culture in Europe and abroad. For instance, in the United States, the TV Series *Law & Order: Special Victims Unit* episode 'Pandora' (2003) wrongly introduced Europol as an instrument of European policing to an American audience.[130] In reality, one of the current challenges is the relation between Europol and external actors, including third states and organisations,[131] which calls for improving the link between the EU's internal and external policies.

The EU is now attempting to build operational relationships with external actors. Europol in developing external cooperation needs to reassure partners that information exchanged and processed via the agency is protected. This is necessary for Europol's effectiveness within and outside the EU. In this context, the status of Europol as an international security actor is to be investigated. Does the development of Europol capabilities make it the most relevant partner to prevent and combat serious crime from an external perspective?

Even before the Europol Council Decision the Council had adopted three regulations concerning the receiving of information from third parties by Europol, the governance of Europol's external relations with third states, and the transfer of personal data by Europol to third states and organisations. The Council Decision then also introduced some changes concerning Europol's means of cooperation with third states and organisations. Among them, legal personality[132] (derived from the EU) allows Europol to establish direct and closer relations with third states such as Canada, India, Israel and the United States and organisations such as Interpol.[133] Unanimity remains required to accept the list of states and organisations with which negotiations should occur when signing agreements.[134]

Cooperation with third states and organisations in preventing and combating crime has strong potential. Europol regulates international data

---

[130] Kaunert, above n 43, 652. See also S Kragh Pederson, 'Fictional Appearances of Europol', Europol Corporate Communications, available at www.europol.europa.eu/content/page/tv-films-and-books-195.

[131] eg, the United States, now considered the most significant external partner of the EU. See, eg, Council of the European Union, Presidency Conclusions, 16-17 December 2004 (2004), doc 16238/04, pt 28; EU Plan of Action on Combating Terrorism (2005).

[132] Article 2 Europol Council Decision; D Heimans, 'The External Relations of Europol—Political, Legal and Operational Considerations' in B Martenczuck and S Van Thiel (eds), *Justice, Liberty and Security—New Challenges for EU External Relations* (Brussels, VUB Press/Brussels University Press, 2008).

[133] Council Decision 2009/935/JHA of 30 November 2009 determining the list of third States and organisations with which Europol shall conclude agreements [2009] OJ L325/12.

[134] Heimans, above n 132.

transfers with a distinction between operational and strategic agreements; the latter said to be 'reserved for countries with a questionable human rights or data protection track record'.[135,136]

With reference to its cooperation with third states, the example of the relationship between the EU and the United States is quite noteworthy. In particular, both Europol–United States strategic (2001) and operational (2002) agreements remain highly controversial, especially because of the differences in data protection standards. However, despite controversies and current negotiations, Europol's relationship with the United States is well advanced and both sides benefit from it.[137]

Regarding its cooperation with organisations, it is unfortunate that Europol does not have any agreement with other regional organisations and/or agencies or other regional organisations' Member States for the purpose of information sharing.[138]

The Europol Regulation Proposal further develops the possibility for Europol to share information with third states or international organisations when necessary to perform its tasks on the basis of international agreements.[139] The proposal highlights the need for the partner to have 'adequate safeguards with respect to the protection of privacy and fundamental rights and freedoms of individuals'. Despite the conclusion of an international agreement with a third party, Europol remains bound by the 'principle of ownership'.[140]

In addition to this cooperation with organisations, transfer of information to third parties not on the list might take place if 'it is absolutely necessary in individual cases for the purpose of preventing or combating criminal offences in respect of which Europol is competent'.[141] The proposal allows Europol's executive director to directly share personal data with third states

---

[135] P de Hert and B de Schutter, 'International Transfer of Data in the Field of JHA: The Lessons of Europol, PNR and Swift' in B Martenczuck and S Van Thiel (eds), *Justice, Liberty and Security—New Challenges for EU External Relations* (Brussels, VUB Press/Brussels University Press, 2008) 323.

[136] Operational agreements allow for the exchange of personal data. They have been established with, for instance, Canada, the United States and Interpol. Strategic agreements are structural agreements, which do not entail the exchange of personal data. They have been established with, for instance, the Russian Federation, Ukraine and the United Nations Office on Drugs and Crime (UNODC). Council of the European Union, Note from the EU Counter-Terrorism Coordinator to COREPER, Brussels (2004) doc 9791/04, 11 available at www.statewatch.org/news/2004/jun/eu-plan-terr-options.pdf; this paper stressed the need for simplification of the procedures establishing structured cooperation between Europol and third States and organisations.

[137] Kaunert, above n 43.

[138] Council Decision 2009/935/JHA.

[139] Article 31 Europol Regulation Proposal.

[140] Ibid, Article 29(4).

[141] Article 13 Europol Council Decision.

or international organisations on a case-by-case basis following a list of situations in which it is absolutely necessary.[142] As for this method of transfer of information by international agreements, the consent of the Member State 'owner' of the information is always required.[143]

Europol's potential information exchange with external actors has been criticised, especially with third parties that are not included on the list.[144] The main concern is that third states and organisations do not always have the same level of data protection, although this is often the case among EU Member States as well. The Europol Council Decision introduced a number of safeguards to ensure a certain protection of personal data. First, it provides that information may only be transferred to external actors with the Member State's consent.[145] Second, Europol shall ensure that an 'adequate level of data protection' is met.[146] Third, an agreement on confidentiality is required for the transfer of classified information to EU bodies as well as to third states or organisations.[147] Europol has to consider the data protection provisions of the entity concerned as well as whether or not this entity has agreed to 'specific conditions required by Europol concerning the data'.[148]

At first glance, the adequacy assessment seems to be based on Directive 95/46. It thus takes into account: the circumstances of the transfer, nature of the data; and the purpose and duration of the intended processing. In this international context, data protection standards are lower, because the assessment over other party's data protection standards is only based on the guarantees provided by the third state or organisation. Moreover, the level of assessment may vary from one agreement to another. In the Regulation Proposal—as modified by the European Parliament and the Council—the EDPS is involved in the negotiation of international agreements and in the decision of the executive director to share information on a case-by-case basis. The proposal also reaffirms the need for adequate human rights protection in the third country or international organisation, to be certified by the EDPS.[149]

An effective fight against serious crime through information exchange would only be possible under the framework of EU data protection provisions

---

[142] Article 31(2) Europol Regulation Proposal.
[143] Ibid, Article 29(4).
[144] Many debates exist regarding the level of protection of fundamental rights required from external partners to authorise the sharing of information. Taking into account the amendments of the European Parliament and the Council, this level should be higher with the future Europol Regulation. See Article 31 Europol Regulation Proposal and its amendments.
[145] Article 24(1) Europol Council Decision.
[146] Article 23(6)(b) Europol Council Decision; see also Boehm, above n 2, 209.
[147] Article 23(7) Council Decision 2009/934/JHA.
[148] Boehm, above n 2, 210.
[149] See Europol Regulation Proposal; European Parliament legislative resolution of 25 February 2014; Council of the European Union, 'Proposal for a Regulation on Europol, General Approach'. Quite similarly, see Article 23(8) Europol Council Decision.

governing international data transfers. Member States will not share information if data protection standards are too low and if information is subsequently used for different purposes, including political ones. The issue of trust is even more sensitive in relation to external partners. The level of human rights protection in third countries is not the same, which nourishes a certain reluctance on the EU side.[150] Information sharing with Interpol is for the same reason not yet fully trusted. In this area, information exchanged between Europol and third parties requires full attention, especially as all parties can develop information-sharing mechanisms with different data protection standards.[151] In this context it is interesting to mention that agreements signed before the Treaty of Lisbon had a very different level of data protection.

Regarding the relationship between Europol and the United States, the EU has been negotiating with the US Government, on the basis of Article 218 TFEU, an international framework agreement (the 'Data Protection Umbrella Agreement') to protect personal data transferred for law enforcement purposes across the Atlantic since 29 March 2011. The scope of such an agreement will cover transfers in the context of the prevention, detection, investigation and prosecution of serious crime, including terrorism. The agreement would introduce a comprehensive framework, ensuring a high level of data protection, by setting out a series of guarantees and safeguards. Future data-sharing agreements would be negotiated more easily once legal data protection standards are adopted within the EU. No consensus has been found yet. Is the agreement to be based on a mutual recognition principle whereby data protection standards are to be considered equivalent? A controversial issue remains for instance that of judicial redress, which is not available for EU citizens who are not resident in the United States. A source of concern is also whether the agreement is to be applied retroactively on previous EU–US data-sharing agreements, although this could lead to a certain level of legal uncertainty.[152]

In the current situation, personal data may only be transmitted under strict conditions (eg, in a 'ticking-bomb scenario' situation). A source of

---

[150] Nevertheless, major concerns have been raised especially about the PNR agreements with the United States, requiring the transfer of European passenger data. See Council Decision 2012/471/EU of 13 December 2011 on the signing, on behalf of the Union, of the Agreement between the United States of America and the European Union on the use and transfer of Passenger Name Records to the United States Department of Homeland Security [2012] OJ L215/1; criticism has been expressed by the European Parliament. See Committee on Civil Liberties (LIBE Committee, Justice and Home Affairs), *Draft Report on the US NSA surveillance programme*, above n 64.

[151] Ibid, 49.

[152] See M Quesada Gamez and E Micheva, 'No Data Without Protection? Rethinking Transatlantic Information Exchange for Law Enforcement Purposes After Lisbon' in PJ Cardwell (ed), *EU External Relations Law and Policy in the Post-Lisbon Era* (The Hague, Springer, 2012) 287.

concern in relation to these agreements from a data protection perspective is that little information exists on where data shared go and for what purpose they are eventually used. The definition of what 'personal data' are for the purpose of the agreements' scope is also vague at times.[153]

Europol could easily be recognised as a strong international actor and thus coordinate and represent the EU common fight against serious crime vis-a-vis third parties. Although the agency's role in representing the external dimension of the EU in security matters is not yet developed,[154] it is clearly under construction.

IV. CONCLUSION

Europol has become a major player within the EU in supporting and strengthening cooperation between Member States in the fight against serious crime. It has developed the legitimacy and trust required to perform effectively. Yet, it is very dependent upon Member States.

Nevertheless, Europol's lack of coercive powers, for instance, does not mean that its action is less effective. In fact, there is a certain causal relationship between effectiveness and legitimacy. The more Europol becomes legitimate and trusted by the competent authorities, the more it will be effective.[155] In this regard, improving the effectiveness of Europol is not incompatible with a human rights-based approach. On the contrary, developing an EU data protection regime and building up trustworthy relationships between Europol, EU Member States, other EU bodies and third states and organisations will eventually transform the EU agency into a vital tool for the fight against serious crime within and outside the EU.

Europol has developed over time to find its place in the EU security landscape and to reinforce its credibility as a competent and credible actor before national authorities. Further developments may improve trust between EU Member States and external actors, but this will take time. In this process, thanks to the fruitful exchange of best practices, meetings are crucial to raise awareness of each EU agency's competence at the national level and develop personal contacts to smooth cooperation. The lack of mutual trust among Member States remains a central issue and a source of concern as it fundamentally hampers Europol's activities.[156]

---

[153] See C Hillebrand, *Counter-Terrorism Networks in the European Union: Maintaining Democratic Legitimacy after 9/11* (Oxford, Oxford University Press, 2012) ch 7.

[154] Kaunert, above n 43.

[155] M Barnett 'Social Constructivism' in J Baylis, S Smith and P Owens (eds), *The Globalization of World Politics. An Introdction to International Relations*, 4th edn (Oxford, Oxford University Press, 2008) 165.

[156] European Council Conclusions, EUCO 79/14, para 11.

8

Building Trust and More: The Importance of Police Cooperation Networks in the European Union

TOINE SPAPENS

I. INTRODUCTION

TRUST IS AN essential prerequisite for effective police cooperation. In this chapter, I will show how police cooperation networks contribute to building trust between police forces of the Member States of the European Union.

Networks such as the *Niederländisch-Belgisch-Deutsche Arbeitsgemeinschaft Polizei* (Nebedeagpol) in the Meuse–Rhine Euroregion and the Cross Channel Intelligence Conference (CCIC) have existed in border areas since the 1960s and are still going strong today.[1] More recently, cooperation networks spanning the entire Union but focusing on thematic issues have also emerged. Aquapol, for example, addresses cooperation on the main internal waterways of the EU. Envicrimenet specifically focuses on cooperation in the field of environmental crime.

From a theoretical point of view the most basic level of trust involves individual police officers who cooperate because they trust each other and not necessarily the state system or the enforcement organisation of which they are a part. At the other end of the spectrum we can distinguish full institutional trust in which the enforcement organisation, and each of the members belonging to it, is trusted.

---

[1] The Meuse–Rhine Euroregion consists of the provinces of Limburg and Liège, as well as the *Deutschsprachige Gemeinschaft* (Eupen–Malmedy) in Belgium, the German Aachen Region with the city of the same name as well as the *Landkreise* Aachen, Heinsberg, Düren, and Euskirchen, and the southern part of the Dutch province of Limburg. The CCIC comprises the regions of Southern Holland, West Flanders, Nord/Pas de Calais and South East England.

Starting from a community perspective, Sztompka for example distin-guishes 'circles' of trust.[2] The narrowest radius covers trust between family members; then comes trust towards people we know personally whom we recognise by name and with whom we interact in a face-to-face manner. The next circle encompasses the members of a small community, which may for instance be a social community such as a neighbourhood or village, but also a company. Police forces of democratic states can to some extent also be viewed as 'communities' with comparable goals, such as protecting the safety of individual citizens, assisting victims, maintaining public order and protecting the state's institutions.[3] The widest circle includes large num-bers of people, for example the inhabitants of an entire country or even the global population.[4]

Studies on inter-organisational cooperation have identified a number of factors that determine trust. Zucker, for instance, developed a well-known typology that identifies three types of trust and the factors contributing to it: characteristics-based trust; process-based trust; and institutional trust.[5] Characteristics-based trust focuses on belonging to similar communities and the sharing of cultural values. Process-based trust refers to trust that follows from interaction.[6] Institutional trust derives mainly from rules, eth-ics and professional standards. Actual cooperation constructs, for example, loyalty and commitment between partners. Obviously, negative experiences will reduce the propensity to seek cooperation in the future. This does not only refer to the material outcomes of the cooperation, but to the process as well. In addition, both negative and positive experiences will be shared with others in and outside the organisation and thus affect a party's reputation.[7]

Police cooperation networks first facilitate different levels of trust by means of promoting 'networking' activities for police officers in the tradi-tional sense, for instance by organising meetings and joint training, but they also increasingly offer operational support to police officers in the field, for example through the internet.

Second, promoting institutional trust is becoming increasingly important in the EU. This is illustrated by the Stockholm Programme in which the

---

[2] P Sztompka, *Trust. A Sociological Theory* (Cambridge, Cambridge University Press, 1999).

[3] In authoritarian states, emphasis will be more on the role of the police as a political instrument. Logically, that will also affect individual police officers' behaviour and ethics. See C Fijnaut, *Opdat de Macht een Toevlucht Zij? Een historische studie van het politieapparaat als politieke instelling* (Antwerp, Kluwer, 1979).

[4] Sztompka, above n 2.

[5] L Zucker, 'Production of Trust. Institutional Sources of Economic Structure 1840 to 1920' Working Paper Series No 82, (Los Angeles, University of California, 1985).

[6] B Nooteboom, *Trust. Forms, Foundations, Functions, Failures and Figures* (Cheltenham, Edward Elgar, 2002).

[7] E van de Ven and P Smith Ring, 'Relying on Trust in Cooperative Inter-Organizational Relationships' in R Bachmann and A Zaheer, *Handbook of Trust Research* (Cheltenham, Edward Elgar, 2006).

European Union (EU) introduced the 'principle of convergence', aimed at streamlining police education and police working methods in the Union. Harmonisation of non-operational police cooperation has been much easier to achieve since the Lisbon Treaty came into effect because the ordinary legislative procedure now applies to directives in this field. 'Informal' police cooperation networks play a vital role in non-operational cooperation. The 'old' cooperation networks—which are still highly relevant and active today—evolved in EU border areas and focused on local problems. Some of the solutions they proposed later found their way into, for example, the Schengen Implementation Convention. The 'new' networks attempt to span the entire Union and aim to influence and harmonise EU legislation more closely from the start.

Until now, non-operational police networks and cooperation have attracted comparatively little attention from academics.[8] The aim of this chapter is to investigate a number of 'new' cooperation networks and how they operate, as well as to discuss their relevance in the context of police cooperation and promoting institutional trust in the EU.

II. OPERATIONAL AND NON-OPERATIONAL POLICE COOPERATION

Before giving concrete examples of cooperation networks and their activities, the question of how to define 'non-operational' police cooperation must first be addressed. How does it differ from 'operational' police cooperation? Furthermore, what is the difference between 'police' and 'judicial' cooperation? As demonstrated below, neither boundary is clear and may vary between countries.

Operational law enforcement cooperation generally refers to the investigation of crimes and the gathering and exchange of information and evidence in this context. Operational *judicial* cooperation refers to requests for extradition and the handing over of suspects, the transfer of proceedings, the recognition of judgments and the transfer of convicted persons. Operational *police* cooperation concerns all other aspects of investigating a crime. However, it refers to the exchange of information that the police already possess; on the other, it concerns specific evidence that foreign counterparts must gather as well as information that is to be presented as evidence before the court. As a rule, operational cooperation involves personal data covered under data protection laws.

---

[8] There exist studies on 'traditional' cooperation networks such as Nebedeagpol and the Cross Channel Intelligence Conference. See S Brammertz, *La coopération policière dans l'Euregio Meuse-Rhin* (Eupen, UCL, 1993); and D Gallagher, 'European Police Co-operation: Its Development and Impact between 1967–1997 in an Anglo/French Trans-frontier Setting' (Unpublished PhD thesis, Southampton University, 1998).

The term 'police cooperation' is misleading as it certainly does not imply that the police are able to seek cooperation and exchange all types of personal data independently. In the EU, the existing legal framework only allows the police to exchange information already their possession, based on Article 39 of the SIC. In 2006, the 'Swedish' Framework Decision further extended this provision to include 'intelligence'.[9] The police require the consent of the competent judicial authorities when the gathering of evidence involves the use of coercive investigation methods. Furthermore, 'independently' exchanged information and intelligence may be used for investigative purposes only and cannot be presented before the court without the consent of the competent authorities of the requested state.

In situations that require the gathering of new evidence abroad, the competent judicial authorities—the public prosecutor, the investigative magistrate, the Ministry of Justice—must file a request for mutual legal assistance (a letter rogatory) with their foreign counterpart. Such a request is necessary whenever the requested state must apply investigative powers, for example summoning a telecom provider to identify a telephone number, hearing a witness, interrogating a suspect, searching premises and wiretapping a suspect. All other information and intelligence that the police exchange independently must also be 'cleared' in a letter rogatory before it is admissible evidence in court.

Operational police cooperation depends on an extensive legal and organisational framework consisting of mutual legal assistance conventions and other legal instruments and international agencies, such as Interpol and Europol, through which the police exchange information. By contrast, regulations for non-operational police cooperation are much less strict. What exactly is non-operational police cooperation then?

To begin with, police officers, particularly those operating in the field of serious and organised crime, regularly meet with colleagues at international conferences. These meetings not only serve to pool experiences and best practices, but also help to develop personal relationships of trust. Such networks therefore play an important role in actual criminal investigations: it is far easier to start by contacting someone you already know and let the paperwork follow, than to immediately go through official channels.

Second, non-operational police cooperation refers to capacity building, joint education and training. In the context of the United Nations, for example, Dutch law enforcement officials have been training the police of South Sudan since 2012.[10] In the context of the EU, the European Police College

---

[9] Council Framework Decision 2006/960/JHA of 18 December 2006 on simplifying the exchange of information and intelligence between law enforcement authorities of the Member States of the European Union [2006] OJ L 386/89.

[10] See United Nations, *Peacekeeping Missions*, available at www.un.org/en/peacekeeping/missions/unmiss/.

(CEPOL) is a good example, offering a variety of joint courses.[11] The Treaty of Prüm and other conventions offer police in border areas—for example in the Netherlands—opportunities for operating on foreign territory. Police officers must, however, comply with the rules and regulations of the partner country. The Police Academy of the Netherlands has therefore set up a joint training programme with its counterparts in neighbouring countries. The final example is joint exercises, for example in handling riots.[12]

Third, countries as well as authorities in border regions may agree to undertake joint action against cross-border crime problems, for instance after a joint threat assessment. The Benelux, for instance, hosts the 'Senningen meetings', in which working groups address cross-border crime and safety problems, including joint disaster management when the emergency also impacts on the neighbouring country.[13] Representatives of police districts in border areas may also convene to discuss the management of events that attract large numbers of foreign visitors, such as Christmas markets, and to agree on exchanging personnel and means if necessary.

Fourth, non-operational cooperation concerns the technical infrastructure for police cooperation. The police in different countries usually work with different equipment for mobile communication. That means that a German patrol car and a Dutch patrol car may not be able to communicate directly. In this specific case, the problem was solved by making technical adaptations, but the solution may also involve harmonising operational procedures. One such case was when the Belgian, Dutch and French police joined forces in patrolling the A16 highway between Rotterdam and Lille to combat drug trafficking.[14] Police officers of different nationalities rode together in patrol cars and stopped suspect cars. The police use specific procedures for approaching a pulled-over car so that two police officers can cover each other at all times. The Belgian, Dutch and French procedures differed, however, which caused confusion and immediately called for harmonisation. The team consequently chose one method and trained all members accordingly.

Finally, the exchange of any information and intelligence not containing personal data and not intended for use in court proceedings may be viewed as non-operational cooperation. Europol, for example, concluded

---

[11] See CEPOL, *About Cepol*, available at www.cepol.europa.eu.

[12] M Bruinsma, M Jacobs, M Jans, J Moors, T Spapens and C Fijnaut, *Grensoverschrijdend politiewerk in de Euregio Rijn-Maas-Noord* (Antwerp/Oxford, Intersentia, 2010).

[13] ibid.

[14] These joint patrols were of course operational in nature and initially based on a bilateral agreement between the Netherlands and France. There were no legal provisions in Conventions on mutual legal assistance in early 1998. By 2005, such provisions had been incorporated in the Treaty of Prüm (see below). See E De Bie, H Ferwerda and I van Leiden, *Op de grens. Evaluatie van het A-team* (Arnhem, Advies- en Onderzoeksgroep Beke, 2004).

strategic agreements with a number of non-EU States that allow for the exchange of information on (1) enforcement actions that might be useful in suppressing offences, in particular special means of combating offences; (2) new methods used in committing offences; (3) trends and developments in the methods used to commit offences; (4) observations and findings resulting from the successful application of new enforcement aids and techniques; (5) routes and changes in routes used by smugglers or those involved in illicit trafficking offences covered by this agreement; and (6) prevention strategies and methods aiding in the selection of law enforcement priorities.[15]

This brief overview makes clear that non-operational police cooperation encompasses a broad array of activities. It also shows that the line between operational and non-operational cooperation is a relatively thin one. As examples in the next sections show, cooperation networks established in the EU address non-operational as well as operational issues.

III. COOPERATION INITIATIVES IN BORDER REGIONS

The failure of borders to repel individual criminals and crime groups is, of course, nothing new. Back in the seventeenth and eighteenth centuries, Dutch bands of brigands operated in what is now Belgium and Germany as well as in their own country.[16] After the Second World War, the police in European border areas increasingly felt the need to cooperate in the area of cross-border crime. This was particularly true in relatively densely populated and economically and socially homogeneous border regions.

One early example of this is the *Polizeichef-Vereinigung Bodensee*, a body founded in 1959 for non-operational police cooperation between Germany, Austria, Switzerland and Liechtenstein in the Lake Constance area. It meets twice a year to share best practices and to discuss cooperation issues as well as solutions to actual cross-border crime problems in the area. It also initiated a joint crime analysis report (*Sicherheitslagebild*) for the region in 2001. In recent years, joint operations in the field of public order policing became common practice, for example during the 2006 and 2008 world and European football championships organised by Germany, Austria and Switzerland, respectively. The fiftieth anniversary of the *Polizeichef-Vereinigung* celebrated the close, direct, informal and trustworthy cooperation that had developed over the decades and set an example for others.[17]

---

[15] See Europol, *External Cooperation*, available at www.europol.europa.eu/content/page/external-cooperation-31.

[16] F Egmond, *Op het verkeerde pad* (Amsterdam, Uitgeverij Bert Bakker, 1994).

[17] Schaffhauser Polizei, *50 Jahre Polizeichef-Vereinigung Bodensee*, 9 September 2009, available at www.shpol.ch.

Another early example of police cooperation in a border area is the Cross Channel Intelligence Cooperation (CCIC), established in 1968 by the Belgian, French and British police forces adjacent to the English Channel. The Netherlands joined this group later. At the time, the British were particularly concerned about illegal immigration, whereas the French and the Belgians worried about the transport of stolen goods across the Channel. Later, drug trafficking also became an issue.[18] The CCIC focused much of its efforts on the operational exchange of information and intelligence outside national and Interpol channels at a time when cross-border police cooperation was still seen as the diplomatic province of centralised bodies within sovereign states.[19] In 1973, the conference agreed to the direct transfer of operational intelligence between the police forces participating in the CCIC, parallel to the Interpol channel. It also agreed to set up multi-jurisdictional meetings to exchange information on possible cross-border crimes proactively. However, before the Schengen Implementation Convention came into effect for the United Kingdom, the question of the direct exchange of information sparked continuous discussion during CCIC meetings.[20] Importantly, the informal network that was built up within the context of the CCIC regularly enabled police officers to respond quickly to crime cases, for example in June 2000, when 58 Chinese nationals were found dead in a container that had been smuggled from the Netherlands to the United Kingdom. The investigating police forces of both countries met within 24 hours after the discovery of the bodies and they continued to cooperate closely during the parallel investigations.[21]

Our final example of police cooperation in an EU border region is Nebedeagpol in the Meuse-Rhine Euroregion, established in 1969 at the initiative of the *Polizeipräsident* (chief of police) of Aachen. As in the Lake Constance area, the initiative followed a long history of cross-border crime problems and past police partnerships at the diplomatic level between Germany, the Netherlands and Belgium.[22] The intentions of Nebedeagpol were to improve the reciprocal knowledge of the various police services; to organise direct radio and telex links between them; to exchange information about crime and criminals; to set up language courses for police

---

[18] J Sheptycki, 'Police Co-operation in the English Channel Region 1968–1995' (1998) 6 *European Journal of Crime, Criminal Law and Criminal Justice*.

[19] E Johnson, 'Case Report Operation Mallard from the Cross-Channel Euroregion' in M den Boer and T Spapens, *Investigating Organized Crime in European Border Regions* (Tilburg, IVA/Tilburg University, 2002) 36.

[20] Sheptycki, above n 18.

[21] Johnson, above n 19.

[22] C Fijnaut and T Spapens, 'The Meuse–Rhine Euroregion: A Laboratory for Police and Judicial Cooperation in the European Union' in F Lemieux (ed), *International Police Cooperation: Emerging Issues, Theory and Practice* (Cullompton, Willan Publishing, 2010).

officers; and to appoint contact officials in the police forces involved.[23] Proposals developed by Nebedeagpol, for example on the direct exchange of information, found their way into Articles 39 and 46 of the Schengen Implementation Convention, which the five original Schengen countries adopted in 1991 and which became effective in 1995. Other ideas, however, such as allowing police officers to go abroad to interview witnesses and interrogate suspects, were not included.[24]

IV. RECENT COOPERATION NETWORKS

The past decade has seen the appearance of new types of police cooperation networks in the EU. The first of these was the Association of Traffic Police Forces (Tispol) in 2000. Aquapol, established in 2002, focuses on inland and maritime navigation (professional as well as recreational), and on transport security and fighting crime on the waterways and in ports. Railpol was founded in 2007 as an international network of police organisations in EU Member States that are responsible for railway-related policing. Airpol was created in 2010 as a permanent and multidisciplinary cooperation network of police services, border guards and other relevant law enforcement services active in and around airports. A final example is Envicrimenet, established in 2011 as an informal network of contacts and a cooperative group addressing environmental crime. This section addresses three networks in more detail: Tispol, Aquapol and Envicrimenet.

A. Tispol

Traffic policing has always been one of the cornerstones of police work. Accident prevention is an important task in and of itself; in addition, information gathered during routine vehicle checks or following a traffic offence is often the starting point for criminal investigations.

Road transport in the EU has internationalised rapidly in the past few decades, particularly since the Schengen *Acquis* entered into force in 1999. It has also led to the stepping up of police cooperation in the field of traffic policing. For one thing, there were all sorts of practical issues. How can a German police officer who stopped a Lithuanian truck establish on the spot whether a transport document presented to him is genuine, for example?

---

[23] C Fijnaut and G van Gestel, 'De Politiële Samenwerking in het Belgisch-Nederlandse Grensgebied' in C Fijnaut, *De Reguliere Politiediensten van België en Nederland: hun Reorganisatie en Onderlinge Samenwerking* (Arnhem, Gouda Quint, 1992).

[24] A letter rogatory may be submitted requesting that foreign police officers be permitted to attend an interview or interrogation abroad, but they are not allowed to ask questions directly.

Second, many of the rules and regulations concerning safety and security on the roads were now being set at the Union level. The EU police forces felt that they had little influence on the policymaking process road traffic and transport. Traffic and transport safety regulations were then part of the First Pillar, whereas policing was part of the Third Pillar. Furthermore, the ministries of Justice and Home Affairs usually governed the police, and they too were often not involved in road safety or transport issues, and maintained no contacts with relevant stakeholders at the EU level.[25] For the police to be on speaking terms in 'Brussels' about these issues required a cooperative effort on the part of the traffic police forces of the different Member States.

The issues described above led to the creation of Tispol. The goal of the cooperation network is to bring the European traffic police units together to improve road safety and, increasingly, security. It includes exchanging ideas on a regular basis and informing the police of new means to enhance road safety, and of new traffic control tactics and techniques. Interestingly, Tispol is a non-governmental organisation set up as a non-profit limited company under UK law.[26] Its members are the traffic police forces, who also govern Tispol.

From the beginning, Dutch police commissioner Ad Hellemons was the driving force behind the organisation. It started as a cooperative effort between only four traffic police forces, but now includes all 28 Member States as well as Norway and Switzerland. Tispol does not have an office and its permanent staff consists of only three persons. The secretariat deals with all communication between its members via the website (www.tispol. org) and email. The website comprises a public part and a section that is accessible to members only. Working groups organise the various activities and meet twice a year. The Tispol Council (the representatives of the member police forces) also gathers twice a year, whereas the executive committee, which manages the network, meets every two months. Three directors take care of day-to-day management: the operational director, the general secretary and the treasurer.[27]

The European Commission immediately recognised the importance of the initiative and funded Tispol from the beginning. Importantly, funding originally came from the Directorate General for Transport and Energy (DGTREN), ie, from the former First Pillar. The Commission funded a variety of projects on road safety such as Lifesaver (training of police officers, compilation of a traffic enforcement handbook) and VERA (exchange of

[25] A Hellemons, 'Cooperation Between Traffic Police Departments in the European Union' in C Fijnaut and J Ouwerkerk, *The Future of Police and Judicial Cooperation in the European Union* (Leiden, Martinus Nijhoff Publishers, 2010).
[26] ibid.
[27] ibid.

information on non-resident traffic violators). In recent years, Tispol also received funding from the Third Pillar so as to address crimes associated with transport and mobility, such as human trafficking and drug trafficking. One example is Depet, a project to develop a new technology for tracking vehicles without infringing on privacy.

The original aim of Tispol was to establish an EU-wide network of traffic police departments. It now includes all the Member States. Working groups address specific topics and Tispol organises regular meetings, such as an annual conference on road safety attended by 200–250 delegates from all over Europe, police officers as well as other road safety stakeholders.[28] Tispol also organises extensive joint training activities and facilitates the exchange of police personnel between different Member States during internships. Operationally, the network organises at least 10 pan-European road safety operations per year, with all members taking part. Practical tools are made available through the website, such as the Transport Document System (TDS). This multilingual database enables checks of foreign transport documents and the detection of forged documents. Another example is the CLEOPATRA database on good traffic enforcement practices.[29]

Starting from road safety issues, Tispol has now also moved into the area of road security and crimes associated with transport, such as trafficking and mobile banditism. Tispol's European inspection operations now also focus on narcotic drugs, illicit firearms, illegal immigration, human trafficking and illicit waste transports. The network also looks into the theft of commercial vehicles and loads, and the security of parking areas for trucks along the main European transport axis.

B. Aquapol

The Aquapol network is a European partnership of water police forces and inland navigation inspectorates. Its areas of responsibility are inland and maritime navigation (professional as well as recreational), transport security on the waterways and in ports, and fighting crime.[30] The network's aim is to promote cooperation between its members and to advise the European legislative and regulatory bodies in the aforementioned areas.

The Dutch and German water police founded Aquapol in 2002. Currently, it comprises nine police forces and three inland navigation inspectorates in

---

[28] ibid.
[29] ibid.
[30] See Aquapol, *Aquapol*, available at www.aquapol.police.com.

nine Member States (the Netherlands, Germany, Belgium, France, Austria, Hungary, Czech Republic, Romania and Slovakia). At first, cooperation in Aquapol focused mainly on the key transport waterways of the Rhine and the Danube, but it wishes to expand its focus and the number of member countries in future. In recent years, for example, Aquapol began addressing port security and environmental crimes.

The contours of the Aquapol organisation are comparable to Tispol's. It maintains only a small permanent office, sharing its secretariat with Tispol, and its main communication tool is its extensive website. Aquapol members regularly meet during thematic seminars and in working groups, such as the working group on security and criminality. All members are represented in the Aquapol Council. The Council is responsible for the Aquapol organisation and all its activities. Council members chair the working groups.

Aquapol organises a number of international inspection operations each year, prepared by the working groups. During these operations, the competent authorities check ships for the presence of illegal and unqualified personnel; for exceeding navigation times; for neglecting safety and security regulations; for navigating under the influence of alcohol and/or drugs; and for breaches of environmental regulations.[31] Another initiative is the overview of stolen boats on Aquapol's website, which the organisation developed in cooperation with insurance companies.

For the practical support of police officers, the website also offers a database with multilingual information on different transport documents ('Documents for Transport over Water' or TDW) used within the EU, which police officers can refer to when they are checking a vessel. The database includes pictures of transport documents and information on specific markers to establish whether the documents are genuine. Another interesting feature is IBISWEB. This is a cross-border reference database for inspections of inland vessels. If, for example, the police have checked a ship in Rotterdam and found unqualified personnel on board, they can add a red flag in this category in IBISWEB. If Romanian police want to check the same vessel three weeks later in the port of Constanta, they can access the website beforehand to see if the ship has any red flags and subsequently pay extra attention to the relevant categories. IBISWEB is a hit/no-hit system; if the police require further information, it must be obtained through the usual channels.

Finally, Aquapol aims to support the development of more common inspection standards in Europe through handbooks, seminars, training, expert exchanges and other forms of dissemination.[32]

---

[31] ibid.
[32] ibid.

C. Envicrimenet

Envicrimenet is a more recent initiative and not as far advanced as Tispol and Aquapol. Envicrimenet is a police network supported by Europol that covers all aspects of tackling environmental crime.

In 2008, the French presidency organised a seminar on the international trafficking of toxic waste, during which participants stressed the need to improve information exchange and the adoption of more efficient tools for combating this particular type of crime. The conclusions were reported to the Council in November 2008.[33] In November 2009, the Netherlands organised an international seminar on environmental crime, during which participants agreed to set up a cooperation platform (Envipol) and formed a working group to prepare the references. This was followed in September 2010 by a meeting of the working group, then consisting of representatives from the Netherlands, Belgium, the United Kingdom, France, Germany and Hungary, hosted by Europol.

Parallel to these events, the Belgian presidency launched the Augias project in November 2008, in which it cooperated with IMPEL (the EU Network for the Implementation and Enforcement of Environmental Law),[34] Europol and Interpol. The project specifically targeted waste trafficking in the EU. The aim of Augias was to develop and experiment with tools to facilitate checks on waste transport. It resulted in a manual and a standardised waste check document. To prepare for the practical application of these instruments, police officers from the Member States attended training courses in early 2010. Then, in October 2010, the police checked 815 waste transports in 16 EU countries over the course of a single week. The results were presented and discussed during a meeting in Hungary in March 2011, where it was also decided to launch Envicrimenet. The Council formalised this in a draft Resolution in May 2011, and adopted it one month later.[35]

The aims of Envicrimenet are: to ensure that Member States become aware of countering environmental crime at strategic level; to identify criminal networks suspected of being involved in illicit waste trafficking in order to determine the links between such networks and other forms of (organised) crime and to identify routes, destinations, modi operandi and trends and types of criminal activities; to identify the indicators of cross-border or

[33] Council of the European Union, *Report of European seminar on combating international trafficking in toxic waste* (Brussels, 24 November 2008).
[34] IMPEL is a cooperation network of regulatory and administrative authorities operating in the field of environmental law and enforcement, such as inspectorates. It is not primarily concerned with issues of policing and criminal investigation.
[35] Council of the European Union, Draft Council Resolution on the creation of an informal network for countering environmental crime—'EnviCrimeNet', doc 10291/11 (Brussels, 20 May 2011).

even domestic criminal activity in connection with environmental crime; to improve the exchange of information and the gathering of criminal intelligence, and to perform risk and threat assessment studies on a regular basis; to gather and share information on trends in environmental crime in close cooperation with the different national and international stakeholders; and to train officers and exchange best practices.[36]

Compared with other police cooperation networks, Europol's supporting role in Envicrimenet is noteworthy. The agency hosted Envicrimenet meetings in October 2011 and 2012. It also opened an online discussion platform within its Europol Platform for Experts (EPE); in 2013, about 125 police officers working in the field of environmental crime were members.[37]

Progress in Envicrimenet has been relatively slow, however. The foremost reason is that the network has not yet received external funding, which would allow it to appoint a director and establish a permanent secretariat. Consequently, all of the organisational work related to Envicrimenet comes on top of the normal duties of the police officers involved.

V. POLICE COOPERATION NETWORKS: BUILDING TRUST AND MORE

The foregoing indicates that non-operational and informal police cooperation networks have always tried to do more than provide a meeting place for police officers working in the same territorial or thematic areas. This section delves deeper into the different activities of the networks, taking the three outlined above as an example.

A. Networks Building Trust

One of the key objectives of cooperation networks is, of course, to build trust between police officers by offering them a meeting place, for example during seminars. This is especially true during the early phase of a network, as we see in the example of Envicrimenet. The members of the network need to become acquainted and to learn about one another's organisations and working methods (best practices) and the particular crime problems that they face. EU-wide cooperation networks often start with a small number of Member States and aim to expand their membership to other Member States over time. After 12 years, Tispol, for example, now includes the police forces of all the EU Member States as well as Norway and Switzerland.

---

[36] ibid, 4.
[37] Envicrimenet also has a publicly accessible website (www.envicrimenet.com), but it was still under construction at the time of writing.

In time, the network may also offer membership to non-police government agencies, such as inspectorates. Furthermore, Tispol has established a network of contacts with the European Commission (transport and traffic-related) and with other relevant stakeholders at EU level in the domains of science, transport industry, road management agencies, the automotive industry, ICT companies, consultants and so on.[38]

B. Joint Operations and Training

Some police cooperation networks organise joint operations and training. Tispol, for example, regularly organises simultaneous traffic inspections in different countries and locations in Europe. During alcohol testing operations, the police test about 1,000,000 drivers; during truck inspection operations, they check about 200,000 trucks within a 24-hour period at about 500 sites all over Europe.[39] Such tests and inspections can be defined as 'working apart together', because every police force organises its own local operations. The findings of such simultaneous checks are naturally shared and discussed during Tispol meetings. The police may share any operational information based on the applicable legal framework, such as the SIC. Apart from this, Tispol also facilitates truly joint inspections in EU border areas under Article 24 of the Prüm Convention.[40] The same provision has been incorporated into the Framework Decision on the stepping up of cross-border cooperation, particularly in combating terrorism and cross-border crime (2008/615/JHA), which the Council adopted on 23 June 2008.[41]

Some informal police cooperation networks have also taken far-reaching measures in the field of education and training. Again, Tispol is a good example. It set up an extensive programme of staff exchanges at the strategic, tactical and operational levels, with 600 traffic police officers participating over the course of three years. Tispol also organises its own training seminars and it developed a European handbook for traffic enforcement officers.[42]

Finally, informal cooperation networks may also disseminate new working methods to partner organisations. One example is the promotion of multi-agency inspection operations (MACO operations) by Aquapol. These

---

[38] Hellemons, above n 25.

[39] ibid.

[40] For an English version of the Treaty of Prüm, see: Council of the European Union, Treaty of Prüm, doc 10900/05 (Brussels, 7 July 2005), available at www.statewatch.org/news/2005/aug/Prum-Convention.pdf.

[41] Council Decision 2008/615/JHA of 23 June 2008 on the stepping up of cross-border cooperation, particularly in combating terrorism and cross-border crime [2008] OJ L210/12. Technically, a joint operation based on this legal framework qualifies as operational cooperation.

[42] Hellemons, above n 25.

inspections may involve the police, customs, waterway authorities or other relevant agencies, depending on the type of check involved (narcotic drugs, waste trafficking, illegal employment, etc). MACO operations may also involve participants from different countries. For example, the Hungarian water police participated in an inspection operation organised in Slovakia in October 2010.

C. Developing Tools for Practical Cooperation

The third important activity undertaken by some of the informal police cooperation networks is the development of tools for practical cooperation. Back in the 1970s, Nebedeagpol developed a system allowing the police incident rooms in the Meuse–Rhine Euroregion to communicate directly. Later, it also facilitated the development of a technical tool to enable patrol cars on either side of the border to communicate directly through their standard mobile communication equipment.[43]

As described above, cooperation networks such as Tispol and Aquapol use the internet to aid police officers working in the field. Examples are the transport documents databases developed for both road and water transport. Modern information and communication technology allows police officers to access this information on the spot during inspections. Aquapol's IBISWEB is taking this principle a step further, by offering the police a database containing the results of inspections of specific ships. That database is also accessible on the internet. Although IBISWEB is password protected and does not contain personal data, it does reveal the names of the vessels. The example illustrates how bottom-up initiatives by police cooperation networks foster the development of cutting-edge instruments to help them cope with the effects of 'open borders' within the EU.

A final example worth mentioning is the DEPET project funded by the EU, in which Tispol plays an important role. DEPET focuses on the use of Privacy Enhanced Technologies (PET) by law enforcement agencies. Such technologies allow for the processing of large amounts of data without violating the privacy of individuals. One experiment involved the use of Automatic Number Plate Recognition (ANPR) to detect traffic violations and crimes. The police may, for instance, try to detect violations of the maximum driving time by truck drivers driving from Spain to the Netherlands. One ANPR checkpoint is set up in the north of Spain and another one on the Dutch border. Say it will take a truck driver at least 24 hours to cover the intervening distance without violating the speed limits and regulations on driving time. The system then uses this information as a search string. It only registers

---

[43] Brammertz, above n 8.

what are pre-defined hits and discards all other information, for instance on a truck that was registered in Spain but did not pass the Dutch checkpoint within the given time frame.[44]

Another example concerns groups that break into trucks parked for the night in a parking lot along the highway. The police know that such groups 'patrol' these parking areas looking for targets and pass by several times on a single night, whereas the chance of a regular traveller visiting the same parking lot twice in one night is relatively remote. Of course, one must be very careful when applying such methods. A search string must always be as precise as possible to prevent the police from casting the net too wide. In addition, more research is needed on how to prevent people who have a perfectly logical explanation—'I returned because I forgot my credit card after refuelling'—from ending up as 'suspects' in the police databases.

D. Informal Police Networks and the EU

The development of the legal framework for police cooperation in the EU is the result of a combination of top-down initiatives, bottom-up pressure from practitioners who require specific tools, and diplomacy. New provisions seldom follow thorough empirical research on the practical problems confronting the police.[45] Informal police cooperation networks, however, can fill this gap to some extent by articulating requirements that are more evidence-based. As explained above, the needs articulated by Nebedeagpol found their way into the Schengen Implementation Convention in 1991, which was incorporated into EU legislation via the Treaty of Amsterdam in 1998.

The newer cooperation networks have maintained a close relationship with the EU from the beginning. The European Commission, for example, heavily funded Tispol and Aquapol as well as specific projects instigated by these networks. In return, the networks offer their information and knowledge 'to those responsible for legislation and policymaking, at the national as well as the EU level'.[46]

---

[44] See www.depet.eu/.

[45] In any case, the lack of a legal framework does not usually represent the biggest hurdle for effective police cooperation. Rather, these are organisational problems (lack of personnel and means, different priorities) and different views on how to apply specific (covert) investigation methods, the result of historical and cultural differences. See, eg, T Spapens, *Georganiseerde misdaad en strafrechtelijke samenwerking in de Nederlandse grensgebieden* (Antwerp/Oxford, Intersentia, 2008).

[46] Hellemons, above n 25.

VI. COOPERATION NETWORKS AND THE PRINCIPLE
OF CONVERGENCE

Strengthening non-operational cooperation between the EU's police forces has been on the agenda since the European Council adopted the Tampere Programme in 1999. This Programme called for the establishment of a European Police Chiefs operational Task Force to share experience, best practices and information on current trends in cross-border crime in co-operation with Europol, and to contribute to the planning of operative actions and the establishment of a European Police College for training senior law enforcement officials.[47]

The 2004 The Hague Programme stressed the importance of 'mutual trust and confidence-building'.[48] It also called for an explicit effort to improve mutual understanding of Member States' legal systems and organisations and to develop training courses for national police officers with regard to practical aspects of the EU, as well as to set up systematic exchange programmes for police authorities. Another aim was to encourage the exchange of best practices on investigative techniques, 'in particular in the areas of forensic investigations and information technology security'.[49]

The 'Informal High Level Advisory Group on the Future of European Home Affairs Policy (The Future Group)' assembled to prepare the Stockholm Programme continued to develop the idea of 'convergence' in the field of police cooperation. Convergence not only includes common training programmes and exchange networks, but also the pooling of equipment. 'The convergence principle would apply to all areas where closer relations between Member States are possible: agents, institutions, practices, equipment and legal frameworks'.[50] The Stockholm Programme itself emphasises the importance of joint training in the area of freedom security and justice, not only for police officers but also for judges, prosecutors, judicial staff, customs officers and border guards.[51] Furthermore, it promotes contacts between senior officials of the Member States in areas covered by Justice and Home Affairs.[52] Finally, the Programme invites the Council to examine 'how operational police cooperation could be stepped up, eg as regards incompatibility of communication systems and other equipment, use of

---

[47] Tampere European Council, 15 and 16 October 1999, Presidency Conclusions.

[48] Council of the European Union, *The Hague Programme: strengthening freedom, security and justice in the European Union* (Brussels, 13 December 2004) 23.

[49] ibid.

[50] High Level Advisory Group on the Future of European Home Affairs Policy, *Freedom, Security, Privacy: European Home Affairs in an Open World* (Brussels, 2008) 10–11.

[51] Council of the European Union, *The Stockholm Programme—An open and secure Europe serving and protecting the citizens* (Brussels, 2 December 2009) 9.

[52] ibid, 26.

undercover agents, and, where necessary, to draw operational conclusions to that end'.[53]

The importance of this becomes clear when we look at the changes brought about by the Treaty on the Functioning of the European Union (TFEU)—better known as the Lisbon Treaty—since it came into effect at the end of 2009. Title V addresses the area of freedom, security and justice. The Treaty introduces a new legislative process, which provides for easier decision-making and more parliamentary rights. The new 'ordinary legislative procedure' requires a qualified majority vote only and applies to most aspects of police cooperation. Until then, all decision-making in the field of justice and home affairs called for unanimity, which slowed progress down considerably and minimised the legal content of many of the instruments adopted.[54]

Now, only measures on *operational* police cooperation require decision-making through the special legislative procedure, in other words, unanimity. If the Member States cannot reach a unanimous decision, a group of at least nine may request that the draft measures be referred to the European Council. If the Council reaches consensus within four months, the draft will be adopted. In the event of disagreement, the group of at least nine Member States may initiate a form of enhanced cooperation in the specific field of action that does not bind other Member States.[55] It is important to note, however, that in the field of police cooperation, this 'emergency brake' does not apply with regard to the ordinary legislative procedure. Member States can only apply the 'brake' in matters of substantive and procedural criminal law.[56]

Article 87 TFEU defines the issues to which the ordinary legislative procedure refers. To begin with, it concerns the collection, storage, processing, analysis and exchange of relevant information. Second, it includes support for the training of staff and cooperation on staff exchanges, on equipment and on crime detection, as well as research into the detection of crimes. Finally, the ordinary legislative procedure applies to common investigative techniques in relation to the detection of serious forms of organised crime.

Of course, the entire chapter on police cooperation does not mention the word 'harmonisation' anywhere, but this is clearly the goal of convergence. Harmonisation of training, equipment and working methods is without a

---

[53] ibid, 41.

[54] V Murschetz, 'European Police Cooperation in the Future Legal Framework of the European Union' in C Fijnaut and J Ouwerkerk, *The Future of Police and Judicial Cooperation in the European Union* (Leiden, Martinus Nijhoff Publishers, 2010) 110.

[55] W Bruggeman and M den Boer, 'Policing and Internal Security in the Post-Lisbon Era: New Challenges Ahead' in S Wolff, F Goudappel and J de Zwaan, *Freedom, Security and Justice After Lisbon and Stockholm* (The Hague, TMC Asser Press, 2012) 143.

[56] Murschetz, above n 54, 111.

doubt a powerful tool. Indeed, there will be far less opposition to a police officer of one Member State working abroad and executing all of his competences in actual investigations if his education, equipment and working methods are interchangeable with those of a colleague operating in his home country.

In the years to come, it will be very interesting to see how broadly we must interpret Article 87. Does it indeed allow for harmonisation of the information and communication systems used by EU police forces? Does it imply that in the future all police officers will receive training according to the same handbooks and standards? Does the ability to exchange equipment not require common technical standards comparable to those applied by the North Atlantic Treaty Organisation (NATO), for example? Must we read the application of common investigative techniques as harmonisation of the principles of subsidiarity and proportionality in the application of special investigative powers?

VII. CONCLUSION

This chapter shows the importance and changing nature of non-operational police cooperation networks. From the 1960s onwards, such networks developed in European border areas and predominantly focused on local cooperation problems and network building, although experiences in the Meuse–Rhine Euroregion, for example, also found their way into the framework of 'Schengen' and via the *Acquis* into the legal framework for police cooperation in the EU. At the turn of the century, new police cooperation initiatives emerged, which from the start aimed to encompass police forces from all the Member States, but which focused on specific policing issues, such as road safety, water police and environmental crimes. Although these too were bottom-up initiatives, the EU immediately gave them strong support, including financially. Starting from a practical perspective, cooperation networks such as Tispol and Aquapol increasingly developed tools for police officers working on the ground, besides taking more traditional initiatives in the field of training, exchange of good practices and networking.

Non-operational police networks may play a key role in the ongoing convergence of training and working methods of EU police forces, one of the key goals of the Union in the field of justice and home affairs. Since the Lisbon Treaty has come into effect, the ordinary legislative procedure applies to directives concerning non-operational police cooperation. I question their impact on police organisation and training in the Member States, however, and doubt whether we will see a cascade of top-down directives emerging from Brussels in the near future. Instead, I expect a continuation of the strategy of supporting existing non-operational networks and developing new ones. These networks will undoubtedly encounter further practical cooperation problems and support new directives from the bottom up. Of course, the process of (minimum) harmonisation will be slow and take decades rather than years, but it is essential if we choose to proceed with the process of integration within the EU.

When we place the two concepts of trust presented in the first section of this chapter in the context of non-operational police networks we can conclude that these networks contribute to widening the circles (or levels) of trust distinguished by Sztompka.[57] We may assume that not many police officers from different EU Member States will be part of the same family, so the first relevant circle of trust is the one of personal relations developed through interaction. At the most basic level, non-operational police cooperation networks provide a platform to develop such relations by organising networking meetings to allow development of personal contacts. Engaging in joint projects of a non-operational nature also offers the opportunity to enhance trust in the community sense in an arena that is far less sensitive than operational cooperation in actual investigations.

However, these networks are also increasingly relevant for building inter-organisational and in the end full institutional trust. It is assumed as a starting point that the EU Member States have a high level of trust in each other's criminal justice systems.[58] However, this is a presumption referring predominantly to legal provisions for mutual assistance. Practical police cooperation is a different matter and the way forward is indeed to 'converge' and also formulate minimum harmonisation standards for qualifications of police officers, operational procedures and technical equipment. We may expect the development of 'standardisation agreements' comparable to those used by NATO. Police cooperation networks are essential in helping to formulate and implement such standards from the bottom up.

[57] Sztompka, above n 2.
[58] V Mitsilegas, *EU Criminal Law* (Oxford, Hart Publishing, 2009) 148.

9

Trust and the International Exchange of Forensic Information

CAROLE McCARTNEY

I. INTRODUCTION

WHILE POLICING AND judicial cooperation across international borders has been an expectation for many years, increasingly, strategies to combat terrorism, organised and serious crime, incorporate the exchange of forensic information. While informal forensic information sharing is not wholly novel, often having been undertaken on an ad hoc basis in response to a particular event, exchange capabilities and initiatives are now numerous and formal bilateral and multilateral agreements to exchange forensic data between countries proliferate apace. Since the Prüm Treaty of 2005, automated exchange of DNA profiles and dactyloscopic data (fingerprints) has become mandatory across the European Union (EU). Such increasing demand and capacity for the extraterritorial exchange of forensic information between law enforcement professionals and agencies means that there are growing numbers of criminal investigations where forensic evidence may have been collected, examined, or interpreted across national borders.

As well as presenting technological challenges, mutual assistance in evidence gathering and utilisation poses important and urgent questions. Attempts to regulate case-based forensic practice across the EU have barely commenced and time is still needed for regulation to 'bed-down'. Those developing the technology (scientists), and those charged with utilising it (police and legal authorities), however, (understandably) focus upon technical issues, rarely interrogating the complex interrelationship between trust, confidence, control, security, inter alia. The social and ethical challenges facing the utilisation of forensic information shall thus be the focus here, considering how the 'integrity' of forensic information plays an essential role in the production and maintenance of 'trust': a critical factor in international policing cooperation.

A. Forensic Data and International Police Cooperation

The significant investment in forensic science over the past few decades reflects political belief in its contribution to both crime detection and risk management creating pressure to expand and accelerate technological abilities to gather and disseminate forensic information within expanding operational boundaries. Thus, domestic law enforcement agencies are working in closer partnerships with their forensic scientific support units, as producers, consumers and purveyors of forensic information. Concurrently, transnational policing strategies have placed 'intelligence' at the heart of law enforcement, while the use of forensic information and intelligence in support of criminal investigations, organised crime control measures and counterterrorism tactics is heralded as an increasingly vital feature of efforts to ensure international 'security'.

While the mascot of formal international policing cooperation—Interpol—is approaching its centenary, exchange of policing information has always taken place, most often informally. Yet both across the EU and internationally, there now exists a number of formal agreements that specifically demand the automated exchange of forensic data. However, there is yet to be any detailed consideration of the multifaceted issues raised by direct access and/or exchanges of forensic data. Traditional parameters restraining the sharing of law enforcement information are increasingly inadequate with merely an expectation that the power to gather, store and share forensic information will be used with 'integrity'. Integrity is essential for generalised trust among not just the direct consumers of forensic information, but the public; yet for trust in forensic information to be maintained, critical attention must be paid not only to the viability of forensic information production and sharing, but also to its legitimacy and acceptability.

i. Why Trust?

Developments in transnational policing rely upon law enforcement authorities trusting both the processes and data produced by extraterritorial authorities. Integrity of data and processes is then essential for the production of trust among law enforcement agencies, and as a 'lubricant' for cooperation. Yet trust across policing bodies nationally and internationally cannot be assumed: an International Centre for Migration Policy Development (ICMPD) survey of police and customs officers across the EU in 2010 found that 89 per cent of respondents put 'trust' as an obstacle to future exchanges of information.[1] The interrelationships between integrity, confidence, justice

---

[1] ICMPD, *Study on the status of information exchange amongst law enforcement authorities in the context of existing EU instruments* (2010) JLS/2009/ISEC/PR/001-F3, 100.

and security, and the significant role these have in ensuring trust both within and outwith justice systems and legal jurisdictions, are thus slowly coming into focus. Research emphasises the necessity of public trust in judicial bodies and systems to maintain commitment to the rule of law and normative compliance with social order.[2] The system of criminal justice thus stands out as requiring trust and cooperation not only from citizens, but equally from other agencies, increasingly from other jurisdictions. As transnational cooperation in policing increases and spreads globally, 'trust' as the foundation for cooperation and exchange of information is critical.

Social scientists have long theorised as to the necessity of trust for functioning relationships, and how trust can be both created and maintained,[3] recognising that trust becomes increasingly problematic with 'virtualised' relations. Trust is more easily established and maintained within personal relationships, which is how policing cooperation has proceeded,[4] but now the trend is for automated or 'virtual' systems of data exchange. Giddens and Fukuyama both argue that faith and security is attainable within 'abstract' systems, but these need to be routinely monitored for competence and effectiveness.[5] They stress that there is an expectation within abstract relations of regular, honest, cooperative behaviour, based on common norms. Similarly, there are clear links between 'trust' and 'control', but in transnational exchange of forensic information, it is not clear who is in control, if anyone. Thus, trust is a crucial yet largely overlooked constituent in cross-border information exchange.

B. Exchanging Law Enforcement Data: Mechanisms and Obligations

One of the first EU mutual assistance treaties was the 1959 European Convention on Mutual Assistance in Criminal Matters,[6] which came into force on 12 June 1962, and provided for the transfer of information on

---

[2] M Hough and M Sato, *Trust in justice: why it is important for criminal policy, and how it can be measured*, Final report of the Euro-Justis project (Helsinki, HEUNI, 2011), available at www.icpr.org.uk/media/31613/Final%20Euro-Justis%20report.pdf.

[3] eg, A Fox, *Beyond Contact: Work Power and Trust Relations* (London, Faber & Faber, 1974); and M Reed, 'Organization, Trust and Control: A Realist Analysis' (2001) 22(2) *Organization Studies* 201.

[4] S Hufnagel, *Policing Cooperation Across Borders: Comparative Perspectives on Law Enforcement Within the EU and Australia* (Farnham, Ashgate, 2013).

[5] A Giddens, 'Risk, Trust, Reflexivity' in U Beck, A Giddens and S Lash (eds), *Reflexive Modernization: Politics, Tradition and Aesthetics in the Modern Social Order* (Cambridge, Polity Press, 1994); F Fukuyma, *Trust: The Social Virtues and the Creation of Prosperity* (New York, Free Press, 1995).

[6] European Convention on Mutual Assistance in Criminal Matters (20 April 1959, ETS No 30).

previous convictions. This Treaty set out the rules for the enforcement of letters rogatory issued by a 'requesting' state, to procure or communicate evidence for the purposes of criminal proceedings transnationally. The 1999 Amsterdam Treaty and Tampere Programme for EU policy development and implementation laid down precise provisions for cooperation between EU police authorities. These instruments boosted intergovernmental cooperation within the EU on policing matters, while endorsing 'mutual recognition' as a cornerstone of European integration. In 2001 a detailed programme of measures was set out in the European Convention on Mutual Assistance in Criminal Matters,[7] which introduced a suite of practical tools for enhancing cross-border cooperation, starting with the European Arrest Warrant, later adding the European Evidence Warrant, and most recently the European Investigation Order.[8] Nijboer predicted that 'the next development will be the EU members' mutual recognition, not merely of court decisions, but also of investigative results such as forensic experts' reports'.[9]

While informal exchange channels remain, more formal and automated exchange channels were originally promulgated by the Hague Programme of 2004 which propounded the 'Principle of Availability' of law enforcement information. This principle, adopted in November 2004,[10] anticipated that the sharing of law enforcement data would take place across the EU under the same principles as those governing the sharing of data domestically. In 2006, the 'Swedish Initiative' marked a significant step towards implementing this Principle of Availability, with the adoption of Council Framework Decision 2006/960/JHA on simplifying the exchange of information and intelligence between EU Member States' law enforcement authorities. Adopting a broad and inclusive approach to information exchange, 49 different types of relevant data were identified, including DNA and fingerprints,[11] the underlying principle being that national parties should apply the same criteria to international exchange across the EU as they do to information sharing between criminal justice professionals at the national level. Transnational exchanges of information could take place through any existing channels of mutual judicial cooperation, including the Sirene Bureaux (utilising the Schengen Information System, (SIS)), the Interpol National Contact Bureaux (NCBs), Europol National Units (ENUs) or Europol Liaison Officers and Bilateral Liaison Officers. Transnational exchanges of forensic data and intelligence between EU Member States thus take place within these evolved institutional frameworks.

---

[7] European Convention on Mutual Assistance in Criminal Matters [2001] OJ C326/1.
[8] V Mitsilegas, *EU Criminal Law* (Oxford, Hart Publishing, 2009).
[9] JF Nijboer, 'Current Issues in Evidence and Procedure—Comparative Comments from a Continental Perspective' (2009) 6(2) *International Commentary on Evidence* 23.
[10] Brussels European Council, 4/5 November 2004, Presidency Conclusions.
[11] CRIMORG 7, 5815/2/05.

i. Sharing Forensic 'Intelligence' and Expert Reports

An important distinction needs to be drawn at this point between the sharing of raw forensic data and exchanges of scientific reports incorporating evaluative expert opinions. Often the two go hand in hand, but data and its interpretation do not always coincide and may not be contributed by the same individuals or institutions. It is far more likely that exchanges of forensic data can be standardised and automated, whereas sharing forensic expert opinions across national borders and legal jurisdictions is significantly more complex. Forensic data might consist of nothing more than raw scientific test results; such information is readily amenable to automatic recording and transmission. For these data to become 'evidence', however, a further vital step is required, that of 'interpretation'. Indeed scientific data are virtually meaningless unless interpreted within the context of other information. It is therefore important to ensure the integrity of systems of accreditation of forensic experts in various countries, and to set appropriate international standards for interpreting forensic data. While efforts to standardise and maintain quality thresholds for expert reports must commence or continue, this chapter shall concentrate on forensic data-sharing as this is currently the focus of activity to date, and efforts to standardise and regulate forensic data are critical and some preliminary moves have been made in this arena. Additionally, any raw forensic data must be capable of trust prior to any interpretation.

ii. Forensic Data Exchange

Cross-border evidence exchange during investigations and pre-trial processes has been increasing for many years, gaining impetus from the terrorist attacks of 9/11.[12] Resort to forensic science by national intelligence services and security agencies is increasingly frequent and there are rapidly evolving strategies to tackle transnational crime which foster the exchange of information across borders as well as the linking of databases of different provenance.[13] Indeed, international utilisation and exchange of forensic information has become a firm expectation of the sector, matched by burgeoning expansion of the mechanisms needed to achieve it.

Interpol initially drove the technological phase of international cooperation involving DNA on a global scale. Resolution No 8 of the Cairo General Assembly in 1998 articulated an aspiration to harmonise DNA profiling and quality assurance systems internationally and recommended that its member

---

[12] R Loof, 'Obtaining, Adducing and Contesting Evidence from Abroad: A Defence Perspective on Cross-border Evidence' (2011) *Criminal Law Review* 40.

[13] C Lewis, 'International Structures and Trans-national Crime' in T Newburn, T Wiliamson and A Wright (eds), *Handbook of Criminal Investigation* (Cullompton, Willan, 2007).

countries should create national DNA databases. The Interpol DNA Gateway, created in 2002, enabled its member countries to search unsolved crime scene profiles and search against DNA profiles from other donor countries using the Interpol Standard Set of Loci (ISSOL). In July 2006, it went online via Interpol's I-24/7 global police communications system. The DNA Gateway does not hold any nominal (demographic) data but acts simply as a conduit between countries who follow up any 'hits' independently. The DNA Gateway is available for use by all 190 Interpol countries. It can only be used by police forces, however, and this excludes from the system countries (eg, Belgium and the Netherlands) in which DNA data are classified as judicial information: that is, the information is collected, managed and used by magistrates or prosecutors rather than police agencies. One consequence of these domestic institutional arrangements is that data can be shared internationally only through judicially controlled mechanisms. For this and other reasons, there has consequently been a low submission rate, possibly also attributable to practitioner scepticism that submission will reap much investigative reward.[14]

In 1997, the EU adopted Council Resolution 97/C193/02 on the exchange of DNA, recommending establishment of national DNA databases and the standardisation of DNA technology to facilitate data exchange between EU Member States. In 2001, Council Resolution 2001/C 187/01 recommended the limitation of DNA analysis to 'non-coding' regions as well as the ongoing standardisation of reporting and recording, and the creation in each Member State of single national points of contact. This programme was designed to promote harmonisation of DNA analysis and the procedures necessary for information exchange and data sharing. Informal exchange of DNA 'in the absence of a supranational authority to govern' was sporadic at this formative stage.[15]

The Prüm Treaty, concerned with increasing the exchange of EU law enforcement data in order to combat terrorism, illegal immigration and cross-border crime, was signed in 2005. The original signatories (Austria, Germany, the Netherlands, Luxembourg, Belgium, France and Spain), were subsequently joined by six others. The Treaty was transposed into EU law in 2007 (Decision 2008/615/JHA; 2008/616/JHA), at which point all EU Member States committed themselves to working within the Treaty obligations by August 2011. The adoption of the Treaty into the EU *acquis* (legal framework) created, for the first time, a requirement that Member States establish an infrastructure to permit the exchange of DNA, fingerprint and

---

[14] P Johnson and R Williams, 'Internationalizing New Technologies of Crime Control: Forensic DNA Databasing and Datasharing in the European Union' (2007) 17(2) *Policing & Society* 108.
[15] ibid.

vehicle registration data. This implies the creation of national databases as a necessary precondition to data sharing, which some Member States still do not have. By January 2012, 12 EU countries were exchanging DNA information (with 10 exchanging fingerprints and vehicle registration data). The Prüm Treaty thus represented a partial step towards the realisation of the Hague Programme's aspiration of free-flowing law enforcement information between EU states under the 'Principle of Availability'. The ultimate objective being 'a virtual EU-wide database for law enforcement that makes an entry loaded onto any forensic database in any EU country potentially accessible to every police force in the EU'.[16]

The Treaty stipulates that automated searches by other Member States are conducted on a 'hit'/'no hit' basis. Only after a 'hit' has occurred will there be an exchange of personal (demographic) details and case information via existing mutual legal assistance channels. The second step of the exchange process then falls back on national legislation, affording discretion to each country to decide whether or not to exchange demographic data. To satisfy the stipulated standard for information sharing, DNA profiles must contain at least six of the seven European Standard Set of Loci (ESSL) for known persons or a minimum of six loci (of any type) for crime scene stains. Mixed profiles are excluded. So, also for speculative searching, are profiles derived from crime stains that have already been 'matched' to a particular person. A country may make some profiles unavailable for searching (eg, profiles of criminal justice personnel compiled for elimination purposes). Declaration of a 'match' requires at least six fully matching loci (one mismatch is permitted, to accommodate 'near' matches; and one base-pair difference is permitted to allow for microvariants that could be artefacts of the profiling process). A report following a Prüm search will include details of: the responding country; the type of 'match' (full or near); the characteristics of both matching DNA profiles; the crime stain or reference sample; and the sample code to facilitate follow-up requests for further details via mutual legal assistance mechanisms.

Introduction of the Prüm automatic information exchange system has been credited with notable operational successes. After less than two months of a trial period of information sharing between Austria and Germany, for instance, the German authorities had obtained 1510 'hits' for DNA profiles from unsolved cases against data held by the Austrian authorities, leading to 710 detections (including, 41 hits in homicide cases, 885 hits in theft investigations and 85 hits relating to robbery or extortion).[17] Advocates, no less

---

[16] Human Genetics Commission, *Nothing to Hide, Nothing to Fear* (London, Department of Health, 2009) para 5.10.

[17] House of Lords European Union Committee, *Prüm: an effective weapon against terrorism and crime?* (18th report) (2006–07, HL 90) 15–16.

than critics, of the Prüm system recognise that these impressive immediate gains partly represent a one-off windfall. When a country first initiates data exchange, large amounts of information about earlier crimes will become available to the prosecuting authorities for the first time.[18] It remains to be seen how effective EU data-sharing will be in terms of producing new 'hits' leading to detections and prosecutions on a more sustainable, ongoing basis.

The biggest practical limitation of the Prüm information-sharing framework is geographical, being restricted to EU Member States (plus a few additional signatory countries such as Norway and Switzerland). There were soon calls for exchanges of DNA data, in particular, to be extended internationally. The UK's presidency of the G8 in 2005 inaugurated a project to identify the requirements for greater international exchange and propose technical solutions. The 'DNA Search Request Network' (DNA SRN) was duly established, utilising Interpol's I-24/7 secure email network to send search requests to other G8 countries. Pilot testing began in 2007 with search requests sent to national DNA Bureaux from the United States, Canada and the United Kingdom. Japan has since joined the original trio and all four countries have commenced sharing crime scene DNA profiles. The nature and extent of these exchanges has not been made public, however.

C. Trust and Integrity

To date, there has been little effort expended in shining an ethical spotlight on forensic science. Touted as an essential element in the fight against crime, it has been widely perceived in the 'public good' and there have been long-standing powers for state agents to take and retain forensic evidence, dating back to the birth of fingerprinting at the turn of the twentieth century. Many states had been meticulous record-keepers for years prior to this, and the collection and use of forensic evidence (particularly bio-information) has often been portrayed as a mere extension of efforts to maintain thorough and accurate records. The police were thus able to take and retain a great deal of information on citizens because there was no real public concern, so consequently, no official concern. However, for a variety of reasons the 'innocent have nothing to fear' argument has lost potency. There is now a greater realisation that there may be social consequences of state powers to take and use bio-information from citizens for forensic purposes. One concern has been an apparent unchecked growth in police surveillance powers (especially retention and scope). Similarly, there has been apprehension about the uses of forensic information, and more controversial techniques and technologies (in particular with DNA, with the development of familial

---

[18] ibid.

searching and phenotyping). These fears accompany questions raised about the possibility of 'function creep': the increased use of information gathered for one purpose, put to another purpose (ie, 'forensic' data being used in research). Much public disquiet was (and still is in many countries) growing at a time when there is a loss of generalised trust in authority and increasing scepticism of state motivations.[19]

Forensic DNA profiling has often grabbed the limelight in such debates, often due to hyperbolic genetic exceptionalism, but concern over DNA has attracted attention to other police databases. In most countries, the legal parameters for use of national collections of DNA, whether or not gathered for forensic purposes, are clearly delineated and legally guaranteed. This affords some certainty about how the DNA may be lawfully used. Laws most often preclude their use in medical or other research, or in paternity disputes. Terminology, however, may be subject to a wide interpretation that expands the range of uses to which the information on the databases may legitimately be put. The immediate question that then arises with automated police exchange of data is: who is routinely monitoring such exchange, and whose 'common norms', essential for trust, are being respected?

i. Essential Elements of Integrity: Viability, Legitimacy and Acceptability

Forensic information exchange typically *precedes* the institution of formal criminal proceedings, since the national authorities will usually have evidence of suspected criminality but at this stage, no identified suspect. Investigators hope that information sharing will produce an identifiable suspect, for example, through a matching DNA profile. Since information shared through mutual judicial assistance is often pivotal to the progress and outcome of an investigation, ensuring its integrity is vital to the proper administration of criminal justice. The need for such guarantees of integrity are all the greater in relation to evidence widely considered inherently reliable (such as fingerprint and DNA evidence), as domestic courts (and juries) may be in the habit of taking its reliability on trust. Thus, integrity is essential for trust among not just the consumers of forensic information, but the wider public. The question is then raised: how do we ensure integrity in forensic information?

ii. Viability

Ensuring harmonious technical systems and processes is critical: data must be intelligible to those receiving and acting upon the data, with no room for

---

[19] R Hindmarsh and B Prainsack (eds), *Genetic Suspects: Global Governance of Forensic DNA Profiling and Databasing* (Cambridge, Cambridge University Press, 2010).

error (both false positives and negatives), or misinterpretation. Exchange of DNA and dactyloscopic data under Prüm arrangements have already struck difficulties with harmonisation of technologies,[20] and problems raised by 'near matches' or mis-typing of DNA.[21] Widespread distribution of automated database searching could also potentially generate candidate match overload. Such problems were anticipated by the European Network of Forensic Science Institutes (ENFSI) DNA Working Group in 2009.[22] The Working Group concluded that while the current ESS loci are capable of handling occasional exchanges of DNA profiles between countries, the much higher volume of profile sharing and searching made possible by the Prüm Treaty means that the chance of adventitious or false matches may significantly increase. An adventitious match occurs when the DNA profiles of two individuals (who are not identical twins) genuinely match (theoretically a rare but not impossible occurrence with the latest, highly discriminating, DNA profiling systems). A 'false match' is a match declared in error, where closer examination shows the result to be invalid (eg, owing to laboratory contamination or interpretational errors).

With increasing horizontal integration of criminal justice data, international liaison officers could be overwhelmed by information and in major investigations may experience considerable pressure to confirm 'near matches' as reliable leads. As Schneider explains: 'When massive exchanges of DNA profiles are undertaken ... the seven ESS loci will not be sufficient because the chance of adventitious matches will no longer be negligible'.[23] Investigators will often be able to eliminate adventitious or false matches when it becomes apparent that the individual concerned had nothing to do with the crime. The reverse situation—a false elimination—may be almost equally damaging for the administration of justice. Yet, false elimination and false inclusion of suspects based on flawed forensic data (both recently occurring in the United Kingdom) are not only damaging to individuals involved, and the success of police investigations, but can lead to a catastrophic loss of confidence among the public. Both Germany and the Netherlands have reported having to undertake extensive re-testing when matches are identified, to exclude adventitious and false matches. The Netherlands now

[20] R Gill, *Study of the obstacles to cooperation and information-sharing between forensic science laboratories and other relevant bodies of different Member States and between the latter and counterparts in third countries* (2008) (JLS/D1/2007/025).
[21] K van der Beek, 'Exchange of DNA Profiles by the Treaty of Prüm' paper presented at DNA Data Exchange in Europe Conference (5–6 June 2008), available at www.dnaconference. eu/ppt/Van%20der%20Beek.pdf.
[22] ENSFI, *DNA-Database Management Review* (2009), available at www.dnaresource.com/ documents/ENFSIdocumentonDNAdatabasemanagement20092.pdf.
[23] P Schneider, 'Expansion of the European Standard Set of DNA Database loci— The Current Situation' (2009) March *Profiles in DNA* 1.

refuses to release demographic data for 'near matches' without the assurance of confirmatory testing.[24] Greater obstacles occur with fingerprint data exchange, where there is no accepted international standard for establishing the validity of matches. However, use of the best quality images is crucial for fingerprint comparison. An international standard for minimum pixel quality would be desirable, for example, but little progress has been made on devising any international standards for transmission of fingerprint data, beyond the specification of an agreed file format. Meanwhile, proprietary search and image capture systems are being developed with little regard for interoperability.

With fingerprint database searches, there were initially large 'fishing expeditions' leading to official limits over concerns that national databases were damaged by overwhelming search volumes. Responding to threats of 'match overload' and excessive strain on examiners required to analyse thousands of prints, the EU placed limits on the number of searches that can be conducted of fingerprint databases.[25] Dror and Mnookin argue that the scale and speed of automated database searching inevitably increases the risk of erroneous identifications by multiplying the number of candidate matches based on incidental similarities, some of which may be artefacts 'both of the relative similarity of the patterns being compared and of the human cognitive architecture involved in pattern matching'.[26] This parallels the problem of DNA 'near matches', and may similarly require significant investment of resources to re-check and eliminate specious 'hits'. Reliance must be placed on national authorities to be diligent in undertaking the necessary re-testing to confirm initial results, before treating shared fingerprint 'matches' as a reliable basis on which to initiate criminal prosecutions.

Laboratories developing imperceptible latent prints from crime scenes must satisfy the rudimentary quality controls required for accreditation under ISO 17025. However, police fingerprint bureaux are exempted, placing Automatic Fingerprint Identification Systems (AFIS) outside this quality framework. The UK Association of Chief Police Officers previously declared its aspiration to ensure that all fingerprint bureaux are accredited to ISO 17025 by 2020. In the meantime, fingerprinting, like DNA profiling, is widely perceived as reliable and routine. This may foster the impression that regulatory frameworks are equally robust and unproblematic, reinforcing implicit faith in these types of evidence. However, the regulation and

---

[24] Gill, above n 20.
[25] Document 5860/5/10 REV 5 JAI 92 CRIMORG 16 ENFOPOL 29.
[26] IE Dror and JL Mnookin, 'The Use of Technology in Human Expert Domains: Challenges and Risks Arising from the Use of Automated Fingerprint Identification Systems in Forensic Science' (2010) 9(1) *Law, Probability and Risk* 56.

governance of both fingerprint and DNA data in England and Wales, and internationally, have attracted critical scrutiny in recent years.[27]

Issues of capacity and technological capability are then not only raised when dealing with smaller or poorer nations who may not have the competence to respond to demands: many EU and other countries are experiencing serious economic pressures, with limited resources to dedicate to the creation and sharing of standardised forensic data (even with the United States 'donating' its CODIS system to many countries). The multiple systems used in the United Kingdom do not yet correspond with those used in the EU, updated in recent years to enable exchange and prevent multiple DNA standards proliferating across the EU. With no internationally accepted standards for DNA, and even fewer standards for other data formats, ignoring for now the more nebulous 'intelligence', the collation of data from multiple sources with varying formats simply exacerbates risk of errors, with the lack of standardisation rendering data transmitted worthless.

Similarly, domestic powers covering the collection, searching, matching and retention of data, particularly sensitive bio-information, varies enormously between countries, meaning that exchange is not undertaken on a level playing field. Domestic governance and oversight of collections of data differ significantly, with very few safeguards in place, and even fewer when data comes to be exchanged. In some countries, staff may be pressured to conform to requirements of data creation and exchange, when proper checks are not in place, a situation already seen with Prüm exchanges.[28] Efforts at standardisation and uniformity have commenced, with the 'Swedish Initiative' of 2009. This Council Framework Decision states that all forensic laboratories must have ISO 17025 accreditation by 2014 (police agencies by 2015). The Decision states:

> The intensified exchange of information regarding forensic evidence and the increased use of evidence from one MS in the judicial processes of another, highlights the need to establish common standards for forensic science providers. Information originating from forensic processes in one MS may currently be associated with a level of uncertainty in another MS regarding the way in which an

---

[27] See, eg, *The Forensic Use of Bioinformation: Ethical Issues* (Cambridge, Nuffield Council on Bioethics, 2007), available at www.nuffieldbioethics.org/bioinformation; Human Genetics Commission, *Nothing to Hide*, above n 16; House of Commons Home Affairs Committee *The National DNA database*: Eighth report of Session 2009–10 vol I report (HC 222-1) (London, The Stationery Office Limited, 2010); and C McCartney, R Williams and T Wilson, *The Future of Forensic Bioinformation* (The Nuffield Foundation, 2010), available at www.nuffield-foundation.org/future-forensic-bioinformation.

[28] K van der Beek, 'Observed and Expected Numbers of (Partially) Randomly Matching Profiles in the Dutch DNA Database, and in International DNA Searches' (2010) 50(1) *Science & Justice* 47.

item has been handled, what methods have been used and how the results have been interpreted.[29]

While welcome, the Decision arguably places too much reliance upon the ISO 17025 standard, which is limited in its ability to guarantee the veracity of data and the quality of 'information' emanating from forensic laboratories. Mistakes still occur in accredited laboratories, and much forensic work is done outside the laboratory, which renders ISO 17025 impotent. The abstract regulation of laboratories via accreditation is also detached from the actual reception of information by law enforcement officials, yet forensic information is highly contextual information. When exchanging forensic data, can caveats, qualifications, or contextual detail be conveyed by the automated sharing of data stored on huge databases and transmission of information across borders via electronic pro formas?

In 2011 the Polish EU presidency called for a 'vision' for forensic science, building on EU efforts to create a 'European Forensic Science Area' by 2020. The policy programme aims to 'ensure the even-handed, consistent and efficient administration of justice and the security of citizens', by accrediting forensic institutes and laboratories and conducting international proficiency testing, establishing minimum competence criteria for forensic practitioners and introducing best practice manuals for laboratory case work. There will be minimum quality standards for examining crime scenes and managing the production of scientific evidence, from the crime scene to the courtroom. Duplication of effort in different countries should be minimised through mutual recognition of testing and processing of forensic data, and the sharing of forensic databases, reducing delays in international crime cases. These objectives are laudable and, if implemented successfully, could go some way towards overcoming obstacles to effective forensic data exchange.

As things stand, enormous disparities in national modes of data production, coupled with markedly discrepant regulatory regimes, conduce to an extremely complex environment.[30] Such issues can be seen in other similar institutions, where standards which are intended to ensure reliability of data are being lowered, or not respected, by submitting authorities. Europol, in formulating their Serious Organised Crime Threat Assessment (SOCTA) report, to inform the strategy from 2013 to 2017, is changing the criteria for accepting intelligence based upon its own 4 x 4 assessment criteria which, when cross-referenced, gives intelligence a code relating its reliability, with attendant risks:

[T]he automatic acceptance of information from Member States and EU agencies provides a way for unsubstantiated or unreliable data to become accepted as 'A1'

---

[29] Council Framework Decision 2009/905/JHA of 30 November 2009 on *Accreditation of forensic service providers carrying out laboratory activities* [2009] OJ L322/14, paras 4 and 5.
[30] Gill, above n 20.

quality at European level. Europol has no powers to examine whether assessment processes at national level or in EU agencies meet the required standards.[31]

iii. Legitimacy

There should be no question that the instruments that permit the creation and exchange of forensic data must be legally binding and authoritative. It would be untenable for individuals or institutions to create their own systems and processes for delivering forensic information, which can then be retained and used domestically or shared internationally. However, at this time, there are no guarantees that this cannot happen. Even the Prüm Treaty itself has had its legality and legitimacy questioned: 'Transferring privately negotiated treaties into the EU *acquis* does not fulfil the requirements of legitimacy. It appears underhanded and dishonest'.[32] Frequently, the introduction of powers to gather, store, manipulate and share forensic data, precedes laws regulating such activity. Even when such laws exist, the diversity of legal instruments across nations, and the interpretation of international treaties and national laws implementing treaties differ, leading to the obstacle of 'legal problems' highlighted as problematic in exchanging information.[33]

Again, it should be indisputable that governing legal instruments will be human rights compliant, but this again is not always the case. The introduction of DNA profiling in a country has frequently preceded laws regulating such activity. Technological development has often outstripped other considerations, with politicians and police having to be reminded that effectiveness is not the sole criterion upon which to base public policy decisions. With many forensic practitioners proclaiming their ability to create forensic information (and a private forensic industry keen to sell such technologies) there must be parallel considerations. The European Court of Human Rights, in the case of *S and Marper* [2008] ECHR 1581 gave official voice to the notion that 'choices' have to be made and balances struck, in criminal justice policy. A unanimous Court ruled that

> any State claiming a pioneer role in the development of new technologies bears special responsibility for striking the right balance between the use of modern scientific techniques and important private-life interests ... the protection afforded by Article 8 ... would be unacceptably weakened if the use of modern scientific techniques in the criminal justice system were allowed at any cost and without

---

[31] 'Europol: "4x4" intelligence handling codes includes "dodgy data"' *Statewatch News* (7 January 2013) 3, available at www.statewatch.org/news/2013/jan/03europol-dodgy-data. htm#.

[32] E Guild, Written Evidence Provided to the House of Lords European Union Committee *Prüm: an effective weapon against terrorism and crime?* (18th report) (2006–07, HL 90) para 6.

[33] ICMPD, *Study*, above n 1.

carefully balancing the potential benefits of the extensive use of such techniques against important private-life benefits.[34]

It needs to be ensured that when deciding to utilise forensic information, important questions of proportionality and necessity are not overlooked. In particular, data protection (to secure privacy rights) is integral yet notoriously vague, patchy in coverage and often disregarded. Individuals are reliant upon states checking, and complying with national laws and upholding international data protection agreements. The European Data Protection Supervisor has been scathing of the 'country-by-country approach' to data protection, with monitoring left to often under-resourced national authorities. Data protection is most notably fragmentary when applied to law enforcement, 'hedged by multiple derogations, allowing significant variation in implementation'.[35] There thus must remain questions over whether states are collating excessive information on citizens and infringing their human rights. This is particularly the case where personal information could be used for discriminatory purposes. There therefore needs to be greater clarity over the information being collated, the uses it is put to and whether any intrusion into privacy is necessary and proportionate.

Traditional parameters restraining information sharing are increasingly inadequate with the proliferation of channels of exchange and the growing diversity of information exchanged. One can normally expect 'boundaries' that law enforcement information is not meant to cross—for example, between police and health or immigration databases and vice versa. Such boundaries are increasingly being dismantled, the latest example being EURODAC, the European wide fingerprint database of immigrants, being made available to law enforcement agencies. With such boundaries often poorly defined and respected at a national level, this is then exacerbated internationally. A lack of formal procedures and legal guarantees exist to prevent unauthorised storage, further manipulation, or exchanges of data. Once created, like the proverbial Pandora's box, databases are open to both use and abuse, and data protection and security becomes an almost Sisyphean task.

iv. Acceptability

With trust in the institutions responsible for forensic information creation, retention and exchange, citizens can expect that respect for human rights and the democratic process remain. However, securing and maintaining

---

[34] *S and Marper* [2008] ECHR 1581, para 112.
[35] S Brown, 'Trading Intelligence' (2009) 3(2) *Policing* 181, 184.

trust requires independent oversight. Citizens must have access to sufficient, reliable, public information in order to trust, but this information is scarce. There are no significant bodies with oversight powers to scrutinise information and yet it must 'require at the very least unambiguous guidelines, close supervision and invasive oversight'.[36] The absence of institutions with either the resources, or the authority to foster greater coordination and collaboration over 'ethical' or social issues, provides no confidence that risks are being monitored. In the United Kingdom, the National DNA Database Ethics Group recommends that the post of 'Commissioner for the Retention and Use of Biometric Material', created subsequent to the *Marper* ruling, should check a sample of subject profiles shared internationally, to ensure that they are based upon the following principles: (a) there must be a policing purpose; (b) exchange has to be subject to proper legal controls; (c) the use must be proportionate; (d) it should meet certain scientific standards; and (e) ethical considerations should be factored in.[37] The Ethics Group voiced concern, however, over the volume of exchanges and how this could be managed, while also failing to articulate what 'ethical considerations' should be 'factored in'.

Inconsistencies in independent oversight are significant and while there is limited oversight of 'quality' measures (in the United Kingdom there is a Forensic Regulator—albeit this role is limited and of questionable effectiveness), 'social' issues are left to Parliament, tasked with 'balancing' individual rights with societal interests. Very often, national governments will take a classic risk-analysis model approach, relying heavily upon scientific risk assessment and actually taking very little (if any) account of social or ethical risks. To complicate matters, consideration of such risks must also be coupled with the encouragement of innovation and development: 'it is a misconception that best practice standard protocols must be set that must then be followed by all. That approach would set forensic science in aspic and be counterproductive'.[38] A difficult balance must thus be struck between strict adherence to quality assured protocols and ensuring that practitioners can innovate and exercise professional judgement to achieve the optimal outcome.

Regulation in the forensic science sector still relies heavily upon the persuasive power of soft law—rules with no legally binding force but which are meant to influence conduct. At the European policy level, there are decisions, resolutions and recommendations, all without much force. Further,

---

[36] ibid, 188.

[37] NDNAD Ethics Group *Annual Report 2011–2012*, available at www.homeoffice.gov.uk/publications/agencies-public-bodies/fsr/ndnad-ethics-group-ann-2012.pdf?view=Standard&pubID=1092485,13.

[38] S Brown and S Willis, 'Complexity in Forensic Science' (2010) 1(4) *Forensic Science Policy & Management* 192, 193.

a risk-based regulatory system does not ensure 'quality' but is aimed at preventing crises. A risk model also relies upon quantification, with practitioners informing regulators of the risks associated with any procedure or practice. Thus, there must be an error rate (and identifiable errors), or known limitations of a method. However, one of the major flaws in applying the risk model to forensic information is that these error rates and limitations remain largely undetermined. Without error rates, how does a laboratory profess to be working within acceptable parameters? For example, what would be the number of 'acceptable' false positives? The second question depends upon the criminal justice system and the public tolerance of such errors. Significant research (and the proper funding of such research) into areas such as error rates, technique and technology limitations, practitioner bias etc all need to take place before the construction of a risk model for forensic information can take place.

There has also been a significant conflation of 'risks'. The Prüm Treaty and other instruments specifically mention organised crime, terrorism and illegal migration for example, but do these pose similar risks? Definitions of each category and their demarcations are contentious. Can forensic information be said to be useful in all these arenas? Is the retention of forensic data and the exchange of information as equally acceptable when countering immigration abuses as with organised criminals? With such conflation there comes the danger of over-inclusion. The European courts have previously warned Member States in both the *S and Marper v UK* and *Huber*[39] cases, that they must resist the over-enthusiastic collection and retention of data on citizens. Concerns are heightened by apparent poor accountability mechanisms (for instance, the sharing of data across Europe under Prüm does not come under the Court of Justice's jurisdiction). There is thus no oversight of process in terms of 'proportionality' and lawfulness at European level and yet we are reliant upon EU political institutions to strike the 'correct' balance between societal, individual and national interests. A consensus approach is necessary but distrust among national and international authorities, with some opting not to share their data, creates a 'loose link' in the data chain, leaving a gap exploitable by criminals.

In a time of austerity, there must also be attention paid to costs and effectiveness. Forensic science requires 'significant pre-investment without any guarantee of short-term quantifiable improvement in performance ... increase[ing] appreciably when it extends into the international dimension'.[40] National policing budgets are under strain, and forensic budgets are easy to cut, being slashed in many police forces across the United Kingdom and EU. Investment has to (quickly) be able to demonstrate its cost-effectiveness and

---

[39] Case C-524/06 *Huber v Germany* [2008] ECR I-9705 (Judgment, 16 December 2008).
[40] Brown, above n 35, 182.

has to be cost-efficient if it is to attract funding or be sustainable. However, it remains unknown what are the parameters of 'success' or 'failure': does excluding a suspect early on in an investigation count as a 'success', or will only a conviction 'count'? Consequently, there is no agreement on how, nor what data should be collected to measure 'effectiveness'. Such limitations limit the ability of forensic scientists to demand greater resources, or for vital investment in research and development and quality assurance work.

The Interpol International Gateway was a relatively low-cost initiative for information searching. The political momentum driving Prüm clearly envisages much greater investment to facilitate multiple database searching and the generation of new data, as well more effective exchange of existing data. Germany claims that it costs less than €1 million to set up its national Prüm data exchange system. However, the UK Government estimated a start-up figure of some £31 million (including £2.5 million first-year operating expenditure).[41] This does not include the additional costs of tracing suspects, their arrest, detention and deportation, following 'hits' identifying foreign nationals or fugitives residing overseas. In 2009–10 UK authorities effected the arrest, detention and extradition of 1032 people under the European Arrest Warrant framework, prompting some commentators to question why UK taxpayers should foot the £25 million annual bill for sending individuals abroad for trial.

II. CONCLUSION

A. Ensuring Trust through Integrity?

Expanding exchange of forensic information makes crucial the need for robust oversight and regulation to ensure integrity. Sensitive personal genetic information warrants advanced levels of ethical and scientific review, but DNA is not alone in requiring superintendence. Given the potential consequences attendant upon the sharing of forensic information, it is imperative that the utility of forensic databases is maximised at the same time as risks of abuse or harmful effects are mitigated. There ought also to be an expectation that the power to gather, store and share forensic information will be 'free from corrupt influence, only when it is lawful, necessary and proportionate to do so'.[42] Yet concerns surrounding extant policing liaison networks[43] are exacerbated when expanding such networks to include

---

[41] HL European Union Committee, *Prüm*, above n 17, 23–24.

[42] C Harfield, 'The organization of "organized crime policing" and its international context' (2008) 8(4) *Criminology & Criminal Justice* 483, 487.

[43] M den Boer, 'Towards an Accountability Regime for an Emerging European Policing Governance' (2002) 12(4) *Policing & Society* 275.

institutions and practitioners producing forensic information. There then needs to be agreement upon prerequisites for integrity: what needs to be ensured to gain and maintain trust in forensic information?

The UK Government has previously explained how the Prüm Treaty would 'speed up and improve the quality and quantity of information exchanged' in order to identify and bring to justice terrorists and criminals. Ministers stated that the government had negotiated hard 'to get an outcome that enables [the UK] to sign up to Prüm and get all the benefits in terms of fighting cross-border crime and counter terrorism where so much depends on good data exchange and intelligence led policing'.[44] In reply, parliamentarians and ethicists emphasised that 'privacy-related issues concerning the use and transfer of DNA and other data for inter-jurisdictional criminal matters must be considered and agreed in parallel with arrangements for availability, exchange and linkage'.[45]

As things stand, there remain enormous differences in national modes of data production and information generation, coupled with markedly discrepant regulatory regimes, overlaid by major differences in national legal traditions and judicial systems, which are far from being comprehensively harmonised (even supposing this to be desirable). For example, in almost all of the initiatives, mechanisms and organisations which seek to build collaborative links and facilitate forensic data and information sharing, the emphasis has been squarely on policing and prosecutorial cooperation. There is almost a complete lack of attention to defence rights and interests. Procedural safeguards for defendants in criminal proceedings and equivalent access to evidence for the defence have largely been ignored in the drive to rearm investigators and prosecutors in the fight against cross-border crime. These deficits are likely to become more salient in the coming years, as the provision of adequate procedural rights for the defence rises up the EU criminal policy agenda.[46]

Pressing issues demand resolution prior to further expansion of international exchanges of forensic data. The existing fragmentary regulatory framework must be developed to set international quality standards to ensure the competency of individual forensic practitioners and the scientific validity and reliability of their results. At a more fundamental level of principle, urgent consideration must be given to implementing procedural safeguards and equivalent powers for the defence to ensure that transnational data and information sharing does not undermine the accused's fair trial rights. Most 'cooperation' instruments are silent on these matters. Robust

---

[44] HL European Union Committee, *Prüm*, above n 17, Ev1–2 and Q8.
[45] Nuffield Council on Bioethics, *The Forensic Use of Bioinformation*, above n 27, 105.
[46] See, in particular, EU Council, *Roadmap for strengthening procedural rights of suspected or accused persons in criminal proceedings* (2009/C 295/01) [2009] OJ C295.

rules need to be in place to ensure that evidence exchanged across borders is relevant, reliable and not obtained through illegal or unfair means. The exchange of evidence between national authorities should not provide an excuse to drive down procedural standards to the lowest common denominator, nor to enable prosecutors to gain access to evidence that would have been legally unavailable to them in their own jurisdictions. To the contrary, mechanisms of mutual judicial assistance should be used to establish and promote best international practice in evidence gathering, production and presentation.

Perhaps most important is the oversight of these transnational flows of law enforcement information. The process lacks transparency, and consequently citizens' ability to challenge exchanges of their personal data is almost non-existent. Simply ensuring that the system 'works' for the law enforcement professionals involved is inadequate for maintaining public confidence. Transparency and accountability are key to the long-term acceptability of expanded networks of data and information sharing across national borders and mutual recognition of judicial evidence. As Professor Spencer explained to a House of Lords Select Committee:

> What is done in trans-border cases has to be acceptable to public opinion, not just prosecutors and people who work the system. If there are dysfunctions in the criminal justice systems of some other Member States ... they are not likely to be sorted out just by people getting to know each other ... Unless these matters are addressed, public opinion will not accept the too ready functioning of cross-border criminal justice.[47]

The international data-sharing landscape is set to become denser, more complex and routine, and will increasingly include forensic information. If this is to be sustained, trust must be ensured and maintained, requiring more than bland assurances of effectiveness from policing and political bodies. While technologies are increasingly interoperable, traditional parameters of debate over law enforcement cooperation are increasingly inadequate: 'Interoperability is more than interconnecting ICT systems, it has technical, semantic, social, cultural, economic, organisational *and* legal dimensions'.[48] Efforts to understand the potential benefits and impacts of forensic information are incomplete without careful consideration of these dimensions. It remains 'a highly sensitive political issue ..., to make it look like a mere technical issue does not create the right context for a serious and in-depth discussion'.[49]

---

[47] House of Lords European Union Committee, *The European Union's Policy on Criminal Procedure* (30th report) (2010–12, HL 288) 11.

[48] P de Hert and S Gutwirth, 'Interoperability of Police Databases within the EU: An Accountable Political Choice?' (2006) 20(1–2) *International Review of Law, Computers & Technology* 21, 23.

[49] ibid.

It is imperative that the utility of forensic databases is maximised at the same time as minimising risks of abuse or other potential harmful effects. However, the requirements for 'good' governance of forensic science are poorly understood. Clarity of purpose and aims are prerequisites to any governance: you need to know what it is that you are aiming to achieve before you can know how then to govern a process. With forensic information, the aims can be many, and unclear, sometimes contradictory. This makes it very difficult to govern, particularly in a privatised marketplace (as in the United Kingdom), where concerns such as profitability also now come into play. Perhaps as Evans suggests, all that we can hope for (at least temporarily), is 'good enough' governance: 'a relative, evolving and culturally defined aspiration—otherwise known in mature democracies as representative, responsible and accountable governmental administration underpinned by the concept of public value'.[50]

Policy in this area is developing rapidly and is highly ambitious and there are increasing demands for evidence of efficacy in all quarters of the criminal justice system, particularly in an era of severe budget constraints. With media enthusiasm for everything 'forensic' yet to wane, it still requires empirical evidence to demonstrate that these technologies are actually assisting in crime detection and prosecution. This evidence is scarce and equivocal. There are also worrying signs that forensic information may be going unchallenged in some jurisdictions. For example, Slovenia responded to a UK Law Society survey in 2009, that the defence in a criminal trial cannot effectively question DNA due to the opinion of the courts that this evidence is 100 per cent reliable. There is clearly a risk that extraterritorial evidence, including forensic information, may be held to a lower standard, and go unchallenged during the criminal process, creating the biggest risk of all: the wrongful conviction of individuals. Until such risks are precluded, caution must be the watchword.

---

[50] M Evans, 'Beyond the Integrity Paradox—Towards "Good Enough" Governance?' (2012) 33(1) *Policy Studies* 97, 99.

Part III

Case Studies of Trust in International Cooperation

10

Law Enforcement Cooperation between New Zealand and the United States: Serving the Internet 'Pirate' Kim Dotcom Up on a 'Silver Platter'?

NEIL BOISTER

I. INTRODUCTION

THIS CHAPTER EXAMINES the law enforcement cooperation between the United States and New Zealand in support of the request by the United States to extradite Kim Dotcom (born Kim Schmitz), a German/Hong Kong/Finnish national resident in New Zealand, for alleged copyright piracy offences based around the activities of his file hosting internet site, Megaupload. New Zealand has assisted the United States by arresting him, searching his premises, seizing his property and intercepting his communications. In the resulting litigation something of the nature and quality of criminal cooperation between New Zealand and the United States has been revealed. It is a story of organisational chaos, illegality, trust on the one part and disdain perhaps on the other. The chapter is a case study of law enforcement cooperation as seen principally through the lens of reported cases. The chapter is broken down into three parts. Part I sets out the background to this litigation in the United States, briefly setting out why the United States is interested in prosecuting intellectual property crime and examining the specific law enforcement actions it has taken against Dotcom and the other alleged members of the Mega Conspiracy. The emphasis, however, is on Part II, which examines the various aspects of the law enforcement action in New Zealand from the granting of bail to electronic surveillance, not in the order they were undertaken but in which they appeared before the courts. Part III reflects on what this litigation exposes about the nature and quality of the transnational law enforcement structures that facilitate cooperation between the United States and New Zealand. Finally the chapter draws some general conclusions.

II. TAKING STEPS IN THE UNITED STATES AGAINST MEGAUPLOAD

A. The Punitive Turn in Intellectual Property Law

Intellectual property (IP) is among the US' largest exports.[1] It is also a promoter of IP 'maximilisation'—the relentless seeking of ever higher standards of IP protection to protect private revenue and tax receipts[2]—penalisation of copyright violation, particularly on the internet. Prosecution of the theft of intellectual property has become a US 'priority'.[3] In 2009 it passed the Pro-IP Act.[4] The Act set up the infrastructure for taking law enforcement action against IP thieves. It made provision for an IP Tsar, the US Intellectual Property Enforcement Representative (IPEC) and an IP Task Force of senior officials chaired by a Deputy Attorney General. The Task Force monitors and coordinates IP enforcement efforts under the aegis of a Criminal Enforcement/Policy Working Group. At an operational level, IP specialist law enforcement agents of the FBI's Intellectual Property Rights Unit (IPRU) and IP specialist prosecutors of the Department of Justice's Computer Crime and Intellectual Property Section (CCIPS) work on complex domestic and international cases. A wave of prosecutions of internet file sharers alleged to facilitate violation of copyright such as Napster, Grokster, Karzaa, Bit-torrent and Pirate Bay[5] has occurred. The 2010 Joint Strategic Plan on IP Enforcement explicitly pursues enforcement action abroad with the cooperation of foreign states as a policy goal.[6] Now Kim Dotcom, the 'pin up pirate for a generation of file-sharers and public enemy number one

---

[1] K Aoki, 'The Stakes of Intellectual Property Law' in D Kairys (ed), *The Politics of Law: A Progressive Critique*, 3rd edn (New York, Basic Books, 1998) 259.

[2] See generally SK Sell, 'The Global IP Upward Ratchet, Anti-Counterfeiting and Piracy Enforcement Efforts: The State of Play' PIJIP Research Paper Series, no 15 (1 October 2010), available at digitalcommons.wcl.american.edu/cgi/viewcontent.cgi?article=1016&context= research.

[3] Interview by S Mercep, Morning Report, Radio New Zealand National (9 May 2013).

[4] Prioritizing Resources and Organization for Intellectual Property Act, *Public Law* 110-403 (10 October 2008).

[5] G Urbas, 'Copyright, Crime and Computers: New Legislative Frameworks for Intellectual Property Rights Enforcement' (2012) 7 *Journal of International Commercial Law and Technology* 11.

[6] Various US Federal Agencies, *2010 Joint Strategic Plan on Intellectual Property Enforcement*, available at www.whitehouse.gov/sites/default/files/omb/assets/intellectual property/intellectualproperty_strategic_plan.pdf, 14.

for the RIAA [Record Industry Association of America] and MPAA [Motion Picture Association of America]'[7] is the target.

B. The Indictment of Megaupload

Federal authorities in the United States took a further step in the execution of this policy when on 5 January 2012 Kim Dotcom, two of his companies, Megaupload Limited and Vestor Limited, and Finn Batato, Julius Bencko, Sven Echternach, Mathias Ortmann, Andrus Nomm and Bram van der Kolk, were secretly indicted by the grand jury in the United States District Court for the Eastern District of Virginia,[8] on five different counts:

1. Conspiracy to commit racketeering under 18 USC § 1962(d).
2. Conspiracy to commit copyright infringement under 18 USC § 371.
3. Conspiracy to commit money laundering under 18 USC § 1956(h).
4. Criminal copyright infringement by distributing a copyrighted work being prepared for commercial distribution on a computer network and aiding and abetting of criminal copyright infringement under 18 USC § 2, 2319 and 17 USC § 506.
5. Criminal copyright infringement by electronic means and aiding and abetting of criminal copyright infringement under 18 USC § 2, 2319 and 17 USC § 506.

The indictment sets out the factual background to the charges at length. It alleges that the defendants—participants in the global 'Megaconspiracy'—had from at least 2005 operated Megaupload.com, an internet site with servers in the United States, Canada, France and the Netherlands, which allegedly 'reproduces and distributes copies of popular copyrighted content over the Internet without authorization' including 'motion pictures, television programs, musical recordings, electronic books, images, video games and other computer software' thus creating revenues of more than US$170 million for the conspirators and loss of more than half a billion dollars to the copyright holders.[9] The prosecution theory is that while the site advertised itself as a facility for the long-term storage of private content uploaded by users, Megaupload was designed to facilitate uploading and downloading of copyright violating music and films. Only a very small proportion of

---

[7] Managing Intellectual Property, 16 April 2012, available at www.managingip.com/Article/3061205/The-most-influential-people-in-Asia.html#Dotcom.

[8] *United States District Court for the Eastern District of Virginia vs Kim Dotcom, Megaupload Limited, Vestor Limited, Finn Batato, Julius Bencko, Sven Echternach, Mathias Ortmann, Andrus Nomm, and Bram van der Kolk,* Indictment, 5 January 2012, Criminal Case No 1:12CR3 (ED Va).

[9] Para 2 ff of the General Allegations of the Indictment. See paras 2–27 for the general allegations.

Megaupload's users had the capacity to store content long term; and only a small percentage had ever uploaded material, while material uploaded by Megaupload itself remained available—the inference being that most users entered the site to download material and that the site's owners had 'purposefully made their rapid and repeated distribution a primary focus of their infrastructure'.[10] The indictment is accompanied by a notice of forfeiture forfeiting all proceeds of the alleged crimes in the event of conviction.

A superseding indictment adding a number of new counts was filed in February 2012 after Dotcom and his co-accused had been arrested in New Zealand.[11] It transformed the single count in count 5 of 'criminal copyright infringement' into four separate counts (counts 5–8). It made entirely new allegations in counts 9–13 of fraud by wire under 18 USC § 1343 and aiding and abetting such fraud under 18 USC § 2. As a result of these additions, count 1, the racketeering count, was amended to include racketeering by wire fraud and allegations that the conspiracy engaged in various acts of wire fraud. Count 3, the 'conspiracy to commit money laundering' count, was also amended to include allegations that the conspiracy engaged in the laundering of the proceeds of wire fraud.

The keystone offences in the indictment are the allegations of criminal infringement of copyright in counts 5–8 and the distribution of a work being prepared for commercial distribution under count 4. Most of the other criminal behaviour alleged flows into or from these infringements. Prosecution in the United States faces a number of hurdles. It will have to establish the mens rea element, which requires either a simple intention to copy or more strictly the intention to violate a known legal duty, which allows ignorance of the specific duty to be a defence.[12] Dotcom et al are likely to argue that they acted in good faith and without a subjective belief that they were violating someone's copyright. Moreover, there is an exception for online service providers within Title II of the US Digital Millennium Copyright Act Title (DMCA), the Online Copyright Infringement Liability Limitation Act (OCILLA). It establishes a safe harbour for online service providers against indictment for criminal copyright infringement provided they meet certain prescribed conditions.[13] General knowledge of unlawful activity is, however, insufficient to disqualify an ISP from using the safe harbour under 17 US § 512(c)(1)(a). The US courts have held that only

---

[10] Indictment, above n 8, paras 7, 8.
[11] *United States District Court for the Eastern District of Virginia v Kim Dotcom, Megaupload Limited, Vestor Limited, Finn Batato, Julius Bencko, Sven Echternach, Mathias Ortmann, Andrus Nomm, and Bram van der Kolk*, Superceding Indictment, 16 January 2012, Criminal Case No 1:12CR3.
[12] See generally E Goldman, 'Warez Trading and Criminal Copyright Infringement' (2004) 51 *Journal of the Copyright Society of the USA* 395, 399.
[13] s 202, codified at 17 USC § 512.

actual knowledge of specific infringements will do.[14] One of these conditions for entry is to remove or block access to infringing material upon notification by the copyright holder. The United States alleges that Megaupload has been purposefully ineffectual in its response to calls to remove material. Finally, and perhaps most significantly, US copyright law 'does not expressly render anyone liable for infringement by another'.[15] The US authorities are going to have to convince the US courts that some form of secondary liability for copyright infringement is possible under US law. From the indictment it appears that the United States already has a lot of circumstantial evidence. It will assist their case significantly if they can gather evidence not publicly available that:

— Supports the prosecution's theory that the website was deliberately designed to facilitate copyright violation and to generate funds from that violation.
— Reveals the defendants uploaded violating material themselves in order for it to be downloaded.
— Reveals the defendants' mens rea.
— Reveals the defendants acted mala fides in not removing material.

C. US Enforcement Action Against the 'Mega Conspiracy'

The indictment of Dotcom and his co-accused is part of an investigation by the FBI working with other federal agencies including the Department of Justice's Organised Crime and Gang Section, Asset Forfeiture and Money Laundering Section, Office of International Affairs and US Immigration and Customs Enforcement (ICE), based in the National Intellectual Property Rights Coordination Centre, Arlington, Virginia. The indictment is the work of specialist IP/computer crime federal prosecutors[16] from the US Attorney's office in Alexandria, Virginia. The FBI led the global action taken against the 'Mega Conspiracy':[17]

> The FBI investigated and led the international takedown of the Megaupload criminal enterprise, one of the largest criminal copyright cases ever brought by

[14] *Viacom Int'l, Inc v YouTube, Inc*, 718 F Supp 2d 514, 529 (SDNY 2010); confirmed on appeal in *Viacom Int'l, Inc, Football Ass'n Premier League Ltd v YouTube, Inc*, US Court of Appeals for the Second Circuit, August Term 2011, 5 April 2012, Docket No 10-3270-cv.

[15] *MGM Studios, Inc v Grokster, Ltd*, 545 US 913, 930 (2005).

[16] *United States Department of Justice PRO IP Act Annual Report FY2012*, US Department of Justice website, available at www.justice.gov/dag/iptaskforce/proipact/doj-pro-ip-rpt2012.pdf,12.

[17] *Congressional Report Federal Bureau of Investigation: Pro IP Act Annual Report 2012*, US Department of Justice website, available at www.justice.gov/dag/iptaskforce/proipact/fbi-pro-ip-rpt2012.pdf, 3.

the United States. ... This investigation was an unprecedented investigative effort involving dozens of FBI SAs [Special Agents], computer forensics experts, professional support staff and others. Approximately 15 FBI legal attaché offices around the world facilitated the cooperation of their foreign law enforcement partners, which led to the arrest of five individuals. Overall, the FBI and its foreign partners executed more than 20 search warrants in the United States and eight other countries, and seized approximately $50 million in assets. 18 domain names associated with the alleged Megaupload conspiracy were also seized and replaced with [sic] Government seizure banner.

In carrying out this take-down US officials effectively killed Megaupload, which arguably was their primary aim. The United States relied on effective cooperation with some of its closer partners, a capacity it has been developing. Urbas notes:

Law enforcement cooperation has been growing among Western states in regard to the suppression of cybercrime, and the US Department of Justice's Computer Crime and Intellectual Property Section (CCIPS) has played an important role in this regard. Relations are so good among some states that actions can be coordinated and information can be shared in real time making simultaneous search warrant executions, arrests and freezing and seizure of property possible around the world.[18]

Ultimately, however, because Dotcom and the others are in New Zealand, the United States has turned to New Zealand for help.[19] John Ip characterises the New Zealand response as 'a series of missteps'.[20]

III. ENFORCEMENT ACTION IN NEW ZEALAND

A. Provisional Arrest and Extradition Request

Dotcom and several of the others wanted by the United States were gathered in January 2012 at his residence in Coatesville, Auckland, in anticipation of his birthday party. They were arrested in an early morning raid carried out on 20 January by the NZ police on the basis of provisional arrest warrants issued at the behest of the United States. A search was carried out on his and van der Kolk's premises, their computers were seized and their assets frozen. Dotcom and the others were remanded in custody. The United States requested Dotcom's extradition on 5 March and the hearing was to be held

---

[18] Urbas, above n 5, 9.
[19] See, eg, report of NZ officials visiting on the *United States Department of Justice PRO IP Act Annual Report FY2012*, US Department of Justice website, available at www.justice.gov/dag/iptaskforce/proipact/doj-pro-ip-rpt2012.pdf, 27.
[20] J Ip, 'Megaupload's Kim Dotcom, US Copyright Enforcement and the New Zealand Legal System' (January 2013) *Public Law New Zealand* 179, 180 ff.

in August 2012, but was repeatedly delayed to allow time for the exhaustion of all prehearing court proceedings.

B. Bail

Dotcom was denied bail shortly after arrest (a denial upheld on appeal), but bailed a month later at the direction of the district court (a decision appealed unsuccessfully by the United States).[21] One of the flight risks identified by the Crown and relied on by the judge in the first bail hearing was unknown bank accounts held by the defendant.[22] Yet at the second hearing Judge Neville Dawson noted that 'the New Zealand police and the Crown knew of the applicant's Rabobank account prior to his first bail hearing and had failed to advise Judge McNaughton and Asher J'. Thus, the police did not seize money they knew existed, first using its existence as a reason for not bailing him, and then when he did get bail (he revealed the existence of the money himself), revealing that they knew about it from the outset. This game of cat and mouse, played with some contempt for the law, has set the tone for much of what has followed.

C. Restraining Dotcom's Assets

Post-indictment restraining orders against Dotcom and Megaupload's assets held in New Zealand were issued by the US District Court for the Eastern District of Virginia on 10 and 25 January. In New Zealand, on 18 January a foreign restraining order was registered under section 54 of the Mutual Assistance in Criminal Matters Act 1992 (MACMA) (which requires notice to affected parties) when in fact it should have been an interim foreign restraining order under section 60 (not requiring notice). The order was declared null and void by the High Court,[23] the mistake was rectified, the interim order granted. Then, on the basis that the Attorney General was satisfied they related to 'tainted property' under section 54(2)—property 'acquired as a result of significant foreign criminal activity' which is defined as an offence under the law of a foreign country carrying

---

[21] Bail refused—*Kim Dotcom and Others v United States of America*, DC North Shore, 25 January 2012, upheld in an unreported High Court Decision 3 February 2012; Bail granted—*Dotcom & Ors v United States of America*, DC North Shore, 22 February 2012; appealed *United States v Kim Dotcom* [2012] NZHC 328, 29 February 2012.

[22] ibid, DC North Shore, 25 January 2012, paras 12, 78.

[23] *The Commissioner of Police v Kim Dotcom, Bram van der Kolk, and Megastuff Ltd*, Auckland High Court, CIV-2012-404-33, 16 March 2012, [2012] NZHC 487.

a penalty of five years or more,[24] the Attorney General authorised the NZ police commissioner who successfully made an application for the registering of the US restraining order on Dotcom et al's assets in New Zealand under section 54.[25] Justice Potter refused to be drawn by Dotcom's counsel into a substantive analysis of how the Attorney General had come to this decision holding that the judge had no discretion in this regard.

In a subsequent case, the High Court ordered the release of some of these frozen assets to pay for various costs including legal fees in the United States and New Zealand.[26] Section 28(1)(d) of the Criminal Proceeds (Recovery) Act 2009, empowers a court to place restrictions on restraining orders to provide for 'expenses allowed by the Court' to be met from the respondent's restrained property. Justice Potter declined to read a requirement that Dotcom's legal costs be reasonable. She held that Dotcom had a right to legal representation and the funds were not money stolen from others but funds in which he had a contingent interest, while the Commissioner only had a punitive contingent interest.[27] It was the US proceedings against Dotcom which had forced him to seek legal defence. Quite clearly the US authorities do not want Mr Dotcom to run down his assets because they are considered forfeitable to the United States.[28] But the litigation war-chest Justice Potter released has made life uncomfortable for the United States and the Crown.

When the original registration order was due to run out on 18 April the United States through the Commissioner of Police applied for an extension of the registration under section 137 of the Criminal Proceeds (Recovery) Act which enables the court to extend the order for up to one year.[29] Although the post-indictment orders remained in force in the United States, an affidavit from the Assistant US District Attorney responsible revealed that because of the delays in the extradition of Mr Dotcom et al the United States was preparing to file an independent claim for civil forfeiture and was not going to rely on conviction-based forfeiture proceedings.[30] The applicant argued that the statutory framework in New Zealand was 'agnostic' as to whether the foreign forfeiture was civil or criminal,[31] but in affidavits supporting the original registration the US Assistant District Attorney had stated that although the United States had both civil and criminal forfeiture systems

[24] s 2.
[25] *The Commissioner of Police v Kim Dotcom, Bram van der Kolk, Megastuff Ltd and Mona Dotcom*, Auckland High Court, CIV-2012-404-33, 18 March 2012, [2012] NZHC 634, in terms of s 60 of the Mutual Assistance in Criminal Matters Act 1992 and ss 128–31 of the Criminal Proceeds (Recovery) Act 2009.
[26] *The Commissioner of Police v Kim Dotcom* et al [2012] NZHC 2190.
[27] ibid, paras 44–48.
[28] ibid, para 15 citing various affidavits by US officials.
[29] *The Commissioner of Police v Kim Dotcom and others* [2014] NZHC 821.
[30] ibid, para 45.
[31] ibid, para 15.

it was only asking New Zealand to temporarily restrain the assets in connection with the US conviction-based forfeiture case.[32] Justice Thomas felt that a request for extension of assistance based on conviction could not be avoided (when by implication a conviction was not forthcoming as Dotcom was resisting extradition) by applying for extension of an order based on a civil forfeiture order.[33] She declined to extend the order,[34] but the Court of Appeal accepted the argument that the original request did not stipulate what kind of order was sought, overturned the decision and extended the orders to 18 April 2015.[35] On 18 April 2015 Dotcom's assets were subject to a new restraining order made by a US court, which Dotcom was unable to stay because of application of the doctrine of fugitive disentitlement which essentially provides for a default judgment based on a civil forfeiture action against a fugitive defendant.[36] This was registered under the MACMA in New Zealand and although a challenge to that registration failed in the High Court, it was alive to the paradox that registration of this order was being made against someone who at the same time had a right under the extradition treaty to challenge his extradition in New Zealand.[37] This twist in the proceedings appears to have been precipitated by a perception among US officials that the extradition was going to take a long time if Dotcom had access to a war chest. They responded by attempting to deny him that money through an essentially ex parte process begun in the United States, a process they must have known the NZ courts would be wary of reviewing.

D. Search and Seizure

There is no bilateral mutual assistance treaty between the United States and New Zealand.[38] However, both states are parties to the UN Convention against Transnational Organised Crime multilateral framework for legal assistance.[39] Article 18(1) obliges New Zealand to afford the United States 'the widest measure of legal assistance' in the investigation of crimes covered in the Convention, which in terms of Article 3(1)(b) includes all transnational crimes carrying a penalty of four years or more carried out by an

[32] ibid, para 57.
[33] ibid, para 62.
[34] ibid, para 65.
[35] *Commissioner of Police v Dotcom* [2014] NZCA 408, paras 41, 55.
[36] 28 USC § 2466.
[37] *Commissioner of Police v Dotcom* [2015] NZHC 1197, para 13.
[38] Article 16 of the 1970 US–New Zealand Extradition Treaty TIAS 7035, 22 UST 1, signed 12 January 1970, in force 8 December 1970, requires only that articles required in evidence shall be surrendered 'if extradition is granted'.
[39] 15 November 2000, 2225 UNTS 209, in force 29 September 2003. New Zealand signed on 14 December 2000 and ratified on 19 July 2002.

organised criminal group. Criminal copyright violation, racketeering and money laundering all meet the punishment threshold in both states, and the United States is alleging that the Mega Conspiracy has engaged in organised transnational activity. The obligation to provide cooperation is implemented through the MACMA. In terms of section 24(1)(a) New Zealand will grant legal assistance to a prescribed foreign 'convention' country. The United States has been thus prescribed.[40] The formalities for such a request are straightforward. Section 25(1) requires that the United States addresses its request to the Attorney General or his delegate. Section 26(1) requires the United States to specify the nature and purpose of the request and the identity of the person making it. In terms of section 26(c) the request must be certified by the US central authority, describe the nature of the criminal proceedings and summarise the relevant facts and law, detail the procedure the United States wishes New Zealand to follow in giving effect to the request, the manner and form in which the thing sought is to be supplied by New Zealand, and the period during which it must be fulfilled. There are various grounds for refusal—mandatory and non-mandatory. Among the latter, section 27(2)(a) preserves double criminality as an optional get-out for New Zealand. It is indicative of New Zealand's willingness to cooperate that this has not been used, because establishing double criminality in regard to most of the offences in the indictment is not a simple matter.

'Operation Debut', the execution of the arrests, involved two helicopters and 76 officers including members of the elite Special Tactics Group (STG) and the Armed Offenders Squad (AOS).[41] A costume drama of heavily armed black uniformed officers, abseiling from helicopters at dawn, it echoed the high theatre of the 2007 Urewera 'anti-terror' raids.[42] The police tried to keep its planning and execution out of the public eye. They approached the High Court[43] to ask that evidence disclosed to the plaintiffs in their claim

---

[40] Mutual Assistance in Criminal Matters (United States of America) Order O1 GN No S 69/2001. New Zealand will also grant legal assistance under s 24(1)(b) of the MACMA to 'convention countries', ie, states that are party to multilateral suppression conventions to which New Zealand is also party (such as the United States), but only for offences listed in those conventions. In terms of s 2(1) of the MACMA the United States is a convention country because it is a party to the UNTOC, and Schedule A lists the following NZ offences that UNTOC offences would correspond to: s 98A participation in an OCG; s 257A money laundering; any offence against any Act if— (a) it is punishable by imprisonment for a term of 4 years or more; and (b) there are reasonable grounds to suspect that it is transnational in nature (as defined in Articles 3(2) and 18(1) of the convention ...) and involves an organised criminal group (as defined in Article 2(a) of that convention). Double criminality is a requirement under s 24A for legal assistance to convention countries, but not to 'prescribed' convention countries such as the United States.
[41] Editorial, 'Kim Dotcom sets off Year of Fireworks for Politicians' *New Zealand Herald* (27 December 2012).
[42] See *Omar Hamed and others v The Queen* [2011] NZSC 101 (2 September 2011).
[43] *Dotcom and others v Attorney General and others* [2012] NZHC 2000, 8 August 2012.

that the police used unreasonable force to effect the arrests—including the methods and identities of specialists of the STG and AOS– be suppressed.[44] Citing public interest in operational effectiveness, the High Court, in the most part, complied.[45]

The legality of the search warrants executed at Dotcom's property in January 2012 was reviewed by Justice Winkelmann in the High Court in Auckland.[46] She painted in the details of the US request for assistance. In early 2011 the FBI made informal contact with the NZ police, and since then the latter had been providing assistance. On 11 January 2012 a formal letter requesting assistance on a government to government basis was sent by the US Department of Justice to New Zealand's Attorney General. It described the nature of the case against Dotcom and the others and asked for 'assistance in the search of property and seizure of evidence located in New Zealand; in the interviewing of witnesses and targets; and in the collection of other business and official records'.[47] The evidence was necessary to demonstrate the accuseds' awareness of the regular use of Megaupload to reproduce and distribute infringing copies of copyright works, to better understand the conspiracy's activities and to identify others involved. The letter requested the search take place during the birthday celebration and that the NZ authorities seize 'all evidence, fruits and instrumentalities of the crime being investigated' and went on to itemise six categories of things and documents. It asked the seizing officials to 'complete the attached Certificate with Respect to Seized Items and forward the seized articles with the certificate to the appropriate authorities for transmittal to the United States'.[48]

Section 43 of the MACMA entitles the Attorney General to authorise the NZ police to apply for a search warrant from a District Court judge on receipt of a request for assistance in obtaining 'an article or thing by search or seizure', so long as she or he is satisfied that the request relates to a criminal matter in that foreign country in respect of an offence punishable by imprisonment for two years or more and that there are reasonable grounds for believing that the article or thing relevant to the proceedings is located in New Zealand. On 17 January 2012, a Deputy Solicitor General, acting with the delegated authority of the Attorney General, authorised the police to apply for a warrant to search for and seize 'evidence, fruits and instrumentalities' including the six categories of things asked for by the United States but not limited to it, in regard to the criminal copyright and money laundering offences. The application for the warrants was made in the North Shore District Court on 19 January 2012.

---

[44] ibid, para 2.
[45] ibid, paras 15–17.
[46] *Dotcom v Attorney General* [2012] 3 NZLR 115.
[47] ibid, para 12.
[48] ibid, para 13.

In order to issue a warrant, section 44 of the MACMA required the judge to be satisfied that there were reasonable grounds for believing that at the premises to be searched there was anything 'upon or in respect of which any offence under the law of a foreign country punishable by imprisonment for a term of 2 years or more has been, or is suspected of having been, committed'. The affidavit of Detective Sergeant McMorran offered to justify the issuance of the warrant, repeated much of the material in the US letter of request but did not mention that the material was to be sent to the FBI in the United States, although the letter of request mentioning this was attached. Neither was this intention to transfer the material mentioned in the accompanying memorandum. The District Court issued warrants for search of the premises and the seizure of the following:

a. Indicia of occupancy or residence in, and/or ownership of, the property.
b. All documents and things in whatever form relating to the reproduction and distribution of copyrighted works, including, but not limited to, motion pictures, television programs, musical recordings, electronic books, images, video games, and other computer software.
c. All records and things in whatever form, including communications, relating to the activities of the Mega Conspiracy, including, but not limited to, Megaupload, Megavideo, and Megastuff Limited.
d. All bank records, deposit slips, withdrawal slips, cheques, money orders, wire transfer records, invoices, purchase orders, ledgers, and receipts.
e. All documents that reference shipments, imports, exports, customs or seizures.
f. All digital devices, including electronic devices capable of storing and/or processing data in digital form, including, but not limited to:
    — Central processing units.
    — Rack-mounted, desktop, laptop, or notebook computers.
    — Web servers.
    — Personal digital assistants.
    — Wireless communication devices, such as telephone paging devices.
    — Beepers.
    — Mobile telephones.
    — Peripheral input/output devices, such as keyboards, printers, scanners, plotters, monitors, and drives intended for removable media.
    — Related communication devices, such as modems, routers, cables, and connections.
    — Storage media, including external hard drives, universal serial bus ('USB') drives, and compact discs.
    — Security devices.[49]

---

[49] ibid, para 19.

A large number of digital devices and a large volume of information (an estimated 150 terabytes) were seized. Appearing before the reviewing court, the police officer in charge of the search, Detective Inspector Wormald,[50] noted that material seized was, following police protocol, not searched on site. It was to be assessed in the United States.

In the High Court the Crown's initial argument was that review of these warrants should be resisted as a collateral attack on a US process; the MACMA was underpinned by international comity and the expectation that the assistance of police will be reciprocated when required should inform its application. Justice Winkelmann responded:

> The obligations of cross-border cooperation do not … require a hands-off approach from the courts, and the MACMA regime only contemplates the provision of assistance permitted by our domestic laws. It would not be consistent with the object of promoting the rule of law internationally, were the domestic courts to refuse to review the lawfulness of warrants obtained under the MACMA regime.[51]

Justice Winkelmann cited *R v Bujak*,[52] where the Court of Appeal noted that in the Act

> the New Zealand Parliament elected to give as much assistance in New Zealand to overseas law enforcement agencies as it would to New Zealand authorities, but no more. For it would be a rather odd result if a foreign law enforcement agency could get more by way of pre- conviction relief here than would be had by a New Zealand agency.

Justice Winkelmann turned to the shortcomings of the search warrants. Sections 44 and 45 relied upon a specific allegation of the commission of criminal offences carrying penalties of two years or more. The warrants were in her view deficient as they did not stipulate the offence or the statutory provision in US law which enacted it, or the maximum punishment that applied (it had to be two years or more).[53] The reason was that the form used was that used for search warrants in New Zealand under the Summary Offences Act not that stipulated under the MACMA regulations. Describing the offences as 'breach of copyright' was insufficient; it only described the type of offence (inaccurately) and not the particular offence or offences alleged. On this basis she held the warrants to be invalid.[54]

---

[50] ibid, para 20 ff.
[51] ibid, para 33.
[52] *R v Bujak* [2007] NZCA 347, para 47.
[53] *Dotcom v Attorney General* [2012] 3 NZLR 115, para 40, referring to Form 5's requirements under reg 3(1) of the Mutual Assistance Regulations.
[54] ibid, para 49.

However, she also accepted the plaintiffs' arguments that the list of items in Appendix A of the warrant was drawn so broadly that it would inevitably lead to the seizure of irrelevant material.[55] In her view,

> it was the intention of the Police to seek warrants that authorised the seizure of anything that might possibly be relevant, in the knowledge that irrelevant material would be caught up in the net that was cast ... [T]he Police needed to seize such broad categories of items because the Police were not able to assess relevance, and indeed had no request to do so. That would have to be done by the FBI and the FBI would do that offshore.[56]

The police practice had grown up of removing digital devices from the scene of the search, a practice which inevitably led to the removal of irrelevant material. Yet the Court of Appeal had held that police officers executing a warrant by the removal of information held on computer devices are not entitled to remove indiscriminately every computer device for sorting at a later date;[57] they are only entitled to remove data they reasonably believe to be evidence in relation to the offence under investigation. In Justice Winkelmann's opinion the police should have undertaken a preliminary sorting exercise at the scene of the search. Given they were not the investigating officers, they should have been accompanied by FBI investigators, something permissible under section 46(1) of the MACMA, which provides for 'such assistance as may be reasonable for the purposes of entry and seizure'. They would then have been entitled to remove any devices that they reasonably believed to have contained evidence of the offences including digital storage devices for necessary sorting off-site. Computers could have been taken off site and cloned, and the originals returned. As to what could be retained, sections 43 and 44(1) of the MACMA dictated that the particular item of 'evidence' must be relevant to the investigation in the foreign country. In her view, the fact that the warrants authorised search and seizure of too broad a category of items defined in such a way that they would inevitably result in the capture of irrelevant material, was a further ground for their invalidity.[58]

She finished by noting that the police were still exceeding their authority by continuing to keep irrelevant material, because of their intention to pass all of this material to the FBI in the United States for sorting.[59] Only things lawfully seized under section 44(1) could in terms of section 49(2) be ordered to be sent to a foreign investigating authority.

---

[55] ibid, para 52 ff.
[56] ibid, para 60.
[57] *A Firm of Solicitors v District Court of Auckland* [2006] 1 NZLR 586 (CA).
[58] *Dotcom v Attorney General* [2012] 3 NZLR 115, para 77.
[59] ibid, para 88.

Justice Winkelmann dismissed a later attempt to re-litigate the validity of the warrants at a remedies hearing held in April 2013,[60] by pointing out that '[w]arrants that purport to authorise fishing expeditions—that are "general" warrants—have repeatedly been held to be nullities'.[61] She ordered the police to sift through all the digital material and return anything irrelevant to their investigation. She recognised that the police would need the FBI's help to do so. Copies of relevant material could be sent abroad, but the material had to be retained onshore within the jurisdiction of the Court.[62]

The Crown appealed Justice Winkelmann's decision successfully in the Court of Appeal.[63] Its starting point on the validity of the search warrants was the need to attain a balance between individual rights and law enforcement. (The need for interpretation consistent with the right to be free from unreasonable search and seizure under section 21 of the Bill of Rights Act was acknowledged throughout this litigation.)[64] The Court of Appeal conceded that the warrants were not in the prescribed form, the offences described only in general terms without reference to the United States and the descriptions of items to be seized in schedule A were broad.[65] The Court of Appeal was, however, prepared to hoist the warrant out of opacity by other means. They began by pointing out that the United States was entitled to assistance and had satisfied the requirements for obtaining it because it had made a request that was 'comprehensive' in all the details of the offending[66] and offered reasonable grounds for the issuance of a search warrant.[67] Thus, if there had been a 'cock-up' in regard to the search warrant, it was on the part of the NZ authorities. The Court of Appeal considered that the question whether defects in a search warrant were so radical as to consider the warrant a nullity, to be a question of degree.[68] It highlighted its own decision in *Rural Timber Ltd v Hughes*[69] that 'inadequate description of the target offending may be adequately explained by the content of the remainder of the search warrant assessed in a common sense way in the particular factual circumstances of the case'.[70] In this case, the necessary buttressing came in part from Appendix A to the warrant which referred expressly to documents and things relating to the reproduction and distribution of copyrighted works, including, but not limited to, motion pictures, television

---

[60] *Dotcom v Attorney General* [2013] NZHC 1269.
[61] ibid, para 27.
[62] ibid, para 58.
[63] *Her Majesty's Attorney General v Dotcom* [2014] NZCA 19.
[64] ibid, para 24.
[65] ibid, para 46.
[66] ibid, para 40.
[67] ibid, para 42.
[68] ibid, para 36.
[69] *Rural Timber Ltd v Hughes* [1989] 3 NZLR 178 (CA).
[70] *Her Majesty's Attorney General v Dotcom* [2014] NZCA 19, para 34.

programmes, musical recordings and 'to records and things relating to the activities of the Mega Conspiracy, including but not limited to, Megaupload, Megavideo and Megastuff Limited'.[71] In the Court of Appeal's view the issuing judge may have blundered in not specifying the offence correctly, but these additional details placed the reasonable reader of the warrant in a position to understand what they related to, especially if that reader was a computer expert such as Mr Dotcom.[72] In addition, the Court of Appeal was also, unlike Justice Winkelmann, willing to rely on the terms of the accompanying arrest warrant which did specify the various charges against Dotcom and his co-accused to patch up the search warrant.[73] A reasonable reader reading the arrest and search warrants together would have had little difficulty in gathering that the offences in the search warrants were those specified in the arrest warrants. Finally, there was evidence from the execution of the warrants that Dotcom had read both and had understood the operation was about copyright infringement. The Court of Appeal concluded that the defects in the warrants were in form rather than substance and not so radical as to require the warrants be treated as nullities.[74] Nor in its view would the practical consequences of these defects have caused the respondent significant prejudice as no more was seized than would have been without the defects, the enormous amount of data in the electronic items meant that these items had 'for practical reasons' to be examined off-site, and 'any subsequent prejudice caused by alleged excessive seizure, retention of irrelevant evidence or alleged breach of s 49 of the MACMA were separate downstream matters not caused by the defects in the search warrants'.[75] Thus, although section 204 of the Summary Proceedings Act entitled the setting aside of a warrant for want of form if there had been a miscarriage of justice, in its view subsequent events showed there had not been.

The final appeal on this question was made to the New Zealand Supreme Court which gave its judgment two days before Christmas 2014.[76] The Majority of the Supreme Court (McGrath, William Young, Glazebrook and Arnold JJ) agreed with the Court of Appeal.[77] They noted that where the defects in a warrant were not so serious that it was a nullity, the test for setting the warrant aside where there had been a miscarriage of justice under section 204 of the Summary Proceedings Act is whether there has 'been prejudice to the person affected', a test where the circumstances

---

[71] ibid, para 52.
[72] ibid, para 53.
[73] ibid, para 59.
[74] ibid, para 66.
[75] ibid, para 70.
[76] *Kim Dotcom and others v Her Majesty's Attorney General* [2014] NZSC 199.
[77] ibid, para 68 ff.

surrounding execution were relevant.[78] They cited *Rural Timber* in support of this view, noting specifically that relevant circumstances could include explanations to those in control of premises.[79] Turning then to whether the warrant was so defective it was a nullity[80] they accepted that it wasn't made on the correct form (which they described as 'most unsatisfactory')[81] and omitted the details of offences and punishment, which they considered could be of potential prejudice.[82] But they were satisfied that there was no significant prejudice in this regard once the circumstances of the explanation to Dotcom of the offences and the details in the arrest warrant were taken into account, because it gave Dotcom the relevant detail about the offences which were the subject of the search warrant.[83] The more serious potential failure was the over broad description of items to be searched for and the absence of imposition of specific conditions in regard to off-site sorting and return. An extensive survey of foreign authority on search and seizure of electronic devices with data storage capacity revealed that many different jurisdictions acknowledged the need to protect special privacy concerns in this regard, and it followed that search of such a device required special authorisation justified by sufficient sworn grounds in the application for the warrant.[84] However, it also revealed that storage of large amounts of data created problems of securing that data, which justified removal off-site. Conditions would have to be imposed in certain circumstances where obvious constraints (such as doctor–patient privilege) were evident, but were not generally necessary: 'Rather, the police will be entitled to search the computer in order to identify any relevant material, generally offsite'. 'Downstream issues' such as preservation of relevant material, storage and return of irrelevant material could be dealt with using the normal legal remedies.[85] The Majority noted rather lamely that where material had already been sent overseas these remedies 'may not be available', and that therefore timely notification was necessary to enable access to the Court to challenge export.[86] But applying these principles to the case before them they found that the warrant had spelled out that computers and other electronic items were going to be searched for offences related to internet-based offending, and that taking the material off-site and cloning it was in the circumstances

---

[78] ibid, paras 115, 130.

[79] ibid, para 125.

[80] The Majority appear to elide the question of whether the warrant was a nullity with the question of whether the defect caused a miscarriage of justice under s 204, by applying the test in regard to the latter to answer the former.

[81] *Kim Dotcom and others v Her Majesty's Attorney General* [2014] NZSC 199, para 141.

[82] ibid, para 144.

[83] ibid, paras 145–46.

[84] ibid, para 192.

[85] ibid, para 194.

[86] ibid, paras 200–01.

the only practical measure that could be taken given that without Dotcom's assistance to overcome encryption they could not be searched.[87] Conditions did not have to be imposed:

> If the police acted unlawfully in carrying out the search, that would be addressed in the normal way, after the search was completed. In the particular circumstances of this case, sending clones of the seized computers overseas may have been the only practical way of effecting the search, but that is not something on which we should express any view as it is the subject of separate proceedings.[88]

They did not consider the warrants to be unreasonably vague and general and dismissed the appeal.[89]

Alone in dissent, Chief Justice Elias thought the warrants were general and invalid because of their failure to specify the offences and the materials to be seized with sufficient particularity.[90] She did not agree that the shortcomings of the search warrant were cured by the details of offences provided in the arrest warrant, because it still left the search warrant unacceptably weak on detail of what was within the scope of the search.[91] For the issuing judge to leave it to the police not to seize anything irrelevant, as the Court of Appeal was content to do, was not good enough from a rule of law perspective.[92] She did not agree with the Court of Appeal (and with the Majority) that excessive seizure and the claims of breaches of section 49 of the MACMA were 'separate downstream matters not caused by the defects in the search warrants'.[93] Moreover, she pointed out 'downstream' was out of New Zealand: 'the fact that under the Mutual Assistance Act subsequent use passes beyond the NZ criminal justice system may be seen as a pointer to a need for more, rather than less, care in the warrants themselves'.[94] In response to the Court of Appeal's comfort with the failure of the judge to impose conditions in the warrant she stated:

> If it was reasonably necessary to seize material likely to be irrelevant … or if it was reasonably necessary because of the scale of the offending for the warrants to be so broad in scope that they were likely to cover irrelevant as well as relevant material (as is suggested here), then the discretion must be exercised to meet the circumstances.[95]

The undefined nature of the Mega Conspiracy, the police's own acknowledgement that they would pick up irrelevant material, and the fact that

---

[87] ibid, para 203.
[88] ibid, para 204.
[89] ibid, para 206.
[90] ibid, paras 8, 27.
[91] ibid, para 38.
[92] ibid, para 41.
[93] ibid, para 51.
[94] ibid, para 46.
[95] ibid, para 60.

sorting would have to occur in the United States, all pointed to the necessity for conditions.[96] Taking the view the warrants were seriously flawed, the learned Chief Justice held that the question of a miscarriage of justice under section 204 was irrelevant, and would have allowed the appeal.

In essence, while the Court of Appeal and Majority of the Supreme Court were prepared to look more broadly than the warrants themselves to make up for its lacunae, they were not prepared to allow this examination to be tainted by contemplation of what was likely to happen to the items once seized beyond merely being taken off-site. Justice Winkelmann and the Chief Justice took a narrower view when looking at the warrant itself, but did allow the likely destination of the items to colour that view. A broad view of the contents of the warrants and the circumstances seems reasonable, but the fact that the material was going to be sent abroad and very rapidly should have required specific conditions be laid down in the warrant for making the sifting process and retaining material. What is apparent is that various policing failures occurred during this search and seizure process.

First, despite claiming in their evidence that they had been heavily briefed about the nature of the case in consultation with the FBI, the NZ police do not appear to have had a clear grasp of the crimes they were policing or the NZ law on which they were relying. This is a matter of clear direction as to the foreign offences concerned and learning to use seldom used processes. Second, they were driven to adopt a method of deciding on relevance versus irrelevance of the digital material off-site, a method of dubious legality (the law has been subsequently amended to permit this)[97] in which they could do little other than deliver the material. Although the United States gave some direction as to what it required for prosecution of the indicted offences, the NZ police took everything knowing that they were not going to search it in New Zealand because that is not what the United States wanted. The NZ police's plea of forensic incapacity echoes the judicially sanctioned US National Security Agency's justification for retaining data gleaned from surveillance for up to five years because of its limited ability to process the data.[98] Although Justice Winkelmann did not consider these operational imperatives and difficulties as being able to expand the scope of police authority,[99] the Majority of the Supreme Court appears to have

[96] ibid, para 62.
[97] s 112 of the Search and Surveillance Act 2012 provides that '[i]f a person exercising a search power is uncertain whether any item found may lawfully be seized, and it is not reasonably practicable to determine whether that item can be seized at the place or vehicle where the search takes place, the person exercising the search power may remove the item for the purpose of examination or analysis to determine whether it may be lawfully seized'.
[98] S Scott and D Sanger, 'Job Title Gave Snowden Special Access to Secrets' *International Herald Tribune* (2 July 2013) 3.
[99] MR Ferrere, 'The Dotcom Saga: Lessons for the Police and Lawyers' 800 *Law Talk* (20 July 2012) 12.

accepted that practical difficulties dictate that in cases of this kind the NZ police could serve as the front line only, with extremely broadly drawn powers to make up for their lack of forensic capacity but also to enable them to do what the United States wanted them to do.

E. Removal of Evidence by US Agents Without Authority

In the High Court hearing on the legality of the search warrant[100] it was revealed that after copying (or cloning) the hard drives seized, US agents had sent them to the United States. An extensive recount of the Crown's futile attempts to get the plaintiff to consent to the copying of the material or the sending of the originals to the United States[101] revealed that the US agents, who arrived on 18 March, had by the end of March cloned the material and sent it to the United States. The arrival of the US agents in New Zealand had precipitated the cloning and transfer of this material to the obvious surprise of the NZ police (the FBI agents Fedexed the copies without asking for permission, then told their NZ police minder, who then went on leave without telling his superiors about the transfer). While the NZ police may not have wanted the FBI to take the cloned material, they had not stopped them from doing so.

In his evidence the officer in charge of the search, Detective Inspector Wormald,[102] noted that the United States had not requested the NZ police to assess the relevance of the material. He had understood that the Attorney General had directed that the items seized be sent immediately to the United States to be forensically examined there; they were not to be examined in New Zealand. The head of the police electronic crimes laboratory deposed that analysis of this material was beyond the laboratory's capacity. A deputy director of the US Department of Justice Cyber-Crime laboratory deposed that it was essential that his laboratory maintain custody and control of the original digital evidence in order to preserve its integrity, to avoid a NZ official having to attend trial in the United States, and to have the material at hand when new issues arose at trial.

In her discussion of the legality of this transfer, Justice Winkelmann relied heavily on the express terms of section 49(2) of the MACMA which provides that the items seized under a section 44 warrant may be kept for one month 'pending a direction in writing from the Attorney-General as to the manner in which the thing is to be dealt with (which may include a direction that the thing be sent to an appropriate authority of a foreign country)'.

---

[100] *Dotcom v Attorney General* [2012] 3 NZLR 115, para 90 ff.
[101] ibid, para 98 ff.
[102] ibid, para 20 ff.

The Solicitor General acting as his delegate had given a direction in terms of section 49(2) on 16 February that any items seized were to remain in the custody of the Commissioner of Police until further notice. There was no direction by the Attorney General directing release to the US authorities. Argument that this requirement did not apply to copies and assurances that the release would have been given had it been asked for did not impress Her Honour. She noted that while the police were entitled to allow the US authorities access to the material, they could not allow it absent a written direction by the Attorney General to be copied and the copies taken abroad because to do so would be to lose control of the material. Brushing aside explanations from Crown Law as to why the Solicitor General had not immediately directed that the evidence be sent abroad, she concluded that the sending abroad was unlawful, commenting:

> The hard drives seized contain information in the form of digital files. Those files are part of the relevant hard drive. The information is the property of the plaintiffs ... Once clones of the digital files were shipped offshore, the police no longer had control over what was done with them. They could not, for instance, compel their return, nor prevent the FBI dealing with them as it chose, even if it was subsequently determined that there was any invalidity affecting the warrant, or that items outside the scope of s 46(1)(d) had been seized.[103]

For the plaintiffs, victory was hollow: all the Court could do in regard to the material already in the United States was to order the Attorney General to 'notify the relevant United States authority of the Court's decision in this matter, and request the voluntary return of the clones removed from New Zealand, along with any copies/clones or data taken therefrom'.[104] It was Winkelmann J's 'expectation' that the FBI would not retain irrelevant material.

The issue was raised again in the Court of Appeal.[105] It interpreted section 49 as 'providing a carefully prescribed process for things seized to be "kept" in the custody of the Commissioner for a short period pending a decision by the Attorney General as to how the thing is to be "dealt with"'.[106] The purpose of the provision was 'to provide a "breathing space"... while the Attorney General or Solicitor General decides whether or not to permit the things to be sent overseas in accordance with the request received from the foreign country'.[107] The Court of Appeal cited as persuasive Canadian authority where the Ontario Superior Court of Justice refused to order the sending of mirror-imaged copies of 32 computer servers seized

---

[103] ibid, paras 96–97.
[104] ibid, para 145.
[105] *Her Majesty's Attorney General v Dotcom* [2014] NZCA 19.
[106] ibid, para 95.
[107] ibid, para 97.

from Megaupload to the United States, adjourning the hearing so that steps could be taken to refine what was to be sent.[108] The Court of Appeal held that section 49 required that the 'thing' to be kept in custody pending a direction from the Attorney General as to how it was to be 'dealt with' was not only the physical thing but its contents including in this case the data it contained; the contrary interpretation would deprive the Attorney General of the power to deal with the thing.[109] It was not for the Commissioner of Police to deal with them by permitting clones to be taken out of the country because to do so would mean New Zealand lost control over them and the ability to refine what was sent; the person whose property was seized lost the opportunity to challenge the validity of the search and seizure; and the constitutional role of the Attorney General and Solicitor General as independent law officers was undermined.[110]

The transfer of the clones has severely limited Dotcom et al's options should he come to trial in the United States. US courts apply the so-called 'silver platter' doctrine[111] to evidence obtained by illegal searches by foreign officials in foreign states holding that neither the Fourth Amendment prohibition on unlawful search and seizure nor the judicially created exclusionary rule apply,[112] and this is so even if US officials are present and cooperate to some extent with the local officials.[113] Dotcom et al's only recourse will be to argue that this evidence should be excluded because the circumstances of the search are so extreme they 'shock the conscience', or that US participation in the search is of such a degree as to convert it to a joint venture with the United States. Neither the search nor the level of US participation, are likely to meet these thresholds. Perhaps Dotcom's best argument is that the NZ police were in effect acting as US agents. US courts have held that where the 'foreign officials conducting the search were actually acting as agents for their American counterparts' the exclusionary rule may apply.[114]

F. Electronic Surveillance

The United States appears to have gathered evidence against Dotcom et al from a variety of sources. Many of the examples of overt action by the accused in the indictment are taken from private emails sent between the

---

[108] ibid, para 98 citing *Canada (United States of America) v Equinix Inc*, 2013 ONSC 193.
[109] ibid, para 99.
[110] ibid, para 101.
[111] See B Zagaris, *International White Collar Crime: Cases and Materials* (Cambridge, Cambridge University Press, 2010) 272–73.
[112] *United States v Barona*, 56 F 3d 1087, 1091 (9th Cir, 1995).
[113] *United States v Rosenthal*, 93 F 2d 1214, 1231 (11th Cir, 1986).
[114] *United States v Behety*, 32 F 3d 503, 510 (11th Cir 1994).

defendants.[115] Sources suggest that more than 22 million emails are in the possession of the FBI.[116] Late in 2012 it was revealed that the New Zealand Government Communications Security Bureau (GCSB), which provides foreign intelligence and protects the security of government communications,[117] had been intercepting the communications of Dotcom and van der Kolk at the request of the NZ police. Dotcom et al then attempted to join the Attorney General in his capacity as representative of the GCSB as a defendant in the judicial review of the unlawfulness of the search of their premises.[118] Section 15 of the Government Communications Security Bureau Act 2003 requires a warrant for the interception of communications, while section 14 prohibits the interception of a NZ 'permanent resident', which Dotcom and van der Kolk both were when placed under surveillance.[119] Intercepting their communications requires a warrant under section 4 of the Security Intelligence Act 1969. It does not appear that a warrant had been asked for, because the GCSB has been told by the Organised and Financial Crime Agency New Zealand that Dotcom was not a permanent resident. Ip explains:

> The GCSB Act defines the term 'permanent resident' to be 'a person who is, or who is deemed to be, the holder of a residence class visa under the Immigration Act 2009'. In fact, Dotcom had been granted a residence visa under the previous immigration legislation, the Immigration Act 1987, in November 2010. He arrived in New Zealand after November 29, 2010, by which time the Immigration Act 2009 was in force. As per the transitional provisions, Dotcom's residence visa became a 'resident visa' for the purposes of the 2009 Act. Section 4 of the Act defines 'residence class visa' to include a resident visa. Accordingly, as the holder of a 'residence class visa', Dotcom was a permanent resident for the purposes of s 14 of the GCSB Act 2003 and hence off-limits.[120]

The Attorney General conceded that the interception was unlawful[121] and Justice Winkelmann granted the order sought. Dotcom et al sought compensation for the illegal search. The GCSB claimed confidentiality on the basis of national security. An amicus had to be appointed to assess this claim. In this regard it is interesting that the Crown was unwilling to reveal details of a FBI briefing given before the arrests were made; the Court had to

---

[115] See Indictment, above n 8, 30–31.
[116] V Robinson, 'Dotcom Extradition Hearing Delayed' *Stuff.CoNZ* (23 December 2012), available at www.stuff.co.nz/technology/7252387/Dotcom-extradition-hearing-delayed.
[117] s 7 Government Communications Security Bureau Act 2003.
[118] *Kim Dotcom and others v Attorney General and others* [2012] NZHC 3268.
[119] Dotcom was granted residence in 2010 under the investor-plus category tailored to those invest NZ$10 million in New Zealand Government bonds. The grant of the visa is itself surrounded by controversy and suggestions have been made it was irregular.
[120] Ip, above n 20, 182.
[121] *Kim Dotcom and others v Attorney General and others* [2012] NZHC 3268, para 2.

order this be disclosed.[122] Justice Winkelmann ordered disclosure of details of the GCSB's surveillance. This included 'Confirmation of all entities to whom the GCSB provided information in relation to this matter. In particular, confirmation is sought of whether any such information was shared with other members of Echelon/"Five Eyes", including any United States authority'.[123] 'Echelon Five Eyes' is the name given to the Signals Intelligence Sharing Arrangement, operated under the UK–US Agreement to do just that, and to which Australia, Canada and New Zealand are party.[124] Under this agreement recovered intelligence appears to be shared with other parties without a specific request. Whether matters such as those involving Dotcom were shared with the United States is unknown but seems likely. Dotcom also requested disclosure by the NZ police liaison officer in Washington of all the termination activity that that officer had monitored in the FBI's multi-agency command centre, something he had revealed witnessing in a journal article,[125] but the Crown argued that revelation would jeopardise police relations with the FBI, and the judge denied it as irrelevant to the case. One of the remarkable features of Justice Winkelmann's judgment was that it had been her questioning of counsel as to why Dotcom et al had not made a compensation claim for unlawful monitoring which precipitated them to do so. When the Attorney General appealed unsuccessfully against the balance of the order,[126] the Court of Appeal made the point that the proceedings became very complex as a result of her observations.[127] When, however, Dotcom tried, prior to the hearing on the legality of the search warrant in the Court of Appeal, to introduce the unlawful surveillance as a further ground for the illegality of the search warrant because it was not disclosed to the judge issuing the warrant, he was not permitted to do so because these grounds were not pleaded or argued in the High Court.[128]

Prime Minister John Key, whose own knowledge of the eavesdropping has been questioned (he denied knowledge of GCSB's surveillance of Dotcom even though he is the minister responsible), ordered an inquiry into it and

---

[122] ibid, para 23.

[123] ibid, para 26.

[124] See the documents opened for public scrutiny by the UK authorities at the National Archives Site, available at www.nationalarchives.gov.uk/ukusa/.

[125] *Kim Dotcom and others v Attorney General and others* [2012] NZHC 3268, para 31 ff: Detective Superintendent Mike Pannet, reported in 'Careful Planning behind Dotcom Swoop' (February 2012) 354 *Ten One New Zealand*, available at www.tenone.police.govt.nz/tenone/February12National1.htm –.

[126] *Attorney General in Respect of the Government Communications Security Bureau versus Kim Dotcom, Finn Batato, Mathias Ortmann, Bram van der Kolk* [2013] NZCA 43, 7 March 2013.

[127] ibid, para 49.

[128] *Attorney General v Dotcom* [2013] NZCA 488.

apologised to Dotcom for the unlawful spying.[129] The inquiry revealed that there have been many similar breaches relating to other NZ citizens or residents.[130]

The debacle over GCSB's eavesdropping again raises the spectre of unauthorised executive actions, which has established itself as a theme of the Dotcom investigation; and once again all in the cause of another very influential and powerful state. Electronic surveillance by security services has always had this potential. The Council of Europe noted in 2004 that, 'Although in principle, the increasing cooperation between law enforcement and national security services can be fruitful in the combating of criminal organizations, extra precautions should be taken to prevent the potential illegitimate gathering of evidence by security services'.[131]

As a postscript, however, the legal barriers to use of the GCSB's services have been dissolved by new legislation that makes it lawful for the GCSB to assist the NZ police in their lawful investigations of residents.[132] Dotcom appeared before a select committee headed by the Prime Minister where he condemned the new legislation as an overreach not a clarification, legalising what was previously illegal practice.[133] This episode provides a very good example of an extension of domestic policing power under external influence and how securitisation of law enforcement cooperation can remove existing domestic legal barriers and penetrate the enforcement of domestic law and order.

IV. WOULD YOU LIKE (ALL THEIR) FILES WITH THAT, SIR?

With the recent thawing of political relations New Zealand can probably be categorised within the closer circle of states with which the United States can engage in law enforcement cooperation and mutual legal assistance. The NZ police's assistance to the US federal authorities in their attempt to extradite Kim Dotcom exhibits many of the developments in recent

---

[129] A Bennett and C Trevett, 'PM Apologises to Dotcom over Basic Errors' *NZ Herald* (27 September 2012), available at www.nzherald.co.nz/nz/news/article.cfm?c_id=1&objectid=10836884.

[130] R Kitteridge, *Review of Compliance at the Government Communications Security Bureau*, March 2013, Executive Summary, para 5, available at www.gcsb.govt.nz/newsroom/reports-publications/Review%20of%20Compliance_%20final%2022%20March%202013.pdf.

[131] Council of Europe, *Interception of Communication and Intrusive Surveillance' in Combating Organised Crime: Best Practice Surveys of the Council of Europe* (Strasbourg, Council of Europe Publishing, 2004) 77, 102.

[132] s15A of the Government Communications Security Bureau Amendment Act 2013.

[133] *3 News*, New Zealand, (3 July 2013).

police cooperation.[134] There has been direct informal personal contact between the police forces involved, and the NZ police liaison officer in Washington appears to have played a role in this regard. More formally, there has been the direct transmission of a request for mutual assistance by US law enforcement authorities to New Zealand's authorities. New Zealand has responded positively, attempting to meet US deadlines and to comply with the formalities and procedures that it has indicated are necessary for successful prosecution.

The problem in this relationship does not appear to be one of trust (expect perhaps an excess of trust). These two sets of enforcement authorities do appear by and large to trust one another. Whether the US authorities' disdain for New Zealand process in regard to the removal of the clones equals disdain for NZ law enforcement is a matter on which one can only speculate. Nor is the problem one of law. There are adequate international and national laws in place. What is missing is a clear understanding of how those rules enable cooperation in an unusual situation involving behaviour on the margins of criminality. The execution of this specific form of cooperation has been marked by capacity on the requesting state's part and incapacity on the requested state's part. Because of New Zealand's forensic incapacity in regard to searching encrypted digital information, the NZ police has found itself in a very similar position to police in a classic developed–developing world situation where all the power lies in the hands of the requesting state except for the power to enforce its jurisdiction. The instrumental nature of this relationship is illustrated in a number of ways. Its seems fairly clear that while NZ officials have been told broadly about what is required to get useful evidence into Dotcom's trial in the United States, neither the NZ officials nor the US officials fully grasped what was necessary to meet the national legal requirements for gathering such evidence in New Zealand. The very broadly drawn search warrant is the obvious example. It is difficult to know to what extent the United States has (i) engaged in increased training and technical assistance to NZ police in order to facilitate this process, while (ii) themselves trying to come to grips with NZ law. One gets the impression that a shopping list was simply presented. In result, the association of the two main actors—the US police and the NZ police—has been transformed by the introduction of the third group of actors—the NZ judiciary, who have attempted to exercise a degree of ex ante oversight, and what was once a relationship of solidarity is in danger of breaking down into party formation: the police (local and foreign) versus the judiciary. One negative consequence has been that what was always going to be a long process,

---

[134] Y Dandurand, G Colombo and N Passas, 'Measures and Mechanisms to Strengthen International Cooperation among Prosecution Services' (2007) 47 *Crime, Law and Social Change* 261, 270–72.

has degenerated into a welter of reviews, appeals and damages claims. The police cannot validly argue that they have been given an unnecessarily difficult time by the courts; the courts have simply insisted on adherence to the fundamental principle that state action be lawfully authorised.

The individuals who reside within a state are subject, in the words of Mathias Risse, to that state's 'unmediated law enforcement'.[135] The state, however, mediates between the enforcement of the law of other states and those individuals. At the centre of the problem is the lack of specificity in the nature of the direction New Zealand has received from the US authorities. The Dotcom case raises the spectre of a long-distance 'fishing expedition', in which the United States is fishing for substance and New Zealand is 'baiting up' for it. Asked about his response to the illegality of these NZ police actions, US Attorney General Eric Holder said he was pleased with the cooperation the United States was getting from New Zealand in regard to this case.[136] One of the interesting questions this raises, which as noted may arise in Dotcom et al's trial where the question of the admissibility of illegally obtained evidence arises, is when, because of the peculiar nature of the subject matter (in this case digital information), does an act of interstate law enforcement cooperation become so heavily directed by the requesting state that the law enforcement authorities can arguably be said to be acting for the requesting state and their behaviour can be attributed to them. If this were a matter of state responsibility under international law, we would examine whether the NZ authorities could in effect be considered to be acting as US authorities—primarily because of their forensic incapacity in the analysis of digital evidence—in these circumstances rather than simply acting on their behalf out of international comity. The principles of attribution serve as a useful prism for exposing the relationship between the NZ authorities and the United States in the Dotcom case. Most appropriate is Article 6 of the International Law Commission's Articles on State Responsibility[137] which provides:

> The conduct of an organ placed at the disposal of a State by another State shall be considered an act of the former State under international law if the organ is acting in the exercise of elements of the governmental authority of the State at whose disposal it is placed.

Is it too fanciful to argue that New Zealand's law enforcement authorities have been placed 'at the disposal' of the US federal authorities in the sense that the NZ authorities are acting under the 'exclusive direction and

---

[135] M Risse, *On Global Justice* (Princeton, NJ, Princeton University Press, 2012) 26.
[136] Interview by S Mercep, above n 3.
[137] See J Crawford, *International Law Commission's Articles on State Responsibility: Introduction, Text and Commentaries* (Cambridge, Cambridge University Press, 2002).

control' of the US authorities?[138] In particular by allowing the cloned copies of Dotcom's hard drives to be taken to the United States they have done their best to serve Dotcom up on a silver platter. This is almost the apotheosis of the platitude, 'international cooperation'.

V. CONCLUSION

International law enforcement cooperation of the kind examined in this chapter is supposed to be trust based. The US law enforcement authorities trust that New Zealand will manage the risk that Dotcom will escape the enforcement of its jurisdiction through the failure to provide them with incriminating evidence; the NZ law enforcement authorities trust that the United States will not abuse its trust by engaging in a fishing expedition that if exposed will expose them to the risk of judicial censure and financial cost. The United States should on the face of it trust the NZ police more as a result of what they have done for the United States thus far; after all they have delivered. But both sides may find that supplication by the requested party in awe of the requesting party is not a trust-engendering exercise. The naive presumption of shared purpose on the one side, and a paternalistic instrumental view on the other, can leave a bitter residue that will harm future cooperation.

---

[138] ibid; ILC Commentary on Draft Article 6, para 2.

11

Transnational Policing and Its Contexts: Flexibility and (Dis)trust

CHANTAL PERRAS

I. INTRODUCTION

TRANSNATIONAL POLICING AND its surrounding infrastructure and support systems have been largely neglected by the field of research focusing on how so-called transnational crimes are dealt with. Rather than using a broad term such as 'international criminal law' or '(international) policing', Boister suggests refocusing on transnational systems, arguing that it is necessary in order to find a doctrinal match for transnational crime.[1] It is also posited that such an approach would lead to a clearer understanding of other concerns such as: the process of criminalising transnational conduct; the question of legitimacy in the development and control of the transnational criminal justice 'system'; doctrinal weaknesses; human rights considerations; and enforcement issues. In other words, the transnational concept is more apt when contemplating such wider issues and can highlight a legal order that attenuates the distinction between national and international.

The reason for a focus on transnational criminal investigation within its surrounding systems is the apparent increase in transnational crime in the last decades. Further, a convenient context has been established. Political authorities around the world, especially among European states, have elaborate specific treaties and conventions to deal with what they see as the problematic state of transnational offending (albeit this is not new in relation to drug matters). The normative framework has been developing since 1961 with the adoption of the Single Convention on Narcotic Drugs. In 1988, the Vienna Treaty[2] was set up to counter trans-boundary traffickers and bestow more power upon police officers.

---

[1] N Boister, 'Transnational Criminal Law?' (2003) 14(5) *European Journal of International Law* 953.
[2] United Nations Convention against Illicit Traffic in Narcotic Drugs and Psychotropic Substances.

This chapter aims to bring clarity to blurred areas of international criminality by adopting an operational perspective of transnational policing and its surrounding network of policies and laws. It looks to two essential components that enable the transnational system to operate, as utilised by system agents: flexibility and (dis)trust.

Law enforcement agents fulfil their roles in an environment characterised by bureaucracy and a judicial system enmeshed in complexity and uncertainties. Strategies and mechanisms are used by system actors to circumvent numerous obstacles to police cooperation. These link operational agent perceptions with edicts that emerge from the surrounding transnational systems, ie, national policies and laws designed to counter transnational crimes. Using Bigo's theoretical framework on security fields (inspired by Bourdieu),[3] and expanding on the analysis and conclusions of Boister,[4] it is possible here to illuminate the transnational policing model with concrete examples.

This chapter details findings from a qualitative study looking at 'what works' in transnational police cooperation. Qualitative interviews were held with Canadian and US crime investigators responsible for transnational investigations. Further interviews were carried out with a sample of their French, Swiss and Dutch counterparts. Formal and informal instruments were discussed and similar means were described as the most useful by both sides (European versus North American). Surprisingly, Interpol and Europol were not considered as useful as might be expected from reading the (legal) literature in this area. Instead, flexibility and (dis)trust are perceived as the essential tools required to achieve goals such as completing an investigation of international reach like those in drug-trafficking operations.

II. UNTANGLING INTERNATIONAL AND TRANSNATIONAL SYSTEMS

Labels such as 'international crime' and 'transnational organised criminals' have been used to describe a large variety of problematic behaviours that transcend national borders. Confusion has thus resulted from the over-inclusive use of rather abstract concepts. There is therefore a need first to differentiate between international, transnational and national measures that have been taken to counter corresponding levels of crime.

International crimes can impact upon the global community. In theory, the jurisdiction is 'mankind' and it has no statute of limitations (or expiry date). Resulting action should prompt maximum solidarity among all people concerned. Such crimes can include war crimes, genocide and crimes

---

[3] See an example of this framework in D Bigo, 'Pierre Bourdieu and International Relations: Power of Practices, Practices of Power' (2011) 5 *International Political Sociology* 225.
[4] Boister, above n 1.

against humanity. International criminal law is responsible for the detection, prosecution and judging of those crimes.[5]

Transnational systems are responsible for so-called 'treaty crimes', which can be considered less serious when compared with war crimes, genocide and crimes against humanity, etc. Trans-boundary crimes such as drug trafficking and terrorism are good examples of what are labelled 'transnational' crimes. They are dealt with only when there is a need, a common interest, and when shared values are being violated.

Boister argues that the distinction between 'international' and 'transnational' is sustainable on four grounds:[6]

1. These are differently constituted systems that project different penal norms.
2. Whereas International Criminal Law (ICL) is for core international crimes and is responsible for instituting action whenever states do not, Transnational Criminal Law (TCL) crimes are dealt with by a more indirect system of state obligations and interests.
3. Because of the different jurisdictions, international criminal systems aim for the application of universality as opposed to more limited forms of extraterritorial jurisdiction in transnational criminal systems. Further, in the fight against transnational crime, bilateral approaches have proven more efficient than multilateral ones.[7] In this case, diverging interests prevent universality.
4. International interests and values are broader than the more limited transnational values and interests.

III. TRANSNATIONAL POLICING AND ITS CONTEXT

Transnational policing policy is formulated by political groups with their own interests. Such policies are then written into treaties and made available for operational use. Law enforcement officers are asked to enforce transnational criminal law with regular investigative resources. Few officers have a detailed knowledge of the full breadth of policies and 'contra-indications' or implications, often resulting in a mutation of policies and treaties in more or less non-corresponding operational practices. These practices are the product of interests, motivations and the discretionary power of officers. They are used to adapt to the context of day-to-day events within the context of specific investigations.

---

[5] ibid.
[6] ibid.
[7] L Guille, 'Police and Judicial Cooperation in Europe: Bilateral Versus Multilateral Cooperation' in F Lemieux (ed), *International Police Cooperation: Emerging Issues, Theory and Practice* (Collumpton, Willan Publishing, 2010).

An analysis of extant literature about transnational systems reveals the existence of at least two different types of agents and systems. Most European literature focuses on treaties, conventions and norms produced by political associations. The North American literature (perhaps understandably) is much less developed in terms of quantity; the focus is essentially on transnational policing in action. The European literature places an emphasis upon theory, legal rules and guidelines, whereas North American literature focuses particularly on policing practices. Few direct links have been made between the phenomena but it is apparent that law enforcement in these geographical regions is responding to different imperatives and logics. The differences between policing policy and practice on the ground have been much studied in criminological studies, with the existence of a 'gap' often expounded. In fact, three different social worlds can be discerned as part of the transnational policing system. The political, judicial and police systems involved are not all working according to shared values and logics. While judicial and police systems are often conceived as being part of the same system, they are constituted of very different professionals who conceive things differently and are reacting to different pressures and priorities. Transnational policing thus needs to be studied with an eclectic view, such as the one used by Andreas and Nadelmann,[8] moving beyond International Relations (IR) traditional divisions. It renders possible the coexistence of liberalism, realism and constructivism with the objective of understanding the whole phenomenon, and with the focus on examining power, values, interests and norms.

Bigo's 'security fields' framework, inspired by Bourdieu's work, includes the study of relationships between individual agents, and can thus assist analysis. First, it recognises the existence of a transnational operational agent club. Also, it allows for a group of professional political agents existing in a parallel social world. The territorial divisions (ie, nation states) are not denied but are minimised to highlight professional divisions.[9] It considers the existing diversity among transnational risk-management professionals and the consequences that arise from their divergence.

Further approaches are also necessary, such as the classical analysis of officers' behaviours, which places an emphasis upon their discretionary power.[10]

---

[8] P Andreas and E Nadelmann, *Policing the Globe: Criminalization and Crime Control in International Relations* (Oxford, Oxford University Press, 2006).

[9] Bigo, 'Pierre Bourdieu and International Relations', above n 3.

[10] The following literature is fundamental with regard to this approach: RV Ericson, *Making Crime*, 2nd edn (Toronto, University of Toronto Press, 1993); RV Ericson, *Reproducing Order: A Study of Police Patrol Work* (Toronto, University of Toronto Press, 1982); RV Ericson, *Making Crime: A Study of Detective Work* (Toronto, Butterworth, 1981); PK Manning, *The Narc's Game: Organizational and Informational Limits on Drug Law Enforcement* (Cambridge, MA, MIT Press, 1980; 2004); WK Muir, *Police: Streetcorner Politicians* (Chicago, University of Chicago Press, 1977).

Also considered are Gambetta's[11] and Luhmann's (1988)[12] trust approaches, to understand the way criminals and people work together in the context of many uncertainties. This can be applied to transnational policing and the surrounding systems. When studying all levels of trust in those systems, ie, interpersonal, institutional and interstate trust, cooperation has to come before familiarity can develop, which is the sine qua non condition for trust-building. Indeed, familiarity, trust and (dis)trust are important elements at every level of the studied phenomenon.

The systems with their own internal logic need to be differentiated to understand the actual working of the transnational system. In Figure 1 states 1, 2 and 3 have different normative frameworks, values and interests. They represent the social world of policy professionals. Those different norms, interests and values are translated into how they approach the issue of transnational crime. Nonetheless, states have joined together in order to develop and establish a common rule base, which should be adapted for use at the transnational level. They work to define common values to protect.

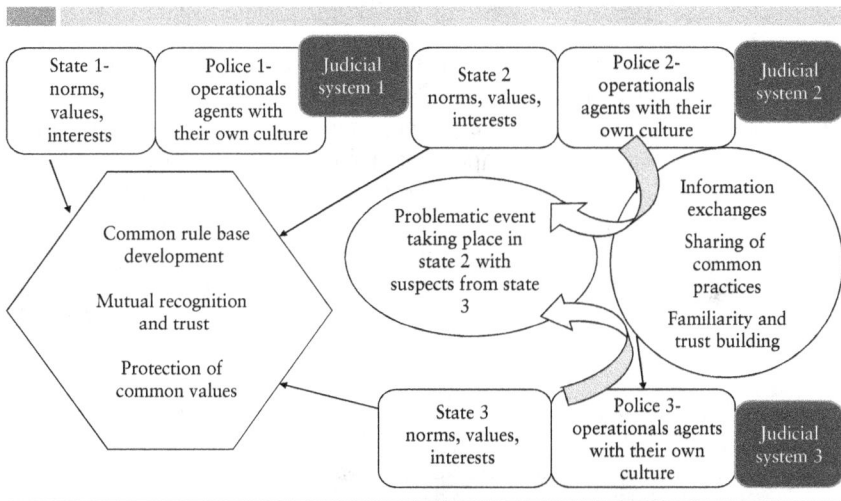

Figure 1: Transnational policing and the surrounding systems

---

[11] D Gambetta (ed), *Trust: Making and Breaking Cooperative Relations* (Oxford, Basil Blackwell, 1988).

[12] N Luhmann, 'Familiarity, Confidence, Trust: Problems and Alternatives' in D Gambetta (ed) *Trust: Making and Breaking Cooperative Relations* (Oxford, Basil Blackwell, 1988).

In the last few years, they also have developed concepts to better cooperate together, such as mutual recognition and mutual trust.

Another part of the system is the social world of policing professionals. Police 1, 2 and 3 represent investigators working in the transnational field. They are operational agents with their own police culture, both national and transnational. Their perspective is based upon concrete events rather than general concepts. They start working on a problematic event taking place in their jurisdiction or concerning citizens of their state. Only those who are concerned work on the case, exchanging information and practices. If they share enough cases, they can come to develop familiarity in their daily working experience with foreign counterparts. Others can benefit from an extended exchange and diffusion of practices. The last part of the justice system is the judicial decision taken after transnational investigations have ended and only when some actions are questioned. Like the other transnational systems, they are embedded in jurisdictions, ie, nation states.

IV. TRANSNATIONAL SYSTEMS: RELIANCE UPON FLEXIBILITY AND (DIS)TRUST

Efficient cooperation in tackling transnational crime is seen to be the first goal of establishing and maintaining transnational systems. It is true for the political, the judicial and the policing system. The analysis will focus on flexibility and (dis)trust as important elements in each of the systems. In transnational politics, flexibility has become increasingly important, especially with the concepts of mutual recognition and mutual trust becoming central. In fact, political agents formulate policies and negotiate agreements by focusing on the protection of national sovereignty. Until recently, the central concept was harmonisation.[13] Calderoni,[14] Tadic[15] and Joutsen[16]

[13] Harmonisation is linked to the European conception of success in cooperation. Cooperation is approached differently in North America, where it is measured by criminal immobilisation. Success in Europe refers to the robustness of legal frameworks and policies. It is then linked to the establishment of legal treaties and the harmonisation of criminal laws. See M Anderson, M den Boer, P Cullen, W Gilmore, C Raab and N Walker, *Policing the European Union: Theory, Law and Practice* (Oxford, Clarendon Press, 1995).

[14] F Calderoni, 'Assessing Harmonization and Approximation of Organized Crime Legislation among EU Member States' (PhD Dissertation, Universita' Cattolica del Sacro Cuore, Milan, 2008).

[15] F Tadic, 'How Harmonious Can Harmonisation Be? A Theoretical Approach Towards Harmonization of (Criminal) Law' in AH Klip and HG van der Wilt (eds), *Harmonisation and Harmonising Measures in Criminal Law* (Amsterdam, Royal Netherlands Academy of Science, 2002).

[16] M Joutsen, 'International Instruments on Cooperation in Responding to Transnational Crime' in P Reichel (ed), *Handbook of Transnational Crime and Justice* (Thousand Oaks, CA, Sage, 2005).

have suggested a wider definition of harmonisation and approximation. The concepts have been interpreted differently by political authorities and researchers, while no legal definition seems to exist.[17] Harmonisation aims at eliminating disparities between diverse criminal justice systems, reorganising different elements using a fixed standard, to avoid or eliminate friction.[18] Approximation uses a similar standard but formulates minimal requirements. Contrary to harmonisation, approximation is more flexible because states are left with the choice of deciding how to establish rules, as long as they conform to European Union (EU) minimal standards.[19] The aim is then to reduce differences between legal systems with minimal interference, as was the aim with harmonisation. The process, however, seems to be more flexible with approximation.

One of the main goals of harmonisation and approximation was to support transnational police cooperation in criminal matters, but the political agents recently recognised the difficulties of achieving this with existing instruments. A suggested alternative was to use the concept of mutual recognition between states, with the hope of reinforcing mutual respect of differences between sovereign states. Mutual recognition was thus recently promoted as a fundamental element of the EU Third Pillar.[20] One advantage of mutual recognition is that it is supposed to resolve theoretical problems with harmonisation, ie, that they actually create conflict and friction rather than eliminating or reducing them. With the mutual recognition concept, differences are maintained and respected because they are seen as essential to the creation of harmony.[21] Flore emphasises that mutual trust between

---

[17] In fact, harmonisation and approximation do not appear in the European Union Treaty. They are used only in the treaty creating the European Community, and they are not linked to criminal law.

[18] Tadic, above n 15.

[19] G Vermeulen, 'Where do we currently stand with harmonisation in Europe?' in AH Klip and HG van der Wilt (eds), *Harmonisation and Harmonising Measures in Criminal Law* (Amsterdam, Royal Netherlands Academy of Science, 2002).

[20] M Joutsen, 'The European Union and Cooperation in Criminal Matters: The Search for Balance' (Helsinki, HEUNI Papers, vol 25, 2006); A Weyembergh, 'Approximation of Criminal Law, the Constitutional Treaty and the Hague Programme (2005) 42 *Common Market Law Review* 1567; J Vogel, 'Why is the Harmonisation of Penal Law Necessary? A Comment' in AH Klip and HG van der Wilt (eds), *Harmonisation and Harmonising Measures in Criminal Law* (Amsterdam, Royal Netherlands Academy of Science, 2002). The 9/11 terrorist events were the turning point in adopting this principle. See JD Occhipinti, *The Politics of EU Police Cooperation: Toward a European FBI?* (Boulder, CO, Lynne Rienner Publishers, 2003). The concept has been discussed since 1998, but is in deadlock because of the lack of trust towards it, as expressed by the Member States. See HG Nilsson, 'Mutual Trust or Mutual Mistrust?' in G de Kerchove and A Weyembergh (eds), *La confiance mutuelle dans l'espace pénal européen* (Brussels, Université de Bruxelles, 2005).

[21] Calderoni, above n 14; S Manacorda, 'Le mandat d'arrêt européen et l'harmonisation substantielle: Le rapprochement des incriminations' in G Giudicelli-Delage and S Manacorda (eds), *L'intégration pénale indirecte: Interactions entre droit pénal et coopération judiciaire au sein de l'Union européenne* (Paris, Société de législation comparée, 2005); Tadic, above n 15.

states has to be constructed with respect for differences. Further, they can be seen as encouraging the adoption of effective practice.[22]

Mutual recognition is seen as a promising concept since it focuses on the criminal justice process. It is less ambitious and potentially less problematic than trying to alter legal doctrine, which is directly linked to cultural values and state decisions. Harmonisation and approximation needs what seems to be an impossible supranational law, while mutual recognition is based on an intergovernmental approach. States can thus safeguard their specificity in this process. Nonetheless, standardising objectives can be accomplished, but with a completely different logic in mind. Mutual recognition has the potential to build a context potentially creating and enhancing mutual trust. In turn, it renders possible the exchange of best practices, possibly creating fewer disparities in terms of results. The concept of mutual recognition thus seems to be better equipped to create consensus where it is desirable. A common rule base can then be put forward to protect shared values.[23] Mutual trust can be, at least in part, built on common values, such as democracy and human rights protection.[24] An important caveat is that trust is not yet established at the transnational political level and chances are that at least some distrust will always be present. Like harmonisation and approximation, mutual recognition and trust are based on the willingness of each state to comply. Thus, the Tampere council has already decided to stress the concept of mutual recognition.

This section focused on the political products and process of the transnational system. Some researchers state that national sovereignty is eroding across the EU. They have then put the emphasis on the creation of a transnational police force to replace the state in transnational matters, but such developments are extremely controversial politically, as well as logistically challenging.[25] Also, such a solution to transnational crime would prove

---

[22] D Flore, 'La notion de confiance mutuelle: "l'alpha" ou "l'omega" d'une justice pénale européenne?' in G de Kerchove and A Weyembergh (eds), *La confiance mutuelle dans l'espace pénal européen* (Brussels, Université de Bruxelles, 2005).
[23] L Frieden, 'Introduction' in G de Kerchove and A Weyembergh (eds), *La confiance mutuelle dans l'espace pénal européen* (Brussels, Université de Bruxelles, 2005).
[24] E Pitto, 'Mutual Trust and Enlargement' in G de Kerchove and A Weyembergh (eds), *La confiance mutuelle dans l'espace pénal européen* (Brussels, Université de Bruxelles, 2005).
[25] M den Boer and N Walker, 'European Policing After 1992' (1993) 31(1) *Journal of Common Market Studies* 3; J Benyon, L Turnbull, A Willis, R Woodward and A Back, *Police Cooperation in Europe: An Investigation* (University of Leicester, Centre for the Study of Public Order, 1993); J Benyon, P Davis and A Willis, *Police Co-operation in Europe: A Preliminary Investigation* (Report to the Commission of the European Community, Leicester, CSPO, 1990/08); N Walker, *Models of European Integration and Models of European Police Co-operation* (European Consortium for Political Research, Limerick, 1992); N Walker, 'The United Kingdom Police and European Co-operation' Working Paper (Department of Politics, University of Edinburgh, 1991); P Van Reenen, *Policing Europe After 1992: Co-operation and Competition* (1989) 3(2) *European Affairs* 45.

incomplete when the challenges are faced by the whole transnational system, including a judicial part (justice and policing), which responds to entirely different norms, values and interests. Within this judicial section, flexibility of law and jurisprudence is utilised to counter transnational crimes.

V. SOFT TRANSNATIONAL JURISPRUDENCE IN CANADA

The legal context retains its importance in law enforcement officer decision-making in transnational investigations.[26] Justice is an inseparable part of the criminal justice process aimed at transnational criminal immobilisation. Rather than rigid rules, there is flexibility within Canadian jurisprudence focusing on transnational crimes. In fact, Canadian judicial agents responsible for writing decisions related to transnational crimes appear to have a comprehensive understanding of transnational police work, albeit there is limited jurisprudence relating to the transnational context produced in Canada. Based on what decisions there are, the state of jurisprudence in relation to transnational crime is similar to other common law countries, with courts aware of the imperative to deal differently with transnational cases. In fact, they have established transnational norms that are more blurred than national norms in order to render possible the use of existing discretionary powers for transnational police agents, recognising the need to counter possible manipulation by transnational criminals, who will manipulate differences among state laws to their advantage. An excerpt from *Libman* [1985] 2 RCS 178 gave us a concrete example of this logic:

> It would be a sad commentary on our law if it was limited to underlining society's values by the prosecution of minor offenders while permitting more seasoned practitioners to operate on a world-wide scale from a Canadian base by the simple manipulation of a technicality of the law's own making. What would be underlined in the public's mind by allowing criminals to go free simply because their operations have grown to international proportions, I shall not attempt to expound.[27]

To judge a criminal case 'foreign' involves taking into consideration elements stemming from at least one other country, such a classification normally following a transnational investigation rather than preceding it. Important general overarching concepts have been repeated in Canadian judgments. Those are sovereign equality, territoriality and interstate comity

---

[26] L Guille, 'Policing and Judicial Cooperation in Europe: Europol, Eurojust and the European Judicial Network: Master Pieces of the European Union's Puzzle in Justice and Home Affairs' (submitted for the degree of PhD, University of Sheffield, School of Law, 2009).

[27] *Libman* [1985] 2 RCS 178, para 42.

(courtesy). With the sovereign equality principle, states are recognised as equal members of the transnational community. Sovereignty is then defined as the power of the state to decide upon its mission, to organise and enforce its authority on its territory.[28] The territorial principle in criminal law was developed to respond to two practical considerations in determining physical boundaries in state sovereignty. Those are described in this way: 'A country has generally little direct concern for the actions of malefactors abroad; and secondly, that other states may legitimately take umbrage if a country attempts to regulate matters taking place wholly or substantially within their territories'.[29]

An infraction can be dealt with by the Canadian courts, as long as there is a real and substantial link between an offence and Canada. This rule can be interpreted in different ways, since this apparently single approach to competency for a crime committed in more than one country is not reiterated in decisions:

> While there were occasional strong expressions of the territorial doctrine, particularly in earlier times, the fact is that the courts never applied the doctrine rigidly. To have done so, as Cockburn CJ noted in *Keyn* p 233, would have meant that a state could not apply its laws to offences whose elements occurred in several countries. This would have provided an easy escape for [trans] national criminals.[30]

This seems to correspond to the notion of a 'blurred' area of law, seeking to maintain an open structure, adaptable to its scalable character.[31] This way of dealing with legal 'foreignness' seems to be intentional, with formulations allowing for broad interpretations.

Interstate comity is a legal concept emphasising the need for courtesy between states. Its evolution has been brought about by necessity but no clear rules seem to exist in this regard. It can also be conceived as a soft concept in law, since no punishments are prescribed in case of non-compliance. This rule is flexible in several ways. Judges in *R v Hape* [2007] 2 RCS 292, 2007 CSC 26 put the emphasis on the fact that it is an interpretation principle rather than a rule of law, because there is no formal obligation attached to it. Interstate comity consists of informal measures taken by states, based on civility and goodwill. This concept is the basis on which so-called international mutual assistance is provided. However, 'acts of comity are justified on the basis that they facilitate interstate relations and global co-operation;

---

[28] L Wildhaber, 'Sovereignty and International Law' in R St J Macdonald and DM Johnston (eds), *The Structure and Process of International Law: Essays in Legal Philosophy, Doctrine and Theory* (Boston, MA, Martinus Nijhoff Publishers, 1983).

[29] *Libman* [1985] 2 RCS 178, para 38.

[30] ibid, para 66.

[31] C Thibierge, 'Le droit souple: Réflexion sur les textures du droit' (2003) (Octobre/Décembre) *Revue trimestrielle de droit civil* 612.

however, comity ceases to be appropriate where it would undermine peaceable interstate relations and the international order'.[32]

Sovereign equality, territoriality and interstate comity are flexible principles and can be categorised as soft law.[33] They can be imprecise in regard to content (blurred law), and non-obligatory with no punishment in case of non-compliance (soft law). This structure permits latitude and is often a guarantee of better acceptance in practice.[34] However, there are examples of Canadian jurisprudence where judges have focused on the utility of the Charter of Rights and Freedoms in transnational cases.

VI. CANADIAN JURISPRUDENCE: A PRECARIOUS EQUILIBRIUM BETWEEN LIBERTY AND SECURITY

To counter transnational crimes, Canadian law and jurisprudence related to foreignness exist in a precarious equilibrium between imperatives of successful transnational investigation and the respect of the Canadian Charter of Rights and Freedoms. For example, in *R v Harrer* [1995] 3 RCS 562, the questions arose whether the Canadian Charter applies outside Canada's boundaries and whether the principles of fundamental justice and the right to a fair trial permit exclusion of evidence obtained outside Canada. The conclusion reached was that the Charter was not directly applicable to police interrogation carried out in the United States, because US police officers were not required to work on behalf of the Canadian Government. An important caveat is that it does not mean the Canadian Charter has to be ruled out whenever a foreign component is present in a criminal investigation. Further, the impugned evidence would not result in an unfair trial:

> Evidence cannot be assumed to be unfairly obtained or to be unfairly admitted because it was obtained in a manner that would violate a Charter guarantee in this country. Different balances may be struck in various countries between the interests of the state and of the individual, all of which may be fair. The accused is entitled to a fair hearing, not to the most favourable procedures imaginable.[35]

Judges in *R v Harrer* are aware of the complexity of the conditions in which evidence is collected in transnational investigations and permit greater lenience for evidence collected during such investigations than those limited to the national jurisdiction.

As with *R v Harrer*, judges in *R v Terry* [1996] 2 RCS 207 state that it is not unfair to deal differently with evidence collected on foreign soil. They

---

[32] *R v Hape* [2007] 2 RCS 292, 2007 CSC 26, para 38.
[33] Thibierge, above n 31, 599–628.
[34] ibid, 613.
[35] *R v Harrer* [1995] 3 RCS 562, para 4.

emphasise that it is the suspect who decides to travel outside the country. Police officers do not therefore have control over subsequent events. Judges thus demonstrate that they understand the different nature of transnational investigations. In *Dynar* [1997] 2 RCS 462, the issue at appeal was whether the respondent's conduct in the United States would constitute a crime if taking place in Canada, thereby meeting the requirement of 'double criminality', which is the precondition for the surrender of a Canadian fugitive for trial in a foreign jurisdiction. The judgment pointed to the US lack of courtesy and respect towards Canadian sovereignty:

> In his report to the Minister of Justice, Keenan J was critical of the conduct of the American authorities. He characterised their actions in investigating Mr Dynar as a cross-border 'fishing expedition' that showed lack of respect for Canadian sovereignty. He condemned the FBI for failing to make use of mutual legal assistance treaties to request Canadian assistance in gathering evidence in Canada, and concluded that '[w]hether deliberately or inadvertently, the FBI agents ignored the principles of international comity and treated Canada as a part of their own jurisdiction for gathering evidence'.[36]

The decision was to extradite the suspect to the United States. It was explained that this decision goes in the same direction as *R v Terry*, where judges have emphasised that extreme prudence should be practised before excluding foreign evidence on the basis of the Charter.

R v Cook [1998] 2 RCS 597 considered the extraterritorial application of the Charter in the case of Canadian police officers interviewing a suspect in the United States on suspicion of a murder committed in Canada. This case is of particular interest since the conclusion was that the Charter was applicable to Canadian police officers, even if they were in the United States when they proceed to interviewing suspects. In their justification, they state that Canadian police officers have directly managed the interviewing, without any intervention by US officers. On this basis, the Charter is applicable. This perspective, combined with the other jurisprudence, permits circumvention of the limits of police discretion.

Judges have also highlighted their understanding of the complexity of the police work:

> In the course of their investigations, police have on occasion been required to lie. In many circumstances this may not only have been appropriate but also necessary and clearly an acceptable procedure. However for police to lie or mislead individuals with regard to their Charter rights is fundamentally unfair and demeaning of those Charter rights. Indeed to countenance it would bring the administration of justice into disrepute.[37]

---

[36] *Dynar* [1997] 2 RCS 462, para 30.
[37] *R v Cook* [1998] 2 RCS 597, para 44.

R v Cook enumerates a number of factual elements to demonstrate why there is no interference with US territorial jurisdiction on the facts in that case. These are: (1) the arrest and interrogation were initiated by a Canadian extradition request; (2) the offence was committed exclusively in Canada and was to be prosecuted in Canada; (3) the US authorities did not become involved in the investigation; and (4) the interrogation was conducted solely by Canadian police officers. *R v Hape* went further, arguing that collaboration necessarily creates breaches in the sovereignty of the other state. Criticising *Cook*, the judge admits having difficulty seeing how these factors establish a 'test'. Rather, this approach is based on a determination that seems as vague as 'We will know what interference is when we see it'. With this logic in mind, cases where the Charter could be applied will be scarce.

Hape decided that there is clearly a need to define a more principled articulation of the rules governing the application of the Charter abroad. Judges have tried to find a rational basis in order to decide upon the applicability of the Charter on foreign soil, considering three options:

1. Who initiates the investigation as determinative of when there is interference with the sovereign authority of a Foreign State. No principled grounds were found as to why the Charter would not apply to Canadian officials who are actively involved in an investigation just because they did not initiate the investigation.
2. The foreign 'control' over the investigation as the limit on the extraterritorial application of the Charter. They concluded that jurisprudence is not clear in this regard, but they state that in most foreign investigations, foreign officers will be in 'control' since Canadian officials must operate in the foreign territory under their consent and guidance, usually relying upon their procedures.
3. Imposing Canadian standards in general as determinative of when there is an interference with the sovereign authority of a Foreign State. This generates objectionable extraterritorial effects.

After rejecting the three options, judges in *R v Hape* explained that adhering to fundamental principles that emanate from the Charter would simply require the Canadian officers to inform themselves of the rights and protections existing under foreign law, and compare them with those guaranteed under the Charter in order to determine if they are consistent. It is not the case that the protections have to be identical. However, differences resulting from different legal regimes and different standards in other democratic societies will usually be justified given the trans-boundary context, the need to fight transnational crime and the need to respect the sovereign authority of other states, coupled with the fact that it is impossible for Canadian officials to follow their own procedures in those circumstances. Flexibility in this case is permitted by section 1 of the Charter. Canadian judges thus recognise that it is the role of police officers to decide on the proper compromise to reach, by using their own professional judgement.

Opinions adopted in the Canadian courts on 'foreignness' emphasise the avoidance of creating rigidity where there is no need to do so. *R v Hape* clearly states that 'the Court should not in this case substitute rigidity to flexibility and, prematurely (and unnecessarily), foreclose Charter options that are now open to it under the flexible principles enunciated in Cook' (para 116). Flexible judicial norms are available to sustain transnational police work. It also arouses concern, however, for instance, about a perceived focus upon security, which can be detrimental to rights protection. It must be borne in mind that police officers are not always aware of the exact limits of their discretionary powers, albeit being careful with what they produce as evidence at trial, indicating a concern that the prosecution not fail because of improperly gathered evidence. This may then be an efficient measure to restrain intentional breaches of rights.

VII. TRANSNATIONAL POLICING

A. Various Instruments and Discretionary Power in Transnational Policing

First, the centrality of flexibility in transnational police work makes decision-making an important aspect of transnational policing, particularly in regard to the selection of appropriate investigative means by officers. Multiple instruments are available for officers in order to obtain information, and analysis elucidates how they choose which method to use. They defer to their own professional judgement, which may not always be in line with the policies laid down in treaties and agreements. In fact, when asked to marry the policies or legal rules with their decisions, it appears that such policy positions did not feature in their deliberations.

Investigative methods such as informal information exchanges with counterparts already known from previous investigations or meetings are prioritised. Predictability is desirable since investigators do not want investigatory leads being discovered or leaked to targets. Direct contact is preferred because, in their view, it enhances predictability and speeds up the process. It may prevent the loss of traces relating to a suspect because formal procedures (and bureaucratic tasks) were not completed (or were late). Such informal means are not valued by states and are often considered undesirable.

Additionally, such methods are more straightforward (less complex and convoluted) for officers working on transnational investigations. In order to avoid lengthy negotiations, the solution is often to resort to liaison officers to ease the process and find a compromise between operational, legal and political imperatives. Bigo first highlighted the importance of liaison officers as a human interface,[38] while Bowling[39] and Block[40] reiterate that liaison officers play a major role as facilitators in complex transnational investigation.[41] Law enforcement officers will often resort to liaison officers to avoid taking inappropriate decisions. Liaison officers can find a trusted interlocutor, and identify the best way to obtain the required information, without being blocked by possible conflicts of interest between national police organisations. Relatively new in the system of transnational policing,[42] liaison officers are a more direct and less time-consuming way of working, particularly when compared with recourse to Interpol or Europol.[43]

Another important agent is the prosecutor, who will be responsible for the redaction of legal assistance demands, using Mutual Legal Assistance Treaties (MLAT). They have the necessary expertise to conform to the other state's demands. When possible, law enforcement officers will avoid or postpone having to use this means. Interviewees explained that it is common for officers to start by using the information obtained by informal means, resorting to a formal demand only when they have to use it for a trial. Contrary to the idea that a formal demand is necessary in transnational investigation,

[38] D Bigo, 'Liaison Officers in Europe: New Officers in the European Security Field' in J Sheptycki (ed), *Issues in Transnational Policing* (London, Routledge, 2000); D Bigo, *Polices en réseaux: l'expérience européenne* (Paris, Presses de Science Po, 1996).

[39] B Bowling, 'Transnational Policing: The Globalization Thesis, a Typology and a Research Agenda' (2009) 3(2) *Policing: A Journal of Policy and Practice* 149.

[40] L Block, 'Combating Organized Crime in Europe: Practicalities of Police Cooperation' (2008) 2(1) *Policing: A Journal of Policy and Practice* 74.

[41] Continental preference was apparent from the interviews. The European tendency is towards Europol or Interpol liaison officers, seen as knowledge brokers, while North America put the emphasis on a less regulated context for liaison officers (see N Gerspacher and F Lemieux, 'A Market-oriented Explanation of the Expansion of the Role of Europol: Filling the Demand for Criminal Intelligence through Entrepreneurial Initiatives' in F Lemieux (ed), *International Police Cooperation: Emerging Issues, Theory and Practice* (Collumpton, Willan Publishing, 2010).

[42] N Bayley, 'Overseas Liaison Officers' in SD Brown (ed), *Combating International Crime: The Longer Arm of the Law* (London, Routledge-Cavendish, 2008); A Goldsmith and J Sheptycki, *Crafting Transnational Policing* (Oxford, Hart Publishing, 2007); Bigo (1996, 2000), above n 38.

[43] Interviewees revealed that the situation has not evolved much since 1991, when Nadelmann explained the low intensity of utilisation of Interpol by the DEA and the FBI. He states that 'Interpol channels have been too slow or unresponsive. Although both agencies do make use of Interpol's facilities, particularly in communicating with countries in which they are not represented, their representatives tend to handle far more incoming than outgoing requests. ... one survey of police chiefs in 1991 found that relatively few had ever found Interpol of assistance to their agencies'. Nadelmann's conclusions apply more broadly than in the United States, since our interviewees have highlighted the same problems. See EA Nadelmann, *Cops Across Borders. The Internationalization of US Criminal Law Enforcement* (Pennsylvania, Pennsylvania State University Press, 1993) 183.

it is apparent that it is instead complementary. In short, direct information exchanges between foreign counterparts, resort to liaison officers and having prosecutors involved in formal requests are the most utilised methods in transnational investigations. However, the communication channel selected is based on an officer's rationalisation, which may not always be in line with other policy or operational considerations. Also, decisions may be taken following some general rules, but they are also often overlooked. First, officers will take into account the nature of the information required from their foreign counterparts. Information can be labelled as documentary or physical. The intended use will also be evaluated. It can be necessary for pursuing the operational investigation or it can be vital from a prosecutorial perspective. This will change the way information is approached. As for the nature of the information required, physical information is created or generated directly by police action, whereas documentary information already exists before officers take action. Physical information is created by investigation techniques like electronic or traditional surveillance. Much is obtained through direct contacts and informal agreements between foreign counterparts. In these cases, officers from the demand country often travel to the country from where they need the physical information. Frequently, they will also participate in some way in the collection of information, supervising its collection or being present when surveillance is carried out. They do so in order to conform to the basic judicial standards of their country.

With regard to documentary information, interviewees state that this should be subjected to formal demands. This is because documentary information is often produced by private organisations, such as hotels and banks for example, and those have confidentiality protection. When not asked by those private organisations, it is nonetheless possible to obtain them without a warrant or a police request coming from the state where the organisation conducts its business. When asked to clarify the rules concerning the way information can be collected in regard to the nature of information, interviewees seem to be confused. They tended to conclude that there is no clear criterion and that they are administrative concerns.

As for intended use, a vital consideration is whether specific information will be used in court or not. An officer from the Netherlands stated clearly that:

> Whenever we were exchanging information, first it's on a police information basis, and when the prosecutors thought they could use it in their files to go to court, we have to send officially, so whenever it's official then you can use it as evidence.

In short, when specific information is to be used as evidence at trial, it will usually have to follow a diplomatic path in order to acquire a formal status. Exceptions seem to exist to the MLAT procedure. Interviewees recount events where a country circumvented a formal agreement but provided the required information by informal means.

Exactly which information will be necessary as evidence in any eventual trial is not the object of a detailed evaluation before trial, except for the rare cases when a prosecutor is involved from the beginning of an investigation. Furthermore, interviewees highlight that suspects often plead guilty when presented with the fact that they were the object of a transnational investigation. As a result, evidence is not scrutinised by a judge, and any breach of rules in the way information was collected is not discovered. Being aware of this fact, it is possible that officers take more short cuts and use simpler procedures, in order to reduce complexity and workload. In summary, multiple means exist to obtain information from foreign jurisdictions. Analysis shows that flexibility and creativity, in combination with professional judgement, are essential characteristics of transnational investigations aiming at criminal immobilisation.

B. Strategies in Uncertainty Management: Trust, Scepticism and Avoidance

As seen, personal relations between investigators are an essential facet of transnational policing. Relationships are vital in order to achieve cooperation, since law enforcement officers have to manage uncertainties to complete specific investigations. In order to reduce uncertainties, they use diverse strategies based upon their evaluation of the reliability of their counterpart as well as the possible advantages and risks related to this alliance. The degree of familiarity and trust shared with their counterparts will influence their every decision. Once again, liaison officers are important to help assess situations, particularly when officers start with few facts needed to evaluate the reliability of their counterparts. Liaison officers have thus been labelled by interviewees as 'protection filters' in transnational investigations.

Having worked together in previous investigations is relatively rare when scrutinising transnational police collaboration. Often officers do not know their counterparts and appreciate their political, legal and working conditions to enable them to have a well-informed opinion. They do not share a common background so they cannot evaluate the risk or advantages of possible cooperation. For example, if they share particularly sensitive information, they cannot be sure whether it will be used (im)properly. The simplest way to assuage such concerns is to ask people they already know and possibly trust about the considered future partner. Reputation is another way for police officers to evaluate the risks and advantages of working with a particular counterpart. In addition, limiting the number of persons involved in the investigation limits risks.

Whenever possible, officers have tried to choose the best location to investigate, keeping in mind the close links already developed. Officers maximise working with the same counterparts, not only because they know and possibly trust them, but because similar drug routes are often utilised by traffickers. By being uncreative, criminals render it possible to enhance familiarity between transnational police officers. Canadian interviewees have highlighted strong links with officers in the US Drug Enforcement Administration (DEA), UK and Amsterdam police. Familiarity develops after repeatedly working together. Similar ideologies also ease the familiarisation process, and social, procedural and technical familiarity is enhanced when counterparts are exposed to each other. This is an important aspect to take into account when understanding why police cooperate, even in situations where scepticism is hard to avoid. It seems to be easier when a known liaison officer has referred police officers to each other. He will also be of importance in helping both to understand the different systems and to adjust to each other's practices and laws.

In sum, common experiences, familiarity and reputation are important factors in officers' evaluations when managing uncertainties created by working with foreign counterparts. The extent of the information and expertise exchange depends upon how officers perceived these uncertainties. In other words, the management of uncertainties is an important rule in the game of the transnational police system. Scepticism is at the heart of the process, aiming at diminishing uncertainties and at its best, possibly achieving results in terms of arrest and drug seizures.

Officers are constantly evaluating their counterparts, and can change their minds at any time. Some may avoid each other, making cooperation impossible. Those officers have decided that it is too risky to share their information, particularly when the counterpart is from another country. They are rather rare, but still exist, particularly when having to work constantly in contexts embedded in corruption. When they cannot avoid working with counterparts, they maintain a sceptical attitude. Officers can obtain some results, even when they do not disclose all information and stay parsimonious in their interaction with the partner. When they trust their partner, results can be maximised, since the exchange of information will be more efficient. Total trust is a rare event in transnational policing, even when the partner is well known. A combination of trust and distrust is more common. In a distrustful relationship,[44] some results can be achieved, but with fewer options than in a trusting relationship. Interviewees focused on a cycle of distrust, reproducing distrustful relationships. Cooperation is nonetheless possible, since agents have interests in common, and know each other. Consequently, trust is not essential in all transnational police activities. In fact, this is highly dependent on the context and on the needed intensity

---

[44] In this chapter, distrust is seen as a type of trust. See Luhmann, above n 12.

of exchanges. Gambetta shows that even in a general context of distrust, a relatively stable social structure can maintain itself and be basically efficient.[45]

Players are introduced one by one, only when needed. If they prove their value and make a positive impression on the rest of the 'team', they will have the possibility of further collaboration, which can result in mutual trust. This description is a synthesis of transnational policing by interviewees. It reveals that trust is not always essential. In some cases where information exchanges have to be sustained, relations have to be good enough to possibly create trust. In other cases, punctual exchanges are enough, and trust is less necessary. Another possibility is that foreign information is not seen as vital in order to complete the investigation. In those cases, relations will be minimal and trust could not be created. Familiarity mechanisms, rather than trust, are fundamental. Familiarity will optimise the benefits of collaboration. Trust is thus a consequence, rather than a precondition of cooperation. Avoidance and distrust mechanisms can serve the same function as trust. Transnational policing agents can collaborate without trust, but they need mutual interest and familiarity.

Finally, clear rules are rare in transnational investigations. Den Boer[46] and Walker[47] introduced the idea of incremental learning processes. Transnational policing is still in a learning phase. Decisions are taken on a case-by-case basis in part because clear procedures have not been laid down. Transnational policing agents are still meeting other counterparts, learning new techniques and applications. Avoidance will be less interesting whenever they start developing relations with their counterparts and notice new advantages. It will enhance trust towards others and themselves, because they will constantly improve their skills in understanding the rules of the game. Thereby, uncertainty will decrease and will permit more concrete results to emerge. Eventually, agents will be able to manipulate the rules, hopefully to the advantage of an investigation that will be respectful of human rights and freedoms. It is nonetheless a possibility that norm deviation may permit better results in terms of arrests and seizures. If it is the case, agents could adopt a more security-oriented way of working, focusing less on human-rights protection.

[45] Gambetta, above n 11.

[46] M den Boer, 'Towards a Governance Model of Police Cooperation in Europe: The Twist between Networks and Bureaucracies' in F Lemieux (ed), *International Police Cooperation: Emerging Issues, Theory and Practice* (Cullompton, Willan Publishing, 2010).

[47] N Walker, 'In Search of the Area of Freedom, Security and Justice: A Constitutional Odyssey' in N Walker (ed), *Europe's Area of Freedom, Security and Justice* (Oxford, Oxford University Press, 2004).

VIII. CONCLUSION

This chapter has distinguished between international and transnational systems, which have been conceived as totally different phenomena. The main reason for using the transnational concept was to make explicit the differences between fighting transnational crimes, such as drug trafficking and terrorism, and international crimes, such as genocide and war crimes.

Using the concept of transnational (systems) helps understand transnational policing and its surrounding systems without the risk of being misunderstood or confused with international systems. It also permits further elucidation of the differences and similarities of transnational systems, such as the political, legal and policing systems. Flexibility, familiarity and distrust are necessary elements in the transnational policing system and the surrounding systems.

An important inclination of transnational systems is flexibility, a concept that characterises transnational systems. Harmonisation and mutual recognition also show how transnational politics have become impregnated by more flexible principles. Canadian soft jurisprudence in transnational criminal law is growing. Also, flexibility in relation to transnational policing is highlighted by the use of discretionary powers. As to the preponderance of the distrust cycle, cooperation diminishes as distrust increases. In fact, and in spite of a context of distrust, a stable social structure is maintained, possibly revealing a collective choice in countering trans-boundary actions of traffickers.

Finally, state relations don't directly influence the nature of the relations between foreign counterparts. The extent of transnational policing does not correspond to the extent of political relations between countries. Officers can act outside directives from their government, either because there are no clear directives or because they consider their choice of action as being more appropriate in order to immobilise criminals. For example, officers can choose to cooperate even if a major political conflict exists between their countries. US and Cuban officers have revealed having collaborated even when their countries prohibited them from doing so. This results in a change of policies between those countries. A reverse example is cases between Canada and the United Kingdom where they won't cooperate in spite of good relationships because of different priorities in regard to their soft drug policies.

12

Intelligence-led Use of International Forensic Exchange Channels

DENISE SULCA

I. INTRODUCTION

F OR A LONG time, it has been recognised that criminals do not cease their activities at national borders. Their mobility and scope of action have augmented during recent decades, together with growing awareness of the increasing globalisation of crime. Police and justice systems have reacted to this globalisation trend by developing different legal and operational instruments for overcoming the barriers of jurisdictions. Centralising, networking and exchanging information, operating in other countries (within limited parameters) and joint investigations have been facilitated during recent years, within the European Union (EU) in particular. These infrastructures are intended to provide a solid basis for responding to evolving criminality recognised to be increasingly mobile, capable of acting in broad territories and in new economical and virtual spaces across jurisdictions. It is however far from obvious that the extreme formalisation and legalisation of exchanges reach their goals of both allowing the efficient identification of criminals beyond borders, and protecting civil liberties.

International police cooperation now also encompasses forensic data exchange. Indeed multilateral cooperation via Interpol, Europol, PCCCs (Police and Customs Cooperation Centres) and bilateral police cooperation agreements have been, and continue to be, strengthened and diversified. With a multitude of available channels, and a large number of countries, each with their own idiosyncratic police system, legal frameworks and databases, international requests for forensic information can be complex. Users of the system may feel insecure in their knowledge about how to process exchanges and unconfident about how their information will be effectively processed. The utilisation of facilities and the reliance upon legal allowances varies widely. Furthermore, the multifarious purposes for which forensic information is requested and the potential relevance of the information sent can mean that exchange channels may be overwhelmed by the quantity and disparate nature of requests and responses. Such glitches are perhaps inevitable given the absence of a global vision that could provide an international strategy to move forensic information exchange beyond a narrowly focused case-by-case approach.

The study detailed here aims to elaborate an intelligence-led framework for orienting forensic case data exchange processes. A regional structure developed in the west part of Switzerland will serve as a possible (albeit limited) model. National and international exchanges and comparison of forensic information have been systematised within this inter-agency crime analysis framework. A novel platform was implemented to improve upon the follow-up of serial offences across jurisdictions. We postulate that this intelligence-led system can aid the decision-making process, by identifying what information, in particular forensic case data, is relevant to be exchanged at an international level, how, when, why and where.

Demands from police and justice systems regarding the provision of an efficient framework for exchanging data and harmonisation of methods in order to facilitate communication are not new. But what has changed is the number of channels made available, as well as systematisation through computerisation. Based on a vision from Switzerland and professional experience, our perception of these systems is that they have dramatically changed the order of magnitude of the flow of information, which becomes difficult to manage and control. The international system already tends to be overwhelmed, thus leading to the question whether there really exists a global vision and strategy on how to use it.

In order to answer this question, we will focus on the decisions made by the users when they exchange data, identify some factors that influence them and study how the choices made are disparate between states, units and even individuals. This diversity will lead to suggest the development of a more intelligence-led style of using the international infrastructures by stimulating the stakeholders to better define and coordinate their objectives and strategies.

II. HYPE FOR INTERNATIONAL POLICE COOPERATION

In 1914, the First International Criminal Police Congress, which was held in Monaco, was the first move towards establishing international police cooperation. Preoccupations then were not so different from today. With the development of more rapid transport and communication systems, mobility of criminals beyond the borders of a country was already to be perceived. Conversely, police officers could not be effective beyond such borders without receiving permission from their nation and without the approval of the governments of foreign states. During this Congress, it was recognised that the police and judicial officers could and should better organise their action at an international level. The obstacles were not only legal; there also existed a lack of harmonisation between information processing systems. Indeed recidivists, more severely punished by laws towards the end of the nineteenth century, were encouraged to settle in countries where they were not identifiable because biometric data-recording systems were not compatible.[1] Some identity recording systems were based upon Bertillon's anthropometrical system, while others relied upon fingerprints, thus making their use only effective within their own borders. This is why Rudolphe Archibald Reiss, the first Director of the Forensic Science School of the University of Lausanne, promoted the idea of harmonising these systems across jurisdictions. Locard even specialised in the comparison of the different forms of recording biometrical data and evaluated and compared the different benefits and drawbacks of each system.[2]

After these initial difficulties, international centres, the first being Interpol, were able to receive any kind of police information and fingerprint exchanges were selected as an efficient way of improving identification capabilities across borders. International channels gradually developed to enable quicker exchanges, initially of fingerprints, but more recently also DNA profiles and photographs (principally facial images). International information processing and exchange now takes place via several different, occasionally redundant, infrastructures, based on different models.

The first such infrastructure was created in 1923 through Interpol. Interpol is primarily a manual and punctual system of data exchange between national law enforcement agencies. Indeed, the requests sent by a police officer, for example, are not direct but pass through a National Central Bureau (NCB), established and managed by the relevant authority of each signatory country (190 members). According to the initial request, any forensic data are distributed to addressee countries through an encrypted system of communication, the I-24/7. Interpol also has a centralised component. The Interpol General Secretariat archives daily information transmitted by the NCBs and makes available forensic data originating from databases of Member States. However, the sharing of data depends entirely on the will of the Member States.

Interpol has been complemented, since the 1990s, by the creation of Europol. In this model, requests for forensic data are centralised at Europol for further analysis. Reports are then delivered as intelligence products. Indeed, Europol can host, organise and analyse data and information voluntarily sent by at least two Member States concerned with a shared criminal

---

[1] J Roux, *Premier Congrès de Police Judiciaire Internationale, Monaco 1914* (Paris, Marchal et Billard, 1926).
[2] E Locard, *Traité de criminalistique: les preuves de l'identité* vols III and IV (Lyon, Joannès Desvigne et ses Fils, 1932).

problem. When the information gathered is sufficiently complete, relevant links between entities crossing the countries can be provided.

Switzerland, even if it does not belong to the European Community, is now part of the Schengen system, and has signed an agreement with Europol.[3] Hence, it participates in both systems, created by Schengen and Europol. Indeed, the initial refusal to enter the Schengen area kept Switzerland out of international decision-making in this arena. To overcome the limitations of this isolation, efforts were dedicated to the development of bilateral agreements with its neighbouring states in the 1990s.

Two bilateral agreements with France and Italy led to the creation of a platform for the exchange of data through two PCCCs. The benefits of this system derive primarily from the proximity between Swiss and French law enforcement officers respectively, as well as Italian police and customs officers. This has considerably improved the sporadic and manual requests. The Centres also operate beyond simple exchange of information; they have an important role in assisting and coordinating cross-border operations and identifying people and objects.

In this context, big changes occurred in the last decades with the development of networked computers, which dramatically impacted upon the global nature of information processing. In the days of Rudolphe Archibald Reiss (1875–1929) and Edmond Locard (1877–1966), at the time of the Monaco Conference, one argument in favour of the use of fingerprints to further the aims of international police and judicial cooperation was that by means of a classification system, numbers of fingerprint cards could be collated and quite easily cross borders.[4] Through the use of computers, the quantity of data and the rapidity of information exchanges between two states has not only grown, it has changed in order of magnitude. This involves new challenges, unimaginable in 1914, such as storage and deletion of data in databases, but above all the analysis and management of a large flow of information. These challenges become concrete, especially with the development of automated or semi-automated systems like those developed within the framework of the European Prüm agreement. Created to strengthen data exchange, this system is not centralised, but databases of each signatory country are meant to be networked. Fingerprints, vehicle licence plates and DNA profiles obtained from crime scenes (and sometimes, those of convicted offenders), are compared against data stored in databases of others Prüm member countries via the secure communication

---

[3] Accord entre la Confédération Suisse et l'Office européen de police (Agreement between the Swiss Confederation and the European Police Office) (RO 2006 1019), (RS0.362.2.2004 (24 September 2004).

[4] Roux, above n 1.

network ESTA.[5] To participate in the 'Prüm' exchange system, each signatory country must establish centralised national forensic databases and use standardised forensic data. This semi-automated system then allows for the exchange of a large amount of data between countries. For instance, in 2008 approximately 25,000 Dutch crime scene profiles from their national DNA database were compared with the German forensic DNA database and approximately 125,000 German profiles were compared with the Dutch database. The automatic exchange results return only in a 'hit' or 'no hit' answer without any nominal data. The number of hits obtained is already unmanageable[6] for the participating countries.[7]

One possible positive effect of Prüm has still not been seriously taken into account. By systematically comparing their forensic data, in particular DNA profiles, a significant number of links between crimes (rather than crime and offender) are detected. These are particularly relevant for detecting the repetition of serious crimes (serial crime), making them, theoretically, of a more strategic interest. An overview of all generated links can potentially provide a global view on the structure of certain types of repetitive crime (eg, the degree of repetition, modus operandi used etc) or the mobility of offenders. This can help provide criminological knowledge on cross-border crime without needing the personal identities of the offenders. This therefore provides intelligence for law enforcement agencies on when, where and how crimes are being committed across borders, without necessarily requiring the detection of the actual offenders in each instance.

III. THE DISPARITY OF DECISION-MAKING PROCESSES

The implementation of these instruments of police and judicial cooperation has changed mechanisms of criminal investigation. Because criminality transcends borders, there is a real will to pursue crimes and criminals beyond the state jurisdiction. Requests to Interpol, Europol, Prüm or PCCCs are on the rise. But although the structure and operation of each system seem clearly established, operators have great latitude about how to use each channel, leading occasionally to redundancies or to the use of the individually best known channel rather than the most efficient one. For instance, the same international request could be transmitted through several channels. This

[5] B Prainsack and V Toom, 'The Prüm Regime: Situated Dis/Empowerment in Transnational DNA/Profile Exchange' (2010) *British Journal of Criminology* 1117.
[6] For instance, the number of relevant hits obtained by the Netherlands on 1 November 2015 through the Prüm system was 8467, available at dnadatabank.forensischinstituut.nl/resultaten/groei_aantal_internationale_matches/index.aspx.
[7] Current users: Austria, Netherlands, Germany, Slovenia, Luxembourg, Finland, France, Bulgaria, Slovakia, Romania, Latvia, Lithuania, Hungary, Poland, Cyprus, Estonia, Sweden, Czech Republic, Malta, Belgium, United Kingdom, Portugal.

complex mess and overlapping of competences may sometimes lead to a certain amount of competition between the different services.[8] There is a real lack of strategy for choosing which specific channel is to be used in regard to a particular international request, and therefore it could be extremely constraining for a police officer to make a request abroad. This creates a certain ambiguity. On the one hand, the policy is to encourage police officers to maximise exchanges with their foreign colleagues, and systems are developed to facilitate these requests. On the other hand, it is not clear which channel should be used. So in practice, the use of these facilities is extremely disparate. We identify, however, several factors that seem influential in the choice of a channel.

IV. DIFFERENT GEOGRAPHICAL SITUATIONS

Some regions are perceived to be more affected by international criminality because of their geographical position. This, in turn, stimulates the use of exchange channels. For instance, in Switzerland, Geneva shares more than 90 per cent of borders with France without having a natural barrier able to inhibit passages. The Geneva police explain that the majority of robberies (banks, post offices and jewellery shops etc) and car-jacking cases are perpetrated by cross-border criminals. In comparison with other Swiss cities such as Zurich and Bern, Geneva is considered to be more attractive to cross-border criminals.[9] Actually, what is observed is that the number of foreign data requests from Geneva through the PCCC is more important than for other regions. Therefore, we postulate that regions that perceive themselves to be particularly vulnerable to victimisation by cross-border criminals will naturally resort more frequently to international channels of forensic data exchange. This tendency may be exaggerated when the efficacy of the communication channel is reinforced by finding solutions to problems through these exchanges.

The proximity between the police and the office operating the exchanges may also be a good indicator of how frequently the service is used. For example, the number of requests sent through the PCCC in Geneva is higher in the State of Geneva than for other states lying in a similar border context (Figure 1). Confidence and knowledge about facilities created through intensive communication or/and regular meetings seem to catalyse the use of such channels.

---

[8] M Alain, 'Les heurts et les bonheurs de la coopération policière internationale en Europe, entre la myopie des bureaucrates et la sclérose culturelle policière' (2007) *Déviance et société* 237.

[9] R Garrote, *La coopération policière transfrontalière franco-suisse: Le cas de la police judiciaire genevoise (1990–2011)* (Geneva, Université de Genève, 2011).

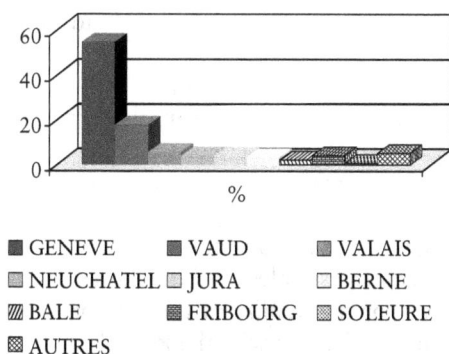

■ GENEVE ■ VAUD ▨ VALAIS
▨ NEUCHATEL □ JURA □ BERNE
▨ BALE ▨ FRIBOURG ▨ SOLEURE
▨ AUTRES

Figure 1: Swiss Exchange requests through PCCC in 2009/Report of activity
PCCC Geneva 2008[10]

V. SLOWNESS OF SYSTEMS

Two surveys have been undertaken in Switzerland gauging the use of international communication channels by police officers.[11] One criterion when
choosing whether to raise a request for information, and the selection of a
communication channel, is the ability to quickly obtain a response. Indeed,
with the opening of national borders across the EU, and the growth of multiple communication technologies, the mobility and organisational abilities
of criminals using transnational communication channels has been greatly
facilitated. This communication can be instantaneous and present asymmetry with the time needed by authorities to exchange data. Forensic information still has to cross jurisdictional boundaries that are paved with obstacles.
For instance, an unidentified trace from a crime scene may be sent abroad
for comparison in the hope of identifying its source. The waiting time for
receipt of a response depends on several factors relating to the country
receiving the request. Political stability is one factor. Indeed, requests sent to
a country suffering a civil war or engaged in a conflict might not be handled
as quickly as desired, or not at all.

The ability and capacity to compare forensic data varies widely from
one country to another. For example, some countries do not yet have a
national forensic DNA database. Others may have multiple DNA databases
increasing the likelihood that they may be able to link a crime scene trace
to its source. The system put in place to analyse forensic data and thus the

---

[10] ibid.
[11] ibid; F Gisler, *La coopération policière internationale de la Suisse en matière de lutte
contre la criminalité organisée* (Freiburg, Université de Fribourg, 2008).

capacity to quickly transmit a response will depend on the technology and the systems established in the country.

Another factor taken into consideration by police officers relates to the languidness of the judicial system. For example, in some countries in order to obtain receipt of a positive link between a crime scene trace and a DNA profile, it is necessary to arrange a letter rogatory. So to obtain a result, sometimes a wait of weeks will be required. In the face of such problems, investigators needing to make rapid progress on a live investigation will prefer what they perceive as the simplest and quickest communication channel. Once again, proximity or the quality of the support obtained from operators may play a great role. This is why the PCCC channel is often favoured over Interpol, which is judged slower, impersonal and potentially may not result in any response or action. Furthermore, simpler and accelerated judicial procedures, as well as direct contacts with police or customs officers, are extra advantages of the PCCC. But such requests are geographically limited to France and Italy.

VI. SERIOUSNESS OF CASES

In Switzerland, international requests and forensic exchanges of data for comparison are not automatic. Each state police force, and ultimately each investigator, takes a decision on a case-by-case basis whether forensic data should be sent for matching. There is thus great diversity in the choice of data transmitted. Some state police will only use international channels for exchanging data relating to serious criminal investigations. In other states, police forces may prioritise cross-border crimes (Geneva for example) and forensic data may be transmitted for almost any offence type. There is no harmonised strategy between the different state police forces and individual law enforcement officers for selecting crime scene traces to be transmitted abroad. But what are the consequences of choices made? Is there an ideal choice? There is no clear answer. Different options have obvious consequences on the number of requests and the intensity of the flow of information crossing jurisdictions through the different communication channels.

Another factor influencing the quantity of information transmitted is the number of addressee countries. All countries with a national point of contact can be solicited in one single request. For each addressee country this has several consequences. First, the forensic data transmitted must be handled and matched. Some countries will transmit results and then delete the foreign forensic data from their databases. Switzerland, on the other hand, preserves all forensic data in its database for 30 years, meaning its national databases are continually growing and, in turn, makes efficient management more difficult. Second, the analysis of the data represents a supplementary charge for laboratories. If there are insufficient resources available, for example to compare fingerprints, backlogs will become frequent, extending response times. National priorities may be threatened when international requests put too much pressure on the operation of forensic data analysis.

When forensic data is sent for matching, the requesting country expects to receive results and hopes for a positive response. To increase the probability of getting a positive match, one strategy is to send the request to the maximum number of countries. For instance, the majority of forensic data requests are sent to the whole European zone. Thus, the number of responses, often negative, increases. Countries like Switzerland must then process these negative responses. This slows down the exchange process and, such is the overwhelming number of negative answers, positive results risk being drowned out. An expected result may be missed or may take a lengthy period before it is brought to the attention of investigators. In serious cases of serial offending, the quick identification of the offender(s) is vital for the investigation, as fast detection can limit potential subsequent victims.

Against this background, one may be tempted to recommend limiting international requests to only serious cases and to suppress negative responses. However, such a generalised strategy may be too restrictive; and what should be considered 'serious' cases? Additionally, a response, even negative, is information that may prove relevant as exculpatory evidence (excluding suspects). There are also many transnational crimes that are not considered individually as serious but, seen as a pattern, may represent a more serious problem. For instance, the PCCC has established a specific team to control a type of itinerant delinquency whose criminal activity covers a broad spectrum of repetitive crimes: assault, theft, burglary, skimming, falsification of documents and so on.[12] In France, an operation carried out by Europol and Interpol led to the arrest of 20 people suspected of being part of a network of Georgian nationals linked to hundreds of burglaries and thefts across Paris. Thus, if international requests are limited to serious cases, there is a risk that the detection and monitoring of certain serial transnational criminals will suffer. There may be the creation of a knowledge gap, hampering the adoption of a global approach to cooperative policing. The critical factors influencing when data should be exchanged are thus not obvious. Therefore, it is necessary to develop strategies to target requests and maximise results, according to well-defined objectives.

---

[12] Garrote, above n 9.

VII. STRATEGY DEVELOPMENT

Since the establishment of Interpol, the focus has always been on the means of quickly transmitting information and the production of useful intelligence. This explains the growth of infrastructures to support forensic data exchange, which have increased the flow of information across borders. But even if forensic information is indispensable at all stages of a criminal investigation, the efficient processing, analysis and the use of such information, is as essential as the information itself.[13] With a continuous growth in flows of data, the number of both positive and negative results has already changed in order of magnitude. This leads to the paradoxical situation where the number of 'matches' reported is growing to a point that becomes overwhelming for systems to process. Once produced, results must undergo a triage process in order to prioritise a response to matches that are considered more important. Identifications thus may be lost in such a triage process. A system for exchanging forensic data without an overarching strategy is essentially 'out of control' and then poses a big problem for civil liberties and data protection. The use of data exchange systems is based on trust between the different partners, including the collection and analysis of traces or fingerprints that will be transmitted. This trust may also emerge with a clearly established methodology. There is an urgent need to regain control and develop a strategic vision of how communication infrastructures can be proactively, effectively and efficiently utilised.

A first step would be to cease less promising or even useless exchanges, and select exchanges according to better defined objectives and selection criteria. A straightforward method for prioritisation would be to narrow the exchange of information to a probable origin or to just a couple of possible addressee countries. In turn, the number of irrelevant comparisons (and answers) should be reduced. However, the ambition must go beyond such restricted measures. They will not dramatically alter the reality of the overwhelming number of obtained matches. This may make the system continuously more reactive and led by the matches themselves. There are already insufficient resources to systematically treat all the positive results from national investigations, thus allowing more time for a more proactive approach to international crime may prove problematic.

There is a need to move beyond case-by-case decision-making and to adopt an intelligence-led policing approach.[14] By combining crime analysis and crime intelligence strategically according to well-defined objectives, international data exchange processes can be more targeted and their usefulness and efficiency improved and more transparent, in turn providing better guarantees for civil liberties. An intelligence system, integrating the Geneva

---

[13] Gisler, above n 11.
[14] J Ratcliffe, *Intelligence-Led Policing* (Cullompton, Willan Publishing, 2008).

PCCC adopted at a Swiss regional level is used in order to test this approach on a small scale.

VIII. A LIMITED STUDY WITHIN THE CONTEXT OF A REGIONAL ANALYSIS CENTRE

Switzerland is a federalist system with 26 states. Swiss police forces are organised into city, state and federal police. The federal police conduct investigations relating to organised crime, money laundering, corruption, economic crime and cybercrime. It is also responsible for the management of national databases such as the AFIS and forensic DNA databases. The federal police office (fedpol) is the single point of contact with the international community. It contains the National Central Bureau and the Sirene office, and acts as national point of contact for Europol. It also handles requests for identification from the PCCC. The federal police have a role of support and coordination including the exchange of information between partner authorities of the Confederation and the cantons. It performs the processing and analysis of information related to organised crime. It should be noted that Switzerland has not signed the Prüm Treaty.

Regarding all other types of crime, the cantons remain responsible for investigations and information requests through Interpol, Sirene (Europol) and PCCC channels. Each canton is autonomous and can decide to send, or not send, forensic data abroad for comparison. This system is not easy to coordinate, because of the fragmentation between the city, state and federal police. Thus, the number of organisations involved is multiplied. Therefore, exchanges of information are sporadic and there is greater contact between people working within the same entity.[15] One challenge during the conception of this structure was to develop a common methodology, which included the sharing and comparison of forensic data. In 2008, in order to facilitate interstate exchange of information and to analyse serial and itinerant criminality, a platform called PICAR (French acronym of *Plateforme d'information du CICOP*[16] *et préventive pour l'analyse et le renseignement*) was implemented.[17] This platform is shared between the states and the

---

[15] O Ribaux, *Le renseignement criminel pour le traitement de la délinquance sérielle dans un système fédéraliste: de l'idée à la mise en oeuvre* (Nicolet, Québec, Colloque international francophone, 2005).

[16] CICOP (*Concept intercantonal de coordination opérationnelle et preventive*) is a French acronym representing the coordination of intelligence for operational and preventive efforts.

[17] Q Rossy, S Ioset, D Dessimoz and O Ribaux, 'Integrating Forensic Information in a Crime Intelligence Database' (2012) *Forensic Science International* 137; S Birrer, 'Analyse systématique et permanente de la délinquance sérielle: place des statistiques criminelles; apport des approches situationnelles pour un système de classification; perspectives en matière de coopération' (PhD Thesis, Université de Lausanne, 2010).

PCCC of Geneva. Each partner state integrates within PICAR information from criminal events, from investigations and other sources of data such as pictures, DNA, fingerprint links and so on. Various types of links between events are systematically recorded in PICAR. They are established on the basis of comparisons between situational information (such modus operandi, spatiotemporal study of cases etc), forensic information (like DNA, fingerprints, footprints, images) and analysis of stolen and recovered vehicles. With information from PICAR, various documents are prepared for decision-makers and police officers. These documents will contain strategic, tactical and operational recommendations. Since the introduction of the concept, CICOP and the interstate platform PICAR, many crime repetitions have been detected (Table 1).

Table 1: Number of series detected according to types of crime and links[18]

Crime types	Number of series				
	Situational information	Shoemark pattern	DNA	Image	Total
Burglary	588 (55.5%)	363 (34.3%)	107 (10.1%)	2 (0.2%)	1060
Theft from a vehicle	71 (83.5%)	3 (3.5%)	9 (10.6%)	2 (2.4%)	85
Robbery	32 (80%)	3 (7.5%)	2 (5%)	3 (7.5%)	40
Property damage	2 (22.2%)	1 (11.1%)	6 (66.7%)		9
Vehicle theft	65 (97%)	1 (1.5%)	1 (1.5%)		67
Aggression-battery-brawl	3 (75%)	1 (25%)			4
Walter's purse theft	4 (57.1%)		3 (42.9%)		7
Arson	10 (76.9%)		3 (23.1%)		13
Sexual offence	9 (81.8%)		2 (18.2%)		11
Paying machine breaking	17 (89.5%)		1 (5.3%)	1 (5.3%)	19
Distraction theft	72 (67.3%)			35 (32.7%)	107
Pickpocketing	33 (56.9%)			25 (43.1%)	58

(continued)

[18] Rossy et al, above n 17.

Table 1: (*Continued*)

Crime types	Number of series				
	Situational information	Shoemark pattern	DNA	Image	Total
Larceny	62 (76.5%)			19 (23.5%)	81
Card fraud	16 (66.7%)			8 (33.3%)	24
Fraud	31 (83.8%)			6 (16.2%)	37
Shoplifting	15 (75%)			5 (25%)	20
Cloakroom/ locker breaking	3 (60%)			2 (40%)	5
Counterfeit banknotes	13 (92.9%)			1 (7.1%)	14
Vehicle plates stolen	33 (100%)				33
Racketeering	17 (100%)				17
Mugging	4 (100%)				4
Chiselling	1 (100%)				1
Murder	1 (100%)				1

With new technologies, interstate police cooperation led to police officers facing a mass of data, including irrelevant information. The use of PICAR and the creation of a common methodology created a new synergy between criminal intelligence units. Repetitive crimes that are analysed by the intelligence structures are mostly international, and do not stop at the Swiss border. Beyond Switzerland, it is difficult to gauge the size, extent and evolution of transnational crimes, at least of those closely neighbouring the border. We postulate that forensic data can be used in order to complete a better picture of different crime problems and assist with finding solutions to mitigate them. We have started a process of potential improvement by studying a single CICOP, domestic burglaries perpetrated along the Swiss border. By analysing the mechanisms, modus operandi, forensic data collected and the solved cases, we should be able to devise a strategy of data exchange, thus proving the validity of a more global and ambitious approach.

IX. CONCLUSION

Organised crime has drawn the particular attention of the media, magistrates and the police. The arrest of international criminals has thus become an important political priority. This can (partially) explain why forensic data exchange processes have multiplied exponentially in recent years. However, information exchange processes have been based upon proposals put forward during the 1914 First International Criminal Police Congress. With the development of technologies and computers, these systems must cope with a new set of problems, and a large flow of information. With no strategy to manage data flows, there is a risk that the systems may be overwhelmed by the quantity and disparity of international requests. To avoid this, it is necessary to create a global picture of international criminality and hence to change the sporadic and erratic case-by-case approach to data exchange. Furthermore, the control of data can better guarantee civil liberties. Indeed, if being more selective considering which forensic data was to be transmitted across borders, and limiting the number of requested countries, with better defined purposes of requests, the control and use of national forensic data in international exchanges can be improved. Thus, processes of international data exchange must be reconsidered. One strategy could be the elaboration of an intelligence-led framework for orienting forensic case data exchange processes.

An important consequence is that exchanges cannot be considered as a flow of information mechanically processed. They are the result of a decision-making process that necessitates knowledge about the potential of each channel and how to use it, according to the context of the demands. Within current legal and managerial procedures, a routine approach to processing, and no express strategy, the necessary framework to inspire confidence in the use of the system has yet to be created.

Index

Page numbers in **bold** indicate information in tables and page numbers in *italics* indicate information in figures.

www.ingramcontent.com/pod-product-compliance
Lightning Source LLC
Chambersburg PA
CBHW050413280326
41932CB00013BA/1842